ALCOHOLISM TREATMENT:
An Integrative Family and Individual Approach

ALCOHOLISM TREATMENT

AN INTEGRATIVE FAMILY AND INDIVIDUAL APPROACH

Donald I. Davis, M.D.

Foreword by M. Duncan Stanton, Ph.D.

GARDNER PRESS, INC.

New York London

Gardner Press, Inc.
19 Union Square West
New York 10003

All foreign orders except Canada and South America to:
Afterhurst Limited
Chancery House
319 City Road
London N1, United Kingdom

Library of Congress Cataloging in Publication Data

Davis, Donald I.
Alcoholism treatment: an integrative family and individual approach.

Includes bibliographies and index.
1. Alcoholism. 2. Family psychotherapy. I. Title.
[DNLM: 1. Alcoholism—therapy. 2. Family Therapy.
WM 274 D26li]
R565.D38 1985 616.86'106 86-1475
ISBN 0-89876-115-8

BOOK DESIGN BY RAY SOLOMON

PRINTED IN THE UNITED STATES OF AMERICA

To my mother and father,
Clara and Aubrey Davis,
who taught me
by the example of their
lives the value of
perseverance with something worthwhile

ACKNOWLEDGMENTS

Chapter 1 is a revised version, used by permission of the publisher, of the article, "The Adaptive Consequences of Drinking," by D.I. Davis, D. Berenson, P. Steinglass, & S. Davis, *Psychiatry, 37* (1974): 209–215. Reprinted in *Annual Alcoholism Review*, New Brunswick, NJ: Rutgers University, 1979.

Chapter 2 is a revised version, used by permission of the publisher, of Chapter 8, "The Family in Alcoholism," in *Phenomenology and Treatment of Alcoholism*, edited by W. E. Fann, I. Karacan, A. D. Pokorny, & R. L. Williams. Spectrum Publications, Inc.: Jamaica, New York, 1980.

Chapter 4 is a revised version, used by permission of the publisher, of a chapter entitled "Special Problems in Family Therapy Posed by Alcohol Abuse" in *Family Therapy and Major Psychopathology*," edited by M. Lansky. Grune and Stratton. New York City, 1981.

Chapter 9 is a revised version, used by permission of the publisher, of the article, "Alcoholics Anonymous and Family Therapy," by D.I. Davis, *Journal of Marital and Family Therapy,* 6 (1980): 65–73.

Appendix B is an article, reprinted with permission of the publisher, by K. Kupetz, et al., entitled "The Acceptance and Validity of the Substance Use and Abuse Survey (SUAS)," *Journal of Drug Education, 9* (2) (1979): 163–180.

Appendix C is an article, reprinted with permission of the publisher, by D.I. Davis, entitled "Differences in the Use of Substances of Abuse by Psychiatric Patients Compared with Medical and Surgical Patients," *Journal of Nervous and Mental Disease,* 172 (1984): 654–657.

FOREWORD

This book is a treasure chest of options. For the therapist or counselor who has become "stuck" in treating an alcohol problem, a wealth of alternatives is provided. The offerings range from a myriad of ways for overcoming the "denial" of an alochol problem to the use of Neuro-Linguistic Programming with alcoholics and their family members. Each display is adorned with instructive clinical vignettes set against a background of skillful technique and solid rationale. Helpful hints and clear guidelines abound in quantity and brilliance sufficient to satisfy even the richest in therapeutic experience. As a sample, consider these:

- "Predicting in front of the whole family what is likely to happen in therapy if drinking does not stop" is usually helpful and sometimes crucial. (*Chapter 4*)
- When a drinking problem is admitted, but denied as the primary problem, asking whether the presence of alcohol "makes any difference" with this "preferred" problem can "open the floodgates to an enormous amount of relevant information about the relationship between alcohol use" and this problem. (*Chapter 5*)
- Calling Alcoholics Anonymous or an Al-Anon group directly during a treatment session can be very effective in actually getting family members to become involved in such self-help opportunities. (*Chapter 9*)
- Accepting that whatever results from a treatment intervention is "feedback rather than failure" helps the therapist avoid defensiveness, maintain a sensitivity to process and retain an openness to alternative ways of intervening. (*Chapter 11*)

Throughout its many options, this book possesses breadth—the staff of a therapist's life. Building upon his earlier, ground-breaking research (with Steinglass and others) on interactions within alcoholic families during both wet and dry states, and extending through his by-now-classic work on the "Adaptive Consequences of Drinking," Davis brings us to the forefront of what is happening in the understanding and the treatment of alcoholic systems. Alternatively, Davis spreads his net laterally, giving us invaluable information on how to treat "exceptions"—the cases that don't, or won't, conform to the more conventional interventions.

There is comfort here. Davis long ago arrived at an integration of family therapy with AA, Al-anon and Alateen. Both family therapists and those from the addictions field should be comfortable with his reconciliation. It invites all in and makes room for each.

Finally, this book provides hope. It shows us that the "impossible" may be possible, and *how* it may be possible. While each of us may have to broaden our perspective and enlarge our repertoire of skills, this book shows us that light does indeed shine at the end of the tunnel. Davis gives us, then, both the light and the compass. He has earned our gratitude.

M. Duncan Stanton, Ph.D. *Professor and Director*
Division of Family Programs Department of Psychiatry
University of Rochester Medical Center

CONTENTS

PREFACE

With some exceptions, this book is not about particular schools of therapy as applied to alcoholism. It is a book, for practitioners and students of any school, about integrating the skills of (family and individual) therapy that one has and utilizing them in the treatment of alcoholism.

Most therapists, in my experience, know more about therapy techniques than they do about how to approach alcoholism—so they apply their methods to whatever other issues they can identify in a family or individual. Therefore, I have emphasized basic ways to broach the topic of alcohol abuse and to confirm that it is a problem in the family. Appropriate transcripts illustrate the method.

The chapters of this book chronicle my own personal odyssey through both the labyrinth that is alcoholism and the maze that is family therapy. Quite recently there have appeared several books relating family therapy to alcoholism or to other drug abuse (1,2,3,4, 5,6,7). Still, whenever I teach, I am asked, "What else can I read?" And when I have offered my own previous papers, I have invariably been told, "These are helpful." Then: "Do you have more?" The last question usually has been followed by certain specific requests, which certain chapters in this book will address.

Basically this work is intended to present a pragmatic, clinical approach to alcoholism, drawing upon the state of the art in integrating available models of therapy with the down-to-earth nuts and bolts of dealing with alcoholics and their families. While no attempt is made to cover the whole fields of alcoholism or family therapy, a clinician absorbing the material in this book should come away with a respect for and comprehension of family issues and family approaches to alcoholism treatment, sufficient to enable him or her to feel confident that s/he now has an approach to alcoholics and their families that s/he is willing to put into practice.

This is not a book about the etiology of alcoholism. There is much in the book, however, that is relevant to the maintenance of alcoholic behavior once it develops and particularly to how to overcome resistances to changes in problem-drinking behavior.

The book is directed toward all individual as well as family and marital therapists, since almost all of them work with alcoholics and/or with clients having an alcoholic family member. Portions of this book are geared toward sensitizing any therapist to the identification of subtler interactional ways in which alcoholism presents itself, as well as to the techniques for dealing with alcoholism in the course of providing therapy for other conditions. It is also intended for alcoholism counselors, especially in the emphasis placed on explaining the benefits—for treatment and prevention—of working with the whole family.

The book is organized to provide just enough theory to support some very specific clinical guidelines. Some readers may want a comprehensive review of all the many different theories about, and approaches to alcoholism. That is not what this book is about; for that the reader is referred to such recent books as Orford and Harwin (Eds.), Alcohol and the Family, 1982 (5), and Galanter (Ed.) Currents in Alcoholism: Recent Advances in Research and Treatment, 1981 (8), which together probably comprise the most complete resources, to date, for a review of the psychosocial and the biomedical, clinical aspects of alcoholism. My book, on the other hand, is based on my own personal clinical experience and on my association with alcoholism clinicians, researchers, and teachers. As such, it is intended to serve more as a handbook for clinicians and for clinicians-in-training than as a comprehensive textbook for the field of alcoholism treatment.

The Introduction offers an opinion about what the competency of an alcoholism therapist should consist of. There follows, in Part I, a section directed at persuading readers—even those comfortable treating individual alcoholics—that interactional thinking is critical to the management of substance abuse. Chapters 1 and 2 draw upon both existing literature and clinical illustrations to support this systems-oriented, theoretical position.

Part II begins with an attempt (in Chapter 3) to convince therapists—including those already adept in thinking at a systems level—that one should not disregard alcohol abuse when dealing with families. Coauthored with Jeffrey Jay, Ph.D., this chapter is largely theoretical, and descriptive of the potential interactions between the behavior of drinking and family-level dynamics. Then Chapter 4 offers a clinical illustration of the pitfalls of ignoring alcoholism and the benefits of addressing it when doing family therapy.

Part III, the final and largest section, delineates treatment techniques (although some theory is included, especially in Chapter 12). Chapter 5 presents some very specific how-to suggestions for what to say and when to say it, when first asking about alcohol use and when first confronting an alcoholic and his family with the need to stop drinking. Chapters 6, 7, and 8 provide actual transcripts of portions of sessions with three different cases. In Chapter 6, a method is offered of eliciting privately, from children, a subtle drinking problem in a parent whose family presented with a child-focused, non-drug-related problem. The transcript in Chapter 7 illustrates a difficult confrontation between highly argumentative spouses about the serious consequences of drinking, where one denies alcoholism is a factor in the problem. Chapter 8 presents a transcript in which I, the consultant, have been observing behind a one-way mirror and enter the latter part of a session to consolidate an agreement for continuing therapy between an alcoholic wife, who is still drinking and wants only marital therapy, and her recently abstinent alcoholic husband, who wants therapy for his wife only, to stop her drinking.

Chapter 9 describes a rationale and method for utilizing simultaneously both Alcoholics Anonymous and family therapy and dispels some false notions about their incompatibility.

Chapter 10 and 11 address what a therapist needs to know about, and to be able to do for, the *individual* alcoholic. Chapter 10 takes into account general conditions, such as the coexistence of another psychiatric condition. Chapter 11 is an introduction to some innovative and still controversial approaches—largely derived from Neuro-Linguistic Programming—to changing certain thought processes and related behavioral patterns of the individual alcoholic.

Chapter 12 represents an attempt to briefly summarize the interrelationships of all the varied aspects of alcoholism treatment. I offer a theory of the stages one must traverse in overcoming a drug-using habit; I also draw connections between the task to be accomplished and the interactional and individual-level interventions now available to help accomplish each task.

Finally, Chapter 13 presents an in-depth case report that illustrates the integration of much of what has been described earlier in the book, while focusing on the post-abstinence phase of treatment.

Included in the appendices are a substance use questionnaire and two previously published papers, in which I attempt to substantiate certain underlying premises of the book. Appendix A consists of a clinically applicable questionnaire, the Substance Use and Abuse Survey (SUAS). Appendix B presents a paper describing the validity of the SUAS and the surprising ease with which its use has been accepted by large numbers of patients. Appendix C offers a study documenting that the heavy use, as well as the clear-cut consequences, of the abuse of alcohol and other drugs is very common, and significantly more prevalent among general psychiatric patients than among a comparable group of people who were patients in a (non-psychiatric) medical or surgical setting. Workers in clinical settings who doubt that they see many people in whom excessive drinking or other drug use is a factor may want to read Appendix C first.

To summarize my own personal history, I went to work full-time in 1972 as a Clinical Associate in the Clinical Research Laboratory of the National Institute for Alcohol Abuse and Alcoholism (NIAAA). My primary interest was family research. Peter Steinglass had recently become Director of the unit and had had the courage to turn a biochemical lab into one of the first live-in research units for the study of couples, all of whom had one thing in common: one or both partners were alcoholic. Thus began my reluctant exposure to the field of alcoholism. My otherwise excellent medical education at the University of Pennsylvania, internship at the Case Western Reserve University Hospitals of Cleveland, and psychiatric residency at the University of Chicago had not really prepared me for dealing with the specifics of clinical management of the behavioral aspects of excessive drinking.

Although my residency training had been individually oriented, with strong psychodynamic as well as biomedical components, I was quite comfortable with systems thinking and with working with couples and families by the time I began working with alcoholics. In part, that comfort reflected a personal bent, which had been cultivated first as a medical student in 1967 with an elective at the Philadelphia Child Guidance Clinic and then nurtured via privately arranged family therapy supervision throughout the rest of my training. An operant behavioral background gained from frequent contact over two years with Israel Goldiamond rounded out my prealcoholism clinical education. Traces of all elements in my educational background can be found in Chapter 1, which is a revised version of a theoretical, clinical paper published in 1974 with David Berenson, Peter Steinglass, and Susan L. R. Davis.

Working for two years with Peter Steinglass and David Berenson, each of whom had been influenced in their psychiatric training by Andrew Ferber and Albert Sheflin and other systems thinkers at the Albert Einstein School of Medicine, I did not find it hard to maintain a systems or cybernetic orientation to the understanding of alcoholic behavior. In addition, Isaiah Zimmerman provided me with clinical supervision in multiple-couples therapy, the intervention format emphasized with the couples in the alcoholism studies. I also maintained a small private practice at my home, in which I occasionally saw couples or families in cotherapy with my wife, Susan L. R. Davis, who had received her social work training at Bryn Mawr while I was at medical school, and who also provided intellectual support for thinking in systems. Of course, our research subjects offered ample reason to apply interactional thinking in and of itself, especially during occasional visits with patients in their homes.

In July 1974 I moved to George Washington University, where for several years I continued almost full-time combining work as well as further training in both substance abuse and family therapy. With a three-year award from the NIAAA as a Career Teacher in Drug Abuse and Alcoholism, I became immersed in clinical research, teaching, and the political aspects of alcoholism and other chemical dependency. At the same time, I had joined with Peter Steinglass and Steven Wolin in following the lead of David Reiss in the creation of the Center for Family Research at George Washington University and for two years was Principle Investigator of a rather large-scale Substance Abuse Survey and Family Study, funded by the National Institute of Drug Abuse. The NIDA grant provided for the convening of an invitational Symposium on Drug Abuse and the Family in Columbia, Maryland, in 1975, which in turn led me to a greater awareness of the then early work in this area of M. Duncan Stanton and others who have more recently had such an impact on the treatment of substance-abuse patients.

During 1975 and 1976 my wife and I each somehow found time to spend at least a day a week for ten months with Jay Haley, who had just moved from Philadelphia to Washington, D. C., and with Cloë Madanes in live supervision of what has since come to be known as Strategic Family Therapy. In the year before starting this training, I had introduced live family supervision, using a one-way mirror, to the psychiatric residents at George Washington University. My own further training made me a zealot of live supervision. My prior eclectic exposure and subsequent training have resulted in an approach to therapy in which I only occasionally take the part of the pure strategic therapist, if such still exists; for years now I have used the term Integrative Family Therapy to describe my particular clinical orientation.

As original grants ended, I accepted the opportunity to apply my peculiar special interests (in those days especially) of family therapy and substance abuse in a *bona fide* clinical setting, as a Team Attending Psychiatrist on the Inpatient Psychiatric Unit of George Washington University Hospital. There I was given the additional title of Director of Family Therapy. Through survey research (the results of which are presented in Appendix B, Part 3, of this book), I already knew that there was considerable heavy use of alcohol and other drugs of abuse among the patients, even though the unit had not generally admitted patients with known chemical dependency. I also knew that although it was assumed that many patients on the unit lacked stable family connections, the survey indicated that most patients had regular contact with one or more first-degree relatives. For the next two years, I probed the mysteries of an inpatient psychiatric system and engaged with director and staff, with some success, in the process of slowly instituting certain changes, principal among which was the treatment of certain cases primarily from a family orientation, including most of the cases now being admitted with a primary diagnosis of substance abuse. I also enlarged my personal practice during this time, seeing as broad a range of presenting problems as possible, knowing that many would involve substance abuse in the identified patient or in some significant other without my having to request substance-abuse cases.

By 1978 I found myself already doing more family-therapy training and teaching than was likely to fit comfortably in my schedule, as my department evolved. Yet my interests lay in expanding this line of work. The resolution of the dilemma was the founding, with Susan Davis, of a private, free-standing, post graduate family therapy training program and clinic in Alexandria, Virginia, which we named the Family Therapy Institute of Alexandria. As Director of the Institute, I have been enormously enriched, both personally and professionally, by Institute association with colleagues, patients, and office staff. One temporary associate, Jeffrey Jay, the co-author of Chapter 3 of this book, was an NIAAA-funded post doctoral fellow at the Center for Family Research. My full-time associates—Susan L. R. Davis, Raymond B. Wertheim, Jean Sidley, and Mervin Moss—have added to my understanding of, and skills with families in profound ways and deserve mention for influencing my thinking in ways that cannot be properly acknowledged in a written text.

Curiously, not long after founding the Institute, my wife and I both formally became students again, this time of a largely new subject, Neuro-Linguistic Programming (NLP). Our exposure to the teaching of Richard Bandler and John Grinder, the developers of NLP, and their closest early associates—Leslie Cameron-Bandler, Robert Dilts, David Gordon, among others—has had a substantial influence on our clinical practice and teaching at the Institute. Of particular relevance to the present book, NLP has enabled me to address rapidly certain factors that reside within the individual without disrupting the flow of, and benefits from, working with the family system in bringing about change in drinking behavior. This influence is evident in portions of chapters 11 through 13, which introduce the readers to a method of integrating the new, largely individually applied model and set of techniques into a systems approach to alcoholism.

Finally, for assistance in editing the final text of this book, special thanks are due Marilyn Moorcroft of Gardner Press, and Caron Fischer, M.S.W.

References

1. Kaufman, E., & Kaufmann, P. (Eds.). *Family Therapy of Drug and Alcohol Abuse.* New York: Gardner Press, 1979.
2. Barnard, C. P. *Families, alcoholism and therapy.* Springfield, IL: Charles C. Thomas, 1981.
3. Wegscheider, S. *Another chance: Hope and health for the alcoholic family.* Palo Alto: Science & Behavior Books, 1981.
4. Stanton, M. D., Todd, T. C., & Associates. *The family therapy of drug abuse and addiction.* New York: Guilford, 1982.
5. Orford, J., & Harwin, J. (Eds.). *Alcohol and the family.* New York; St. Martin's, 1982.
6. Lawson, G., Peterson, J. S., & Lawson, A. *Alcoholism and the family: A guide to treatment and prevention.* Rockville, Md.: Aspen, 1983.
7. Kaufman, E. (Ed.). *Power to change: Family case studies in the treatment of alcoholism.* New York: Gardner Press, 1984.
8. Galanter, M. *Currents in alcoholism: Recent advances in research and treatment.* New York: Grune & Stratton, 1981.

ALCOHOLISM TREATMENT:
An Integrative Family
and Individual Approach

INTRODUCTION: CLINICAL COMPETENCY WITH ALCOHOLICS AND THEIR FAMILIES

In the middle of a therapy session, mother joked about how husband sometimes drinks in the morning. Nearly drowned out by the general laughter was daughter's petulant reply that he drinks too much. Therapist and family returned to the previous topic, the timing of father's depressive moods. Soon mother complained that in the evenings husband can get into a mean mood and at those times has been known to hit her. The family therapist followed up with an exploration of the links between depressed mood and conflicts between the spouses.

As they watched the videotape replay of this session, the therapist asked his consultant how to deal with the issue of drinking when it came up, as in this case, as a constant diversion whenever the family began to talk about something conflictual. The family is bright and verbal, the consultant was told, and they ought to be getting somewhere in therapy, but the first few sessions seemed to have gotten bogged down. Previously, a month or so of hospitalization and a year of outpatient individual psychotherapy also had failed to make a sustained dent in father's depression. It seemed now that if the family could just overcome a certain resistance to dealing with core family issues, therapy would just take off. Alcohol use, which had never been considered a major issue, seemed to be one of the more frequent vehicles for expressing resistance. The therapist reiterated that what he sought through consultation was ways to dispose of the alcohol-related diversions.

The consultant told him, however, that he was asking the wrong question, that he, like so many other therapists, might be ignoring the horse (alcohol) while trying ever so hard to budge the cart (the family). The therapist had been assuming that the drinking resulted from marital conflicts, that depression led to more drinking, and that if drinking were really a primary problem, someone, either in the family or a previous therapist, would have said so. Wrong, wrong, wrong, the therapist was told. It was usually the other way around (or at least it was more useful to think of it that way). When one spouse is drinking frequently, mental conflicts don't go away; they smolder and deepen. As for depression, alcohol is a depressant. Most alcoholics eventually become depressed. It may be impossible without a period of weeks or months of abstinence to tell if the depression has a life of its own. Finally, it is untrue that others would have made the diagnosis if it were there. Alcohol abuse frequently goes largely ignored. Family members and previous therapists may have missed the diagnosis, or failed to make it stick. In fact, in this family we already know that daughter thinks father has a drinking problem, but her opinion has been ignored or overruled. The therapist was asked to pose a different question, "How can I assess how much alcohol abuse is a factor while doing family therapy?" Also, "What do I do with that information once I have it?" The answers to these questions are the subject of this chapter.

In the case presented, some important information had already been elicited, but not used. Based on the same videotaped session, the consultant reconstructed the family's story as follows. Some mornings, father begins drinking shortly after arising. By evening, he is often intoxicated and capable of acting violently with his family. He misses work at times, ostensibly for depression and anxiety. His daughter thinks he has a drinking problem. This man is an alcoholic, but neither his family nor his therapists are acknowledging the fact.

In family therapy, it is likely that he will continue to show promise of improvement but never quite recover. That will happen for several reasons. One is that he continues to drink daily enough of the sedative drug—alcohol—to perpetuate a chemical basis for feeling depressed. Another is that, since nothing is being done to change his drinking habits, he will continue to miss work or perform poorly on occasional mornings, thereby generating covert or overt reprimands and lowered self-esteem. Under the sanction of intoxication, he may strike his wife some evening, further scarring their already wounded relationship. When they have problems to resolve, as all couples do, they will fail to work them through to a mutually acceptable conclusion. This failure may stem from either the expectation or the reality of his wrath or his fatigue, when drinking, or to her overreaction when he has been drinking. When their teenage children are exposed to heavy peer pressure to be truant or to take drugs, parents will have little moral clout with which to restrain them because of the parents' hypocrisy concerning alcohol misuse.

Of course, all of the above may become moot, if father is killed or maimed or harms somebody else while driving under the influence of alcohol. But father may not have an accident. He may not even drink and drive. His work may suffer imperceptively to others than himself. It may be years before an organ in his body fails as a secondary effect of alcohol, and he may die of other causes before that occurs. It may be that the only consequences of alcoholism in evidence will be that relationships suffer. This is particularly true of people who come to see a family therapist. Hence, the family therapist must know the more subtle cues to alcohol abuse. Fortunately, she* has the tremendous advantage over other therapists of seeing and hearing first-hand what role alcohol has come to play in the alcoholic's relationships, and of being able to make use of these relationships to bring an end to the drinking problem. If she capitalizes on these aids, the odds are very good for successful outcomes in family therapy with families having an alcoholic member. If not—if the drinking continues—it is likely that therapy will not progress to the desired end-point.

Background

Alcoholism is a frequently occurring disorder in our society, with incidence figures generally ranging from five to ten percent of the population (1). If these were the percentages among a therapy population as well, it would be significant. It appears, however, that alcoholism is found with much greater frequency among certain groups, groups that are also more likely to be seen in family, marital, and individual therapy. For example, alcoholism has been identified in 20 to 40 percent and more of hospitalized patients in some urban hospitals (2).

If one also considers heavy drinking and job or social problems associated with drinking, as opposed to only the confirmed diagnosis of alcoholism, the frequency with which alcohol misuse is found to be a potential complication in therapy is very high. My colleagues and I have found heavy or problem use of alcohol and/or some other substance of abuse in nearly 40 percent of all patients in even a largely middle-class, general, psychiatric, out-patient population (3). Alcohol

*We shall often use the feminine, "she," for therapists, to accurately reflect the majority in many therapeutic settings, and the masculine, "he," for patients, for similar reasons. I should also note that for both therapists and patients the opposite sex is running a close second, and everything in this book that applies to one applies as well to the other.

is the most frequent drug abused in these populations. Much of the other drug abuse involves various tranquilizers or sedative-hypnotics. While this book is about alcohol abuse, it should be understood that most of what is said here about the problems posed by alcohol abuse in therapy is applicable to sedative-hypnotic abuse as well.

These surmises apply most to identified patients. They do not begin to take into account the number of identified patients who have alcohol-abusing spouses, parents, and children. Statistics are lacking in this area. We do know that there is a greather-than-normal frequency of alcoholism among parents of disturbed children who are patients in child psychiatric settings (4). Beyond that, we can only say that it is not uncommon to find, if one inquires, that spouse abuse of alcohol is a major factor in a man's or woman's seeking therapy or that a young adult's parents' abuse of alcohol figures prominently in his or her current mental conflicts. In short, if a clinician does not deal with alcohol abuse frequently, it is not for want of opportunity.

A recent outpatient psychotherapy clinic study has revealed an increased rate of incorrect diagnosis on the part of therapists when dealing with substance-abusing patients (5). That is, therapists were more likely to mislabel patients especially in the cases of major diagnostic categories, such as depression or schizophrenia, if the patients misused drugs. These findings relate to other recent studies that predicted but failed to find higher-than-average rates of symptomatic depression in newly abstinent alcoholics (6). Even though most alcoholics eventually appear clinically depressed, once they stop drinking the incidence of primary depression is not greater than that in the general population, perhaps 10 to 15 percent. Similarly, sex problems that may not persist post-abstinence (though may also) can arise from heavy drinking. These include impotence, diminished libido, decreased sensory pleasure, and partner distaste for sex. In general, the ability of a therapist to assess a situation accurately will improve after a period of abstinence on the part of the heavy drinker. This constitutes one very good reason for the family therapist to learn to identify and to address alcohol abuse in a family member.

In the treatment literature, there is support now for the application of family therapy techniques to the treatment of alcoholism. While conclusive data are lacking, comparisons of family and marital approaches with other approaches to the treatment of alcoholism have yielded either equal or favorable results for family-relationship approaches (7,8) and have indicated that these can, at times, be sufficient treatment in themselves (9). However, family therapy can also become another means of forestalling the treatment of alcohol abuse if the drinking is not adequately addressed. This latter fact will lead some family members to lack confidence in their therapist. These people will have seen or heard about individual, family or marital therapy failures who finally got help through the self-help groups of Alcoholics Anonymous (AA), Al-anon (for the alcoholic's mates or adult significant others) and Alateen (for the teenage children of alcoholics). Family members may test indirectly or directly the therapist's ability to address the fact that a drinking problem exists. If the therapist fails the test, they will lose hope or confidence. The surest way to fail the test is to label the alcohol abuse as a mere sympton of family conflict that will go away as faulty communication is removed from the family.

The hope that alcohol abuse will go away with an effective family intervention that disregards drinking is an impractical strategy on pragmatic grounds. It also is squarely at odds with the disease concept of alcoholism espoused by AA and Al-anon (10). The disease concept holds that alcoholism is a primary illness, one with typical symptoms and a predictable course, and one that requires outside intervention. More than an act of will power is needed for adequate treatment. And in family treatment more is needed than changing those significant others who are somehow to blame for the systems aspects of the problem. Therapists are ill-advised to take sides on the issues of cause versus effect when it comes to alcoholism; but in working with families it cannot be smugly assumed that emphasis on the system alone will be effective without some attention paid to alcoholism as a disease (10).

Also useful is to conceive of alcoholism as a final common pathway disorder; i.e., one can get there from a multitude of origins—social, physiological, or psychological; but once a pattern of alcohol abuse develops, the family adapts to it. It is these self-reinforcing adaptive consequences, a concept developed in Chapter 1, that the family in successful therapy must provide a substitute for, alter, or give up. The special problems posed by the need to treat a drinking problem and adaptations to it are discussed further in Chapter 4.

There is an extensive literature examining the premise that the spouses of alcoholics, who invariably feel like either forlorn victims or frightful villains (11), are, in fact, disturbed personalities themselves (12). Paolino and McCrady have reviewed the entire literature and, in the process, questioned the whole notion of characteristic, pre-existing "alcoholic" personalities. They conclude that the chaos, high-disease rate and higher-than-average rates of physical and emotional disturbances seen among alcoholics and their families are the consequences of years of disruption caused by heavy drinking. This is felt to be supported by their finding that marital interaction tends to improve when heavy drinking stops (7). Overall, there is support in the literature for treatment approaches that do not stem from etiologic presuppositions and take advantage of multiple-treatment resources, including AA self-help groups and family therapy. The latter is more effective if the therapist can comfortably reconcile the systems point of view with a disease model. How to do this is described in Chapter 9.

There is much arising from clinical research, clinical experience, and concerns about prevention that supports taking a family-therapy approach to the treatment of alcoholism. An added task for the family therapist treating alcoholism is to become adept at identifying alcohol abuse itself in an individual and the adaptation to it on the part of the family. Signals and cues are discussed at some length in the Treatment section (Part Three) of this book. Briefly, if a person comes into a therapist's office with alcohol on his/her breath, the therapist should not shrug it off as a one-time event. The National Council on Alcoholism has even concluded that such behavior in an inappropriate setting, such as a doctor's office, is presumptive evidence of alcoholism (13). Many family therapists are not yet adept at creating some opportunity to catch a whiff. Without the odor, one may have to watch for subtler cues of mild intoxication. (The chronic heavy drinker has a tolerance to alcohol and can hold a great deal without acting grossly drunk.) A little increased irritability, silliness, or sleepiness, or the accentuation of usual idiosyncratic behaviors may be all that there is to go on. A hint of any such signs should lead the therapist to inquire whether the person has been drinking in the previous few hours. If anyone in the family confirms the fact, it should be taken as a signal of alcohol misuse until proven otherwise.

Among other more blatant cues, sometimes concern is raised by other family members about someone's drinking. In the case cited earlier, in which a daughter's suspicions were ignored, these should have been taken seriously. Detailed questions about the extent and timing of the drinking and the immediate effects on the family should be asked on the spot, or shortly thereafter. To do so serves two purposes. It permits the rapid identification of a drinking problem and serves to model appropriate concern for the problem. In rare instances, it turns out that the concerned person has a very low threshold for seeing alcohol use as an abuse—that is, even only one or two drinks scares him or her. The therapist can then use that as an opportunity for education and move one. More often, unfortunately, therapists as well as family members have an unwarranted high threshold for being able to identify alcohol use as a problem. Therapists are likely to lower their thresholds if they begin to probe into what happens between family members when someone is drinking and then compare that with what happens when no one is drinking.

Any symptom should be taken as a cue to look for alcohol abuse in a family: Psychosomatic disorders, low self-esteem, vague marital and life-stage complaints all indicate a careful look for alcoholism in the spouse as well as in the identified patient. Of course, drug abuse in children requires an alertness for alcoholism in parents or siblings; but underachievement in school is also a symptom. Purely relationship symptoms should also trigger questions about alcohol. Couples whose conflicts escalate to physical fighting or intense shouting are a prime example. Often it is easy to determine that the arguments go out of control only when one spouse has had at least something to drink, however little. Similarly, sexual incompatibility may relate to the use of alcohol by one spouse at times of lovemaking, although alcohol is less frequently the culprit with sexual complaints than with complaints of physical violence. Finally, the frequent statement, "My husband (or wife) drinks a lot, but he (or she) won't come to therapy" should not be taken as a blithe endorsement to work only on the presenting problem. The presenting patient must be treated as part of an alcoholic system. To make the point, he (she) might at least be encouraged to attend Al-anon long enough to be exposed to others in a similar situation and learn from them something about how not to help perpetuate the problem by overreacting in the presence of alcohol.

All therapists, not just alcoholism counselors, deal with alcoholism. Some are more aware that they do than others. Unfortunately, awareness alone is not enough. A therapist's level of awareness of the role of drinking as a factor maintaining the presenting problems of an individual and his or her family does not alter the actual role that drinking plays. A therapist's ability to address drinking problems does impact greatly on the efficacy of treating behavioral disturbances that occur in association with drinking problems. Hence, therapists of all schools and disciplines owe it to their patients and clients to become as skilled as possible in identifying and treating alcoholism. The truly dedicated, however, will find this a monumental—but not impossible—task.

A comprehensive knowledge of the management of alcohol dependency and all of its complications comprises much of the biochemistry, physiology, and psychopharmacology that is taught in four years of medical school and several years of psychiatric training plus, a comprehensive knowledge about therapy within family systems and with chemically dependent individuals—subjects often not even offered in all those years of training. Many physicians who know a great deal about the organic complications of alcoholism know little or nothing about the treatment of the primary condition. Regarding the medical aspects of alcoholism, it is probably sufficient for most therapists to know that excessive drinking can impair the function of just about any organ system one can think of and can bring about behavior that replicates most psychiatric diagnoses; plus, it is important to have some idea of the likelihood that a given condition, such as depression, in the presence of excessive drinking is either a primary condition or a secondary consequence of drinking. Beyond acquiring at least this minimal medical knowledge, the therapist seeking competence with problem drinkers should learn what is unique to dealing with individuals who drink excessively and what is unique to the systems in which they live, and integrate this information with the broad range of family and individual approaches to therapy currently available.

The biological aspects are clearly beyond the scope of this book. Let us reduce the remaining clinical aspects to their parts. "How do you talk to them about it?" "When should I bring it up?" "Isn't it better to wait and see what happens for a while in therapy rather than take the chance of blowing the whole thing wide open?" "How will I know if he drinks too much anyway?" "What do I do if I do find out he has a drinking problem?" These are a few of the typical questions asked by therapists at all levels of experience—questions that have led to the preparation of this book. A therapist should have some effective ways of finding out to what degree people use alcohol (and other drugs). She must be able to obtain that information without driving away clients and without apologizing unnecessarily or in other ways diminishing the importance of the findings. She needs to know how to elicit the consequences that have already occurred because of drinking, and elicit them at all levels: individual, marital, parental, family and community network levels.

Therapist competency requires even going beyond the sophisticated identification of problems associated with drinking. It requires the skill of utilizing oneself and others to convince an alcoholic and his family that alcohol use is a central problem. Even for the alcoholism counselor with those skills, competence also requires learning to incorporate, in productive ways, the wider system of people interacting with the alcoholic, and in all phases of therapy: the identification of alcoholism, the commitment to therapy, the achievement of abstinence, and during post-abstinence.

In this book, considerable attention has been paid to treating the individual alcoholic. Yet, as we say in other parts of the book, the family must be taken into account, not just as casualties of alcoholism but also as resources in its treatment. It is an essential objective to convey here just how these different emphases are reconcilable. Every extant approach to alcoholism has worked well for some alcoholics. None has worked for all. The task of modern therapists (generalists as well as alcoholism specialists) is to broaden their base of knowledge and skills sufficiently to offer (directly or in collaboration with other helping resources) the full range of what is currently available for the treatment of a given condition, taking into account the unique aspects of *every* case. Sometimes the individual can change, but the family cannot handle it. Sometimes through family therapy the family as a unit and each of its nonalcoholic members learn to function in a much healthier fashion, but the alcoholic cannot stop drinking. And who is the patient? Are we as therapists responsible only to carry out that which we (narrowly) define as our prescribed task, be it treating individuals one at a time, helping recovering alcoholics, or providing family and marital therapy? Fortunately, those drinking-reducing interventions beneficial to the wider system in which the alcoholic interacts are usually also helpful in the recovery process of the individual alcoholic. That is, engaging the family (or wider, extended network) in the process—of identifying alcoholism; confronting it about alcoholism; applying leverage and otherwise generating a commitment to seeking help for, or stopping, the drinking; and dealing with the consequences of stopping the drinking—is consistent with good management of the individual alcoholic. The reverse is not so true: Working exclusively with an individual alcoholic, even using some of the more innovative approaches described in this book, is less likely to provide family members with the help they need in dealing with the impact of alcoholism on them (even successfully treated alcoholism)—the help they are entitled to from a therapist, given the state of development of family therapy concepts and skills, and given the known impact of alcoholism on spouses and children.

Therapist competency, where problem drinking is concerned, often requires that one operate for a time purely on faith. To have the faith that persistence will pay off, one probably must first acquire certain beliefs. Some beliefs that have usefully sustained my curiosity about an inquiry into alcohol use, at times when nothing short of faith would seem to justify it, are the following:

1) The number of people denying that there is a drinking problem is irrelevant. A family physician, a surgeon, a sweetheart, a parent, a child, a colleague, a policeman and forty million Frenchmen *can* be wrong (and, in the case of French patterns of wine consumption, were, for many years).

2) Intermittently acceptable functioning, even in the presence of alcohol, does not invalidate alcohol use as a problem.

3) When there is an alcoholic in the family, alcohol use becomes a central organizing principle of family interaction.

4) If alcoholism is present, it must be identified and overcome, in order to deal well and lastingly with other family problems.

5) A therapist treating alcoholism can make a difference. This book

unabashedly has, as an underlying agenda, the installation of these beliefs.

The challenge to the therapist who treats alcoholism is great. It involves becoming an integrative therapist, integrating individual and family treatment approaches and varieties of individual and systems-level theories. Hopefully, case material in this book will offer some guidelines. How to learn a broad enough range of theories and skills to fully implement an integrative approach is a larger topic than can be addressed by reading this book, although the chapter references to some of the more innovative literature would also be a useful starting point.

Alcoholism is the great leveler. Treating it generates humility in practitioners of all individual schools. But the sum total of knowledge currently available is probably sufficient to deal helpfully with nearly all alcoholics and their families.

References

1. U. S. Department of Health, Education and Welfare, NIAAA. *First Special Report to the U. S. Congress on Alcohol and Health*. 1971.
2. Whitfield, C. L., & Williams, K. *The patient with alcoholism and other drug problems*. Carbondale, Ill.: Southern Illinois University Press, 1976, pp. 8-10.
3. Davis, D. Differences in the use of substances of abuse by psychiatric patients compared with medical and surgical patients. *Journal of Nervous and Mental Disease, 172* (1984): 654–657. (Reprinted in Appendix of this book.)
4. Haberman, P. Childhood symptoms in children of alcoholic and comparison group patients. *Journal of Marriage and the Family, 28* (1966): 152–54.
5. Hall, R. C. W., Popkin, M. K., DeVaul, R., & Stickney, S. K. The effect of unrecognized drug abuse on diagnosis and therapeutic outcome. *American Journal of Drug and Alcohol Abuse, 4* (1977): 455.
6. Schuckit, M. A. The identification and management of alcoholic and depressive problems. *Drug Abuse and Alcoholism Review, 1* (1978): 1–8.
7. Paolino, T. J., & McCrady, B. S. *The alcoholic marriage: Alternative perspectives*. New York: Grune & Stratton, 1977.
8. Steiglass, P. Experimenting with family treatment approaches to alcoholism, 1950–1975: A review. *Family Process, 15* (1976): 87–123.
9. Janzen, C. Families in the treatment of alcoholism. *Journal of Studies on Alcohol, 38 (1977): 114–130.*
10. *King, B., Bissell, L., & Holding, E. The usefulness of the disease concept of alcoholism in working with wives of alcoholics. Social Work in Health Care, 3* (1978): 443–455.
11. Bailey, M. *Alcoholism and Family Casework: Theory and Practice*. New York: Community Council of Greater New York, 1968.

12.Burton, G., & Kaplan, H. M. Marriage counseling with alcoholics and their spouses: The correlation of excessive drinking behavior with family pathology and social deterioration. *British Journal of Addiction, 63* (1968): 161–170.

13.National Council on Alcoholism, Criteria Committee. Criteria for the diagnosis of alcoholism. *American Journal of Psychiatry, 129* (1972): 127–135; also in *Annals of Internal Medicine, 77* (1972): 249–258.

PART ONE
WHY THINK ABOUT THE FAMILY?

CHAPTER 1

THE ADAPTIVE CONSEQUENCES OF DRINKING*

by Donald I. Davis, M.D., David Berenson, Peter Steinglass, M.D., and Susan L. R. Davis, M.S.S.

Of all the questions that can and have been asked about chronic alcoholism, the most elusive question seems to be the one most basic to a psychiatric understanding of the condition—namely, "Why do people continue to drink when everyone knows it's so bad for you?" In other words, what are the factors that maintain or support the behavior of alcoholism? No previous theory has gained wide acceptance; and, more importantly, no hypothesis has led to a conclusion that has widespread therapeutic application. (1). In this chapter a theoretical model of the maintenance of drinking behavior is presented, derived primarily from a synthesis of systems analysis and operant behavioral analysis. It is hypothesized that the maintenance of drinking behavior is under the control of its adaptive consequences, and clinical vignettes are offered as illustrations. This theoretical framework offers opportunities for broadly applicable research and clinical work on alcoholism

Historically, there have been two premises underlying much of the therapeutic approach to alcoholism. The first is that excessive drinking is maladaptive. The second is that there are ultimate causes that lead to alcoholism, be they essential personality or biological traits.

These premises have led to certain therapeutic approaches. The stress on the maladaptive, destructive nature of drinking has led to moral exhortations and scare tactics by physicians, punitive legal approaches, and generally aversive therapeutic approaches, such as

*Chapter 1 is a revised version of a paper with the same title, first written with David Berensen, Peter Steinglass, and Susan L. R. Davis, in *Psychiatry, 37* (1974): 209–215. Revision reprinted with permission.

the use of disulfiram (Antabuse), apomorphine injections, or video tape self-confrontation. Therapeutic approaches based on ultimate cause hypotheses rather than multidetermined hypotheses have led therapists to apply uniform techniques to all "alcoholics." These approaches, while sometimes leading to short-term improvement, usually lead to relapse and increased frustration for both patient and therapist.

The search for ultimate causes has led to concepts such as biochemical sensitivity, genetic predisposition, and oral dependency, which are interesting and perhaps valid in some cases (2), but our clinical experience leads us to a conclusion of a different order: That alcoholic behavior is more profitably thought of as a final common pathway and that excessive drinking can therefore be put to a wide variety of uses by a wide variety of people.

In addition to those who see ultimate causes in the nature of individuals who become alcoholic, there are those who attribute the primary cause to drug effects themselves. For example, some researchers turn to the concepts of "addiction" (3,4) or of "blackouts" (5) to explain the persistence of the behavior of excessive drinking. These concepts derive from a medical-disease model of alcoholism in which research emphasis is placed on describing what seems maladaptive (pathological) about behavior and on finding the involuntary or addictive (disease) process that produces the disturbed behavior. Working with this model, some people treat an "addiction" as having qualities that remove the control of behavior from behavioral contingencies.

In contrast, we have been studying alcoholism from the perspective of a behavioral-adaptive model in which emphasis is placed on finding what seems adaptive and reinforcing of drinking behavior. Using this model, it is not necessary to postulate that the addictive process serves as the mechanism for the persistence of largely aversive behavior. Rather, we take the view that a seemingly aversive dysphoria (a feeling of being unwell) or other unpleasant conditions resulting from alcohol use will not necessarily make the overall experience of drinking aversive.

By "overall experience," we do not mean each and every drinking experience. "Overall" refers to the composite effect of many drinking episodes, the sum total of which is reinforcing. Only occasional drinking experiences will be strongly rewarding. It is a well-established behavioral tenet that intermittent, rather than continuous, reinforcement leads to the development of the most tenacious habits; this tenet also applies to alcoholic behavior.

HYPOTHESES

As an alternative to the two premises mentioned at the outset, the following is proposed as a model for conceptualizing alcoholism with the following characteristics.

1) The abuse of alcohol has adaptive consequences. It must be emphasized that, by using the word "adaptive," we are not implying "good" or any other moral value. There is certainly precedent—within psychoanalytic explanations of symptom formation, learning theory descriptions of positive reinforcement, and systems theory assessments of levels of functioning—for asserting that behavior may be adaptive, yet not necessarily desirable.

2) These adaptive consequences are sufficiently reinforcing to serve as the primary factors maintaining a habit of drinking, regardless of what underlying causation there may be.

3) The primary factors for each individual differ and may be operating at an intra-psychic level, intra-couple level, or at the level of maintenance of homeostasis in a family or wider social system.

IMPLICATIONS FOR THERAPY AND RESEARCH

There are two main therapeutic implications that can be drawn from our central hypotheses.

1) In each individual or family that presents with an alcohol problem, it is important to ascertain how the drinking behavior is serving an adaptive function. The maladaptive aspects are readily apparent and can usually be recited quite easily by doctor, patient, and family members. Usually, in spite of the mutual agreement of how terrible drinking is, the drinking pattern continues, with a concomitant increase of feelings of frustration on everybody's part. Care must be taken to avoid this trap and to concentrate, during the history-taking and clinical observation, on what is adaptive about the drinking. In this way more useful information can be gathered, and a better therapeutic alliance established.

2) Once the adaptive consequences of drinking have been ascertained, therapy may be structured around helping the patient to manifest the adaptive behavior while sober, instead of only during

drinking, and to learn effective alternative behaviors. In a well-equipped, in-patient clinical research lab, we found video tape self-confrontation very helpful in this regard, although care must be taken to ensure that the confrontation focuses on the adaptive consequences of drinking and doesn't become another aversive experience contributing to the frustration of self-help efforts.

Similar considerations must be kept in mind in designing a research strategy. An awareness of the variety of systems operating will be essential. Peter Steinglass developed a naturalistic research design to allow for in-home evaluation of behavior both sober and intoxicated at the family level. The presence or absence of adaptive consequences were indirectly measured. The most salient findings were that there were predictable stereotypical interactional patterns, but different ones depending on whether alcohol was present or absent. These patterns, while unique to each family, were quite rigid or inflexible, particularly in the presence of alcohol. (6)

CLINICAL ILLUSTRATIONS

In each of the clinical vignettes that will be presented in this chapter, the use of alcohol has an ongoing, adaptive function. Originally, there may have been psychological or pharmacological reasons for the drinking behavior; yet the behavior persists because it is currently being reinforced at least intermittently.

Case One: A Marital Couple

In the case of a couple in psychotherapy with one of our colleagues, the wife was labeled by herself, by her spouse, and by her neighbors as the alcoholic in the family. She was frequently drunk, and when drunk, was quite outspoken and verbally aggressive. When sober, she was typically quiet and demure. Both drunk and sober behaviors were observed numerous times in therapy. After some weeks of weekly family therapy, a pattern emerged in which it appeared that in a session following a stressful therapy hour, the wife predictably arrived acting drunk and argued with the therapist, while her spouse sat quietly, as was his custom. Upon careful inquiry, it was discovered that the woman had drunk no more than two ounces of alcohol before these sessions (while her husband had been drinking at least twice as much).

That this pattern of behavior within the therapy setting was typical was supported by historical evidence that a similar pattern had been used by the couple in handling conflictual situations between the family and the outside community. For example, in an episode occurring 15 years prior to therapy, their daughter developed an acute fever and abdominal symptoms late one evening. The pediatrician who was called advised antipyretics and an office visit in the morning. However, the child appeared to her mother to be seriously ill, and after several hours with no change in symptomatology, the wife wanted to call the pediatrician back. Her husband urged her not to, saying that doctors know best and that it wasn't right to be bothering the doctor at two A.M. But his wife persisted, an argument ensued, she started drinking, and when behaviorally drunk, called the doctor back, insisting that he see the child that night. He acquiesced, the child was taken to the local Emergency Room, was found to have an intestinal intussusception and was operated on that night, with a positive outcome.

Using the medical model, the wife's "drunken behavior" would probably be seen as obstreperous and obnoxious, and treatment would likely consist of disulfiram, aversive conditioning, or admonitions. From our perspective the wife's "drunken behavior" served an adaptive role in allowing the couple to respond to a perceived threat from the outside world. It would appear, in this case, that the alcohol has served as a prop in the presence of which assertive behavior becomes expressible by the wife and, perhaps, tolerable for the husband. The consequences of drinking for the wife appear to involve both assertiveness in the face of a perceived threat and tacit approval from her spouse, both of which reinforce her drinking behavior. Treatment, then, is focused on bringing to the attention of the couple the role alcohol has been seen to serve and on teaching more successful means of interacting without alcohol.

In this case, therapy never progressed to the point of learning more successful modes of interacting. The therapist found himself accepting the family belief-system that drinking is the problem and drinking is intractable. Before adequately helping the couple to see the reinforcing, systems aspects of their drinking, he prematurely fell back on his familiar methods of therapy and began making observations on how the couple related to one another and to him. Soon the couple panicked. They informed him, with some wisdom, that they appreciated his interest in them, that they "knew" their way of doing things made no sense, but that it was their way, they had no other, and it would be best not to tamper with it anymore.

Case Two: Two Brothers

Another case in which alcohol serves an adaptive function within a family has been reported by Steinglass and colleagues (7). Two brothers, both chronic alcoholics, who were admitted together to a research program which involved experimentally induced intoxication, gave the following history of their drinking relationship with each other. The older brother had led a life characterized by frequent changes in job and geographic location and a peripheral relationship to the family. The younger brother's life, by contrast, seemed externally stable. He had been married for 15 years and maintained close ties to the extended family. However, whereas his external life suggested relatively greater strength and stability, his reaction to alcohol was one of increasing violence. After a particularly violent, drunken episode, during which he severely beat his mother, his older brother was called home in the hope that he would act as a stabilizing and controlling element for him.

Although both were heavy drinkers, they would rarely be drunk simultaneously. The typical drinking bout would be initiated by the older brother after considerable encouragement from his sibling. The younger brother would then follow suit, but the older brother would simultaneously decrease his drinking, and, being relatively sober, function as a watchdog for his more provocative and aggressive brother. Exactly this sequence of behaviors occurred during the research study when these men were allowed to consume alcohol together on a voluntary basis.

From the perspective of a medical model, these two brothers would be of genetic interest as siblings now living apart, yet having the same addiction. In their treatment, the brothers would likely be seen separately and each exposed to some aversive responses to their drinking conditions.

Looked at from the point of view of the adaptive uses of alcohol, however, these brothers had established a drinking relationship that offered the opportunity for the controlled and manageable expression of aggressive, even violent, tendencies. It seemed likely, in addition, that this drinking relationship, at least on some occasions, allowed a perpetuation of a system in the family, the maintenance of which was reinforcing for each brother.

This formulation might lead to a very different treatment model from the medical one alone. The two brothers would be seen together at times; their drinking situations would be analyzed retrospectively and as they occurred; their uses of alcohol would be elucidated and clarified; and a more viable family system and means of reducing, coping with, or expressing aggression would be sought, along with all necessary means being applied to helping each individual achieve sobriety.

Case Three: A Family

Another example of adaptive consequences maintaining the use of alcohol within a family is provided by the following observations. A family was videotaped twice: first when the husband, the identified alcoholic, was sober, and second, during a session of experimentally induced intoxication for the husband. Most striking was the increased animation by all the family members during the intoxicated interview, even though only one of them was drinking. Although there were many verbal complaints about the husband's drinking, there was a great deal of laughing and joking by family members during the second session. Interestingly, while viewing the two tapes in a subsequent session, there was again a great deal of hilarity when watching the "drunken" tape. The complaints and other pointed comments made only during the drinking session seemed quite accurate expressions; yet they were spoken as if they would not be remembered because they were said in the presence of alcohol. Thus, the family had established a system in which affective communication was present during the husband's drinking and not while he was sober.

One might be tempted to use these observations to show the alcoholic how maladaptive his drinking was. After all, his drinking laid him open to criticism from his family. From an adaptive standpoint, however, we might see the greater intensity of relating and more open contact with the father when drinking as serving to reestablish bonds in the family and justify current roles in the family system.

In any case, what is most important about the comparison of drinking and nondrinking conditions in this family is not simply that the family behaved differently, but that their changed behavior probably was a reinforcing consequence of the drinking behavior for the alcoholic.

Case Four: Mr. A.

The following clinical example will help illustrate the therapeutic implication of our hypotheses within the context of a preliminary, naturalistic research design. Peter Steinglass, David Berenson and I worked with psychotherapy groups of five or six alcoholics, when they were drinking as well as when they were not drinking, while they were hospitalized on the clinical research ward of the NIAAA Laboratory of Alcohol Research. The experience of one man in one of these groups will help illustrate the formulation of, as well as the potential application of, the hypotheses in this chapter.

Briefly, Mr. A. was one of five men who spent four consecutive weeks as inpatients on the hospital unit and who took part in a one-and-one-half-hour group psychotherapy session every weekday throughout the four weeks. The first ten days, alcohol was not available. During the next ten days, alcohol was made freely available to each man, and group sessions continued. The last week, drinking was not permitted. Most sessions were video taped, and sessions during drinking as well as nondrinking periods were played back to the group during the final, sober week.

Mr. A. took part in the group verbally from the start, but his voice was barely audible the first week. When disagreed with, he uniformly acquiesced to the other person. A tall man, he usually sat back, deep into his seat, head low, with his back bent over. During the ten days of drinking, Mr. A. drank increasingly heavily throughout, reaching a peak of 32 ounces of 100-proof alcohol in one day. During the first few days of drinking Mr. A.'s verbal participation in the group increased only moderately. His effectiveness in terms of audibility, being listened to without interruption, and actively defending his position to the point that others listened to him increased greatly. At least when talking, he now sat upright or forward. As days of drinking progressed, Mr. A. became so intoxicated that he had difficulty keeping his eyes open in the group or putting words together, though when he did participate, the qualities of increased assertiveness were still evident.

In viewing video tapes of drinking sessions during the subsequent sober phase, Mr. A., like the other men, first looked at his drunken demeanor. As was typical of the group, he had expected to be shown, for shock value, evidence of lack of control and general sloppiness while drinking. Instead the adaptive elements of his drinking, before his level of consciousness was affected, were pointed out. He seemed genuinely surprised to see his own increased assertiveness and concomitant increased effectiveness in the group. Several times in the last week, Mr. A. was encouraged to discuss again issues that he had discussed in the drinking session and to express opinions on current issues. Increasingly, he seemed to be reproducing the more effective elements of his drinking behavior without drinking, and this fact was repeatedly pointed out to Mr. A. by therapists and by other group members. At termination, Mr. A. elected to be referred to a new group psychotherapy program.

DISCUSSION

The idea of alcoholism as a final common pathway (8) and of alcoholism as the expression of an intrinsic logic for the individual alcoholic (9) has been raised before. Steinglass first drew attention to the apparent systems-maintenance aspects of drinking operating between familial pairs (7). MacAndrew and Edgerton have illustrated how differing social expectations may have maintained a wide variety of drinking patterns, especially among different Indian tribes. (10) Hunt and Azrin reported quite successful outcomes with a small number of alcoholics using broad-scope manipulations of environment combined with some training in making use of these changed living and work conditions. (11)

Thus, by the early 1970s, a small but increasing number of workers were treating the abuse of alcohol as if they assumed it was an adaptive behavior, subject to the usual rules of reinforcement governing most other behaviors. Others had not dealt directly with the question of what had been maintaining the use of alcohol prior to the use of modification procedures nor with the value of attempting, in therapy, to discover significant reinforcers of alcohol use. It was with the idea of generating a hypothesis, therefore, that my colleagues and I first presented, in 1974, the clinical observations discussed in this chapter, illustrating both what we believe to be examples of reinforcement of drinking and the broad range of interactional situations that can be examined fruitfully in treatment and research with alcoholics.

References

1. U. S. Department of Health, Education and Welfare, NIAAA. *First special report to the U.S. Congress on alcohol and health*. 1971.
2. Goodwin, D. W., et al. Alcohol problems in adoptees raised apart from biological parents. *Archives of General Psychiatry, 28* (1973): 238–243.

3. Mendelson, J. H., et al. Experimentally induced intoxication and withdrawal in alcoholics. 3. Psychiatric findings. *Quarterly Journal of Studies on Alcohol: Supplement, 2* (1964): 40–52.
4. Tamerin, J. S., & Mendelson, J. H. The psychodynamics of chronic inebriation: Observations of alcoholics during the process of drinking in an experimental group setting. *American Journal of Psychiatry, 125* (1969): 886–899.
5. Nathan, P. E., et al. Comparative studies of the interpersonal and affective behavior of alcoholics and non-alcoholics during prolonged experimental drinking. In N. K. Mello & J. H. Mendelson (Eds.). *Recent advances in studies of alcoholism: An interdisciplinary symposium* (HSM Publication No. 71–9045). Washington, D. C.: U. S. Government Printing Office, 1971.
6. Steinglass, P. The alcoholic family at home. *Archives of General Psychiatry, 38* (1981): 578–584.
7. Steinglass, P., et al. A systems approach to alcoholism. *Archives of General Psychiatry,* 24 (1971): 401–408.
8. Chafetz, M. Fact and myth in alcoholism: A call for high-quality research. In F. A. Seixas (Ed.). Nature and nurture in alcoholism. *Annals of the New York Academy of Sciences, 197* (1972): 8–10.
9. Bateson, G. The cybernetics of "self": A theory of alcoholism. *Psychiatry, 34* (1971): 1–18.
10. MacAndrew, C., & Edgerton, R. B. *Drunken Comportment*. Hawthorne, NY: Aldine, 1969.
11. Hunt, G. M., & Azrin, N. H. A community-reinforcement approach to alcoholism. *Behaviour Research and Therapy, 11* (1973): 91–104.

CHAPTER 2

THE FAMILY IN ALCOHOLISM

Alcoholism does not occur as an isolated event affecting one individual. For every case, there are multiple victims. The primary victims are usually the alcoholic and his/her immediate family, although colleagues, unknown pedestrians, and many others may at times feel the consequences as well. This chapter will focus on the more compelling reasons for including the family when dealing with an alcoholic.

FAMILY ISSUES IN ALCOHOLISM

It is becoming common knowledge that only a very small percentage of alcoholics are living on skid-row; nonetheless, the bias toward dealing with alcoholics as isolated individuals persists. Therefore, it seems worth stating that most alcoholics do not live alone. In our own recent survey of the drinking and other drug-taking habits of several thousand general medical, surgical and psychiatric patients in a university medical center, we found that the majority of heavy and problem drinkers were still living with at least one family member. Of those who were not, most were living in a stable relationship with at least one significant other and had been for three or more years. Furthermore, most of the problem drinkers either living alone or without such long-term relationships were young adults.

A special word is in order about alcoholics in their twenties and thirties—those we refer to here as "young adults." Clinically, we have usually found it a mistake to assume that young adult problem drinkers, regardless of domicile, are independent of their families of origin. As has been more rigorously documented by Vaillant (1) and Stanton (2) regarding adult male heroin addicts, young adult alcoholics are usually found to be in frequent contact with one or both parents, either by telephone or in person. Further, it is common to find that they move back into the home of their parents intermittently. More importantly, even when they do not move back into their parents' home, the degree to which they include their parents in the process of making important decisions about their own lives is often extensive.

The fact that alcoholics live with, or in some important way are in contact with significant others is only one dimension of the rationale for looking to the family for help in treating alcoholism. Along more functional dimensions, all aspects of family life are compromised when a member of the family is abusing alcohol. The marital relationships, parenting, and often development of the children suffer.

It is doubtful that there are any good marriages in which one or both spouses are alcoholics and still drinking heavily. Studies recently reviewed by Paolino and McCrady have shown that divorce is higher in marriages with an active alcoholic than in marriages without an active alcoholic (3). There is no data from which to conclude either that alcoholism causes a greater number of divorces or that bad marriages cause alcoholism. From a treatment standpoint, however, it is enough to know that in the family system of an alcoholic there is an unusual risk of disruption in members' lives and of morbidity. Divorce itself has these consequences. Divorce among actively drinking alcoholics leaves a family system less well-prepared to weather a marital breakup than most family systems. Thus, the assessment of the need for help in the marital relationship of married alcoholics seems indicated.

Clinically, what I and many others who have shared their clinical and personal experiences with me have found is that chronic alcoholics and their spouses often have great difficulty resolving their differences if the alcoholic continues to drink heavily. This applies not just to issues unique to alcoholism but to any of the broad range of inevitable dilemmas that arise in any marriage. When there is a difference of opinion, and one spouse has the option of an altered state of consciousness, couples do not stay at the task of problem-solving until differences are reconciled.

Such a marital deficit can become a serious factor in the early phases of abstinence. The clinician frequently observes a disillusionment during the period just after abstinence is initiated. It seems to have to do with the discovery that, while individuals are recovering and less tense, the marriage remains unsatisfactory or stressful. Lack of mutual problem-solving mechanisms is probably a major contributor to this disillusionment. In fact, abstinence is often associated with heightened awareness of interpersonal conflict as the couple carry their talks further, no longer constrained by one partner's falling asleep or becoming uncontrollably angry. Soon they discover that they are truly at an impasse. For example, couples come to realize that they still do not agree, or no longer agree, on such matters as when to have children, how many children to have, whether to buy a house, whether to ask a grandparent to move in or out, when to have sex, and on numerous other issues of significance for that particular family.

Parenting suffers as well as the marital relationship when alcoholism is present in a parent. It is well known that a high frequency of alcohol use has been associated with the physical abuse of children by parents. Not all of that abuse is by chronic heavy drinkers, and not all alcoholic parents physically abuse their children. There are, however, more subtle areas of child neglect that many would say are inevitable consequences of chronic alcoholism. A description of an interview with the mother of a four-year-old girl will help to illustrate this point. As a consultant, I was asked to interview a woman in her mid-twenties who had been hospitalized for two weeks for an acute depression. She had just been abandoned by the man with whom she had been living for several years, who was the father of her four-year-old daughter. The problem for the consultant was to understand the role of alcohol in this woman's depression. It was originally thought that the patient had been drinking a pint of hard liquor a day since becoming depressed in the few weeks previous to hospitalization. Her history showed that a similar pattern had apparently emerged following the same man's departure two years earlier. But a brief but persistent inquiry led to the finding that this young mother had, in fact, been drinking a pint or so of hard liquor daily for at least eight years. Subsequent probes readily uncovered the myriad ways in which alcohol had interfered in her life, affecting her performance on her job, driving, socializing, and in fact directly contributing to her mate's two decisions to leave. She was proud, though, that she had protected her little daughter from the ravages of drinking. There she drew the line. She was a good mother and clearly loved her daughter dearly. Still, it soon became apparent that she was unwittingly neglecting her daughter. When asked how she, mother, was able to stay awake long enough in the evening to be with her daughter, she replied with genuine pride, "Oh, she's a very independent little girl." It emerged that mother was increasingly taking daughter to grandmother to be cared for, both because mother worked later to make up for her poor work in the morning hours and because she could not handle her child to her own satisfaction. Grandmother, however, did not want to care for a small child. After once again claiming that the four-year-old could "take care of herself," mother began to cry and acknowledged that she was an alcoholic and that her alcoholism was even leading her to become a poor parent.

Children of alcoholics become victims in ways that are even harder to document than neglect is (4,5). Two such ways were highlighted in a broadcast featuring a panel of alcohol educators, of which I was one (6). The first way is that the children of alcoholics commonly take responsibility for their parent's alcoholism (just as children often describe ways in which they think their behavior is responsible for their parents' divorce). They feel and act guilty, and they may also feel and act angry at having to bear the burden of this guilt. They may sulk and retreat socially, or they may achieve highly. There are many different reactions to perceiving that one's parent is an alcoholic. Some common, clinically observed characteristics of these children, which they describe in therapy sessions and share among themselves in Alateen (an organization for teenagers who have an alcoholic parent), are that they believe they are in some ways responsible, that they dwell on the issue, that they sometimes go to great lengths to either make their parent happier or compensate for what that parent can no longer do, and that they are not very happy in their own lives. The research to back up these specific clinical impressions is lacking, although there is ample evidence of hardships and high risks of behavioral consequences for the children of alcoholics (7,8,).

Other important consequences of alcoholism to children of alcoholics are apparent only when they reach maturity. The second consequence highlighted on the panel mentioned has to do with the frequent limitations in the capacities of these children even as adults to experience pleasure and to maintain intimate relationships. Having lacked competent parental models for mutual problem-solving, and having adapted often with denial of their own natural childhood impulses in the absence of reliable parental figures upon whom to lean when necessary, even otherwise highly successful adult children of alcoholics are in need of guidance to develop self and mutual pleasuring skills (6).

Another major adult-onset consequence to children of alcoholics is their predisposition either to develop some substance abuse problem themselves or to marry someone who has or develops alcoholism. The reference here is to familial, nongenetic factors. Goodwin has reviewed the state of the knowledge of the role of genetics in the development of alcoholism and concluded that some genetic factor may contribute to at least a predisposition toward alcoholic behavior and the severe complications of alcoholism when heavy drinking is present (9). We cannot do justice here to the issue of the role of genes in the transmission of alcoholism, except to say further that Goodwin and others have also concluded that genes alone do not explain fully the distribution and variety of alcoholism problems arising in the offspring of alcoholics. Environment clearly contributes to the documented increased incidence of alcoholism in the children and the grandchildren of alcoholics when compared with offspring of nonalcoholic parents.

There are two types of issues to keep in mind in assessing the risks to the next generation. One is that of increased drug use. The other deals with behavior that may facilitate or foster alcoholism in the family system of offspring but not necessarily in the child. The latter is more theoretical as yet. Clinically, it appears that nonalcoholics who grew up with an untreated (and often unacknowledged) alcoholic adult often seem to have a high threshold of tolerance for heavy or problem drinking in a spouse. When the spouse of an alcoholic has such a background, the whole family is more ready to deny the existence of alcoholism.

One does not have to postulate deviousness on the part of such spouses to understand how they have come to put up with heavy drinking and drunken behavior for as long as they have. In fact, in their recent extensive review, Paolino and McCrady appear to have debunked the theories of disturbed personality in spouses of alcoholics as significant contributors to alcoholism (3). That does not detract from the impact of alcoholism in the spouse's family of origin on the maintenance of an alcohol problem in the present family. The experiences in the family of origin alone is often reason to include the spouse in the educational process of the early phase of intervention with alcoholism without fear that the clinician is necessarily up against a personality in need of basic change.

One more aspect that may justify inclusion of the family in the treatment of the alcoholic is the family interactional consequences of alcoholism. A number of both clinical research and laboratory research studies have now appeared on the interaction of the members of families that have one or more alcoholics or other drug abusers. In our own review of this literature we concluded that what stands out from these studies is the important role that family interactional processes seem to play in maintaining the alcohol or other drug-abuse behavior of an individual (10).

We are not addressing the issue of causality. There is nothing in this literature to either support or disprove that there is a role for family interaction processes in the etiology of alcoholism. Rather, we are talking about how problem behavior involving the use of alcohol may actually be sustained by family interaction, even after the drinking behavior has become clearly destructive. We are talking about the ways alcohol abuse and drunken behavior seem to come to serve a function for a family regardless of whether the family can be seen to have played a role in the development of the problem in the first place. As discussed in Chapter 1, we have employed the term "adaptive consequences of drinking" to describe the functions that alcoholic behavior may come to serve in a family (11).

A case example of a research situation with a family of an alcoholic will help illustrate the concept of how a family can adapt to a drinking problem and in turn how the family's adaptation can come to serve as a source of resistance to change in the drinking behavior. The father in this family was a chronic heavy drinker of many years' duration. He still had his job, however, and continued to live with his wife. Their adult daughter had recently been discharged from a psychiatric hospital for depression. She alternated between living in her parents' home and living on her own, but only a block away. Just prior to taking part in the research, the three had entered family therapy, which was the last of many attempts, including a trial with Alcoholics Anonymous, to get help for father's drinking problem. One part of the research study involved the use of the largely nonverbal psychodramatic technique of family sculpting. In this case, each family member was instructed by a research psychologist, who was not involved in their therapy, to characterize or portray a typical family situation, using the other two family members and themselves as the characters. They were asked to do this under two conditions, first when alcohol was not present and then, again, when alcohol was introduced into the scene.

Only mother's response will be described. Without alcohol in the picture, mother had her husband sit in a chair right next to her, but sitting parallel to her rather than looking directly at her. She further instructed father that he was to "put up a barrier" whenever she either spoke to him or turned to look at him. He was to do so by raising his jacket up and holding it between them. At the same time, daughter was instructed to walk both toward and away from both parents, back and forth, apparently without making conversation or having eye contact with her parents. When mother was told, "Now alcohol is introduced; what is it like now?", she immediately sent father to the farthest corner of the room and said he was out of the picture. She then moved to the opposite corner of the room from him and had her daughter come sit in a chair right next to her, facing her; and she indicated that she and her daughter were in conversation. Mother also indicated that all three of them were having at least a little something to drink.

The family members were asked to describe their feelings in these situations. But even if we ignore the descriptions of their affect, the simple changes in position and activity offer us a poignant example of the differences in this family under drinking and nondrinking circumstances. The most prominent observation was that when alcohol was not present in this family, no one was really in contact with anyone else. When alcohol was introduced, at least the daughter was no longer vacillating between leaving her parents and staying with them.

Both father's and daughter's portrayal of their family with and without alcohol were quite similar to mother's, with the exception that each of them showed daughter becoming more connected with her father, as well as with mother, when father was drinking. We would speculate from this example that father's drinking, regardless of how it got started, has come to serve in this family at least the function of keeping their adult daughter in more direct contact with her parents. We would further speculate that, should father succeed in becoming abstinent, the family would serve as a source of resistance to sustaining his abstinence, unless either (1) mother and father were helped to find an alternative way of keeping daughter connected with them, or (2) mother and father were helped to find new ways to tolerate their relationship together once daughter had finally moved out.

This illustration from research experience provides us with an example of how we might find evidence that the drinking behavior of an alcoholic has come to serve a significant function within his or her family. The resistance to giving up such a function could be great, even among well-intentioned family members, unless the family is helped to either substitute for the function or make the function unnecessary.

Readers familiar with recent family systems terminology might think of this change in function in terms, as described by Stanton (12), of the daughter's "orbit" among her family members becoming altered. It should be emphasized that, while the above example was derived from a research experience, within a different context the same experience might have occurred in the course of family therapy, and often does. Of course, the particular role the drinking may have come to serve is likely to be different for each family.

The family and marital issues discussed above provide a theoretical basis for including family interaction in the treatment of the alcoholic. Drawing upon this material, one could posit an argument that, with such pervasive interpersonal consequences of alcoholism, would it not be productive to treat alcoholism with a family/marital technique most of the time? If these family issues are usually operating, one should be able to accomplish several things through family interaction that one cannot accomplish through treatment of the identified alcoholic patient alone. First, a concomitant marital disturbance can be treated. Second, the negative emotional and behavioral consequences in children can be treated or prevented. Third, the resistance from other family members to the alcoholic's sustaining an effective therapeutic change (abstinence, in particular) can be avoided. The alternative to each of these expectations is that the successful treatment of the individual alcoholic alone will just as frequently and effectively deal with each of these concerns. These are all testable arguments and hopefully, in the future, will be adequately examined. Only rudimentary direct testing of these alternatives exists to date. For example, there is evidence from studies with widely used marital inventories that marriages do improve some when an alcoholic simply stops drinking (13,3). On the other hand, there is also evidence that interpersonal stress (such as marital stress) is more likely than other life stresses to lead to a renewed bout of heavy drinking among abstinent alcoholics (14,15).

However, research simply does not yet thoroughly answer these important theoretical questions. There do appear to be, though, some pragmatic reasons for bringing family approaches to an alcohol problem. For example, working with families, even at the most peripheral level, has been shown to offer benefits in the treatment of alcoholism. It has been shown that, regardless of the type of treatment offered ultimately, just having a family member accompany an alcoholic patient at the time of an initial interview was associated with alcoholics staying in treatment longer (16).

Experience to date with *bona fide* family therapy approaches to alcoholism also provides a substantial pragmatic basis for attempting more family work in the field, even in the absence of definitive outcome data. In the past decade, there has been a rapprochement between the two rapidly developing fields of alcoholism treatment and family therapy that has not always existed. In fact, the widespread adaptation of the many recent advances in family therapy to the field of alcoholism treatment was quite slow in developing (17). The literature that exists on family therapy for alcoholism has been reviewed recently by several authors. Briefly, all reviewers concluded that methodologically definitive studies comparing the outcome of family therapy with other approaches to the treatment of alcoholism have not yet been done (17,18,3,19). However, Steinglass emphasized that there is in the literature a sound basis of support for more conclusive treatment outcome studies in the future (17); while Janzen found that there is, at the very least, evidence that family therapy for alcoholism has, at times, been a successful mode of intervention in and of itself (18). Paolino and McCrady note that the several behavioral marital therapy studies in the literature provide a combined treatment outcome success rate of 70 percent or better (3), which compares favorably with success rates in the range of 60 percent for alcohol treatment outcome studies in general (20). These outcome comparisons are based solely on the evaluation of the drinking behavior of the identified alcoholic. Abstinence and usually also decreased drinking at follow-up are taken as indicators of successful outcome. Measurement of family, marital, and child behavior in the family of the alcoholic are not yet a strong part of even our best treatment outcome studies. However, Harwin has reported on one extensive outcome study by Gacic at the Center for Family Therapy for Alcoholism in Belgrade, Yugoslavia, in the late 1970s which did include measures of both family functioning and drinking behavior and which did show significantly better results on both measures for family treatment when compared with their own traditional, non-family treatment for an earlier, comparable population (19). That study also showed a close correlation between the achievement of abstinence and improvement in family functioning. Seventy-eight percent of the family therapy treatment group (50 cases) achieved abstinence, and 90 percent improved in family functioning, while in the control group 38 percent improved on both drinking and family measures. Improvements for the family therapy treatment group were sustained at both one-year and five-year follow-ups. Unfortunately, comparable follow-up data for the control group were either not done or not made available. The family therapy offered was quite extensive, all on an out-patient basis. There was an initial preparatory stage lasting "one to a hundred" sessions. This was followed by a two-month period of intensive daily treatment. A third and final phase, other than follow-up interviews, consisted of weekly family-therapy sessions for a year or more. Larger network contacts by therapists were also made with friends, other relatives, and employers.

Going beyond the literature and into the field, Coleman and Davis have found additional support for bringing family therapy into the mainstream of alcoholism treatment (21). This report on a National Survey of over 2,000 treatment programs in the United States which offer treatment for the abuse of drugs, including alcohol, revealed a high level of enthusiasm for family approaches to addictive disorders among at least some of the staff of most of the programs surveyed. To summarize briefly, the survey revealed a high level of intuitive interest in the appropriateness of family therapy approaches to substance abuse, whether of alcohol or other drugs. Unfortunately, there was not a comparable, consistently high level of family therapy expertise found with which to implement this intuition. Even so, those therapists who were already using some form of family approach answered uniformly that they would continue doing so; and those programs with the least family therapy expertise, rather than being pessimistic about the benefits of family work, indicated a strong desire to be offered family therapy training.

There is no data yet to demonstrate a primary prevention outcome for the treatment of alcohol problems. There has been a study that documented that family therapy can serve a primary prevention role. Klein, Alexander and colleagues (22) conducted a well-controlled treatment-outcome study with court-referred, delinquent adolescents. One of their most remarkable findings was that, two to three years later, there was a significantly lower incidence of court appearances for delinquent behavior among the younger siblings of those delinquent adolescents whose families had been offered therapy, but not among those whose families had not been. Like children in the families of a delinquent, children in families with an alcoholic member have a high incidence of both drug-related and non-drug-related behavior disturbances. In both cases, these families are much in need of preventive intervention. Since there is evidence that family therapy has served a *bona fide* preventive function, it would seem wise to consider family therapy with families of alcoholics for its possible preventive benefits as well as for all the other reasons discussed. Future problems of the children of alcoholics, or the transmission of alcohol-related behavior problems to future generations, have never been assessed as outcome variables in a prospective, comparison-group treatment-outcome study, but they should be. There is ample reason to warrant such a study on a large scale, without which it would be impossible to document what may turn out to be the single most substantial reason for treating the family when dealing with alcoholism.

Family and Marital Intervention

Working with the family of the alcoholic is the province of the family practitioner or any other provider of health care services. There are interventions with other family members, short of family work by therapists trained in family and marital techniques, that can be of considerable importance. Simply questioning others in the family can provide needed confirmation of an alcohol problem. A family member present at the outset of treatment can be a great help not only in clearly identifying an alcohol problem but also in effectively confronting a person with the problem. Having a spouse confirm that he or she, as well as the therapist, sees the problem as alcoholism can be a major step in overcoming the denial that both alcoholic and spouse have been living with for many years. Direct contact with family members is also the best way to detect substance abuse or other serious problems in others in the family. Undetected substance abuse in the spouse, parent, or child of an alcoholic can add immeasurably to the length and inefficiency of treatment.

The likelihood that spouses will attend Al-anon and children Alateen is greater if the therapist has direct contact with the family to allow for its education and encouragement. Attendance at either may have the benefit of reducing excessive reactions by spouses or children to the alcoholic's drinking, thereby reducing time wasted on fights and decreasing the excuses for further drinking as well. Along a similar line, another practical way a nonfamily therapist might choose to reduce conflicts and excuses is to prescribe that *disulfiram* (Antabuse) be taken in front of the spouse daily. In selected couples, this has appeared to decrease fear in the spouse and to speed the restoration of mutual trust. Certain precautions should be taken, of course. For some couples, the latter approach would only replicate numerous previous solutions that have failed and would therefore be inappropriate. It is also true that, while Al-anon and Alateen for family members and AA for the alcoholic may increase the self-sufficiency of each individual, they may do so without improving family relationships at all. In these situations, and when there are clear-cut marital conflicts or child-neglect issues, family therapy should be considered.

There are several approaches to family therapy that have been applied with some success in these situations. From their extensive review of the literature on the marital treatment of alcoholism and from their own work, Paolino and McCrady have leaned toward the use of behavioral marital therapy techniques (3). They draw particularly upon the work of Weiss, et al. (23) and of Stuart (24) on the application of conflict resolution techniques and on the means of making relationships more mutually rewarding. Berenson (25) has described approaches to family therapy for alcoholics that are taken primarily from the structural family therapy techniques of Minuchin (26), as well as the strategic and often paradoxical approaches described by Haley (27) and by Watzlawick, Weakland, and Fisch (28). As he indicates, these approaches are compatible with behavioral marital therapy techniques and often combined with them. He also integrates Bowen's family systems theory (29, 30) with these approaches, either as an alternative or as part of a second phase of therapy. As was noted earlier in this chapter, young-adult substance abusers seem to be surprisingly involved with their families of origin. Bowen's emphasis on the use of therapy to help the person more successfully individuate from his family of origin would seem to many in the field to go right to the heart of the issue for the alcohol- or other drug-abusing young adult. Nevertheless, techniques that focus more on immediate problem-solving (31) may need to come first if the drinking is to cease. These include structural techniques for altering roles in coalitions and thereby shifting the structural context of the family, leaving more flexibility in roles and behaviors for the alcoholic to attempt.

Using the strategic approach, there is often an essential paradox introduced, in that alcoholism is clearly defined as the number-one problem, and then, having done that, the therapist shifts the focus to problems in other members of the family and within relationships. Then it becomes possible to achieve a redefinition of people's roles in the family. For example, the alcoholic may be seen as protecting an obese wife from depression through calling attention to his own problems, thereby placing the alcoholic's behavior into a caring context. Similarly, it may be possible to show that the spouse, whose behavior has been experienced by the alcoholic as critical and domineering, is in fact in need of and desirous of help. Children who have come to see the alcoholic parent as someone not to be taken seriously, and therefore lacking in authority over them, may find themselves surprisingly acting out the role of children in need of help who are turning to the more experienced and caring (alcoholic) parent. Sometimes families need to experience such redefinitions of the meaning of their family's interaction in order to dare to give up alcoholic drinking behavior. As Watzlawick, et al. (28) have indicated, often the solutions that families have come up with are in themselves the problem. Alcohol abuse, or behaviors that have the effect of maintaining alcohol abuse, can be seen as solutions that have become the problem. When this is the case, alternative behaviors which may be brought about by surprising or paradoxical interventions are often called for. The effects of these interventions must be accepted by all the members of the family system in which the alcoholic lives. A therapist may need family therapy techniques in order to guide family members to and help them tolerate the new and therefore unpredictable family situation.

There are a few points to be made about family therapy used for alcoholism that apply without regard to the type of family approach used. A very practical role for family therapy that is seldom written about but has much to offer is the use of family therapy in a complementary way with AA, Al-anon and Alateen. This is the subject of Chapter 9, a brief preview of which follows.

Family therapy can be used effectively to get previously recalcitrant alcoholics into AA and their spouses into Al-anon. It has been a great help in maintaining their participation in AA self-help groups. Family therapy and self-help groups can each reinforce the other's emphasis on taking responsibility for one's own behavior. What family therapy adds particularly to the approach of the self-help groups is direct work on relationships. Often disillusionment occurs when abstinence is newly achieved and the marital or parenting relationships are found to be no better, or sometimes even to be generating more anxiety than before. This can be anticipated, planned for, and modified through the addition of family therapy to an otherwise successful approach to change in AA.

There has been much fear and resentment about psychotherapy among many of the proponents of the AA self-help groups. Many of the misgivings have stemmed from the experiences of alcoholics with, first individual and more recently also family, therapists who failed to explicitly address the drinking problem. Their concern is that, with the growth of the family therapy field, family therapy, like individual therapies before it, may also be offered as an alternative to the self-help groups and that ignorance of alcohol combined with zeal for a new therapy will again fail to appropiately address the alcohol problems.

A family therapist who fails to explicitly set the elimination of the drinking problem as a first priority is making a mistake. Altering roles or improving communication or the expression of affect among family members in and of itself is not likely to proceed well if the drinking of an alcoholic in the family continues. It is unrealistic for family therapists to assume that, if they forget about the alcohol problem and somehow deal effectively with other underlying problems, the alcoholic drinking will go away. On the other hand, when the family therapist is knowledgeable about the problem of alcohol and establishes a clear agreement with all members of the family that overcoming the drinking problem is an objective of the first priority, family therapy has much to contribute; and it can be used in conjunction with self-help groups.

Finally, here are a few practical suggestions. First, the earlier the family is brought in to see the therapist, the more likely members are to cooperate with the family approach and, as was stated earlier, the more likely the abuser is to stay in treatment. Second, alcoholics and their families are among the most difficult of all psychotherapy patients to get into the office. Direct phone calls to each family member, especially from the eventual therapist, are often critical. Repeat calls may be necessary, but it is worth the initial effort because once the family gets involved the odds are good that they will continue. It is often critical to include in family sessions the parents of young-adult alcoholics, even if the latter are living away from their parents and with a spouse. The restoration or establishment of a traditional parent-child hierarchy around the issue of the irresponsible behavior that goes along with alcohol abuse is a key step, without which the abuser's further individuation from his parents aborts and drinking is likely to resume. When the alcoholism resides in an older parent, the children should be incorporated into therapy at least temporarily. As with a spouse, children will automatically resist the changes when drinking behavior stops, unless they are helped to adapt well to the change.

Finally, in family therapy for alcoholism, as in family therapy for other conditions, the control in sessions must be firmly established in and by the therapist. An aspect of control that is critical in therapy for alcoholism is the control over medication. Besides alcohol, the alcoholic is often using and abusing tranquilizers, pain medications, antidepressants or amphetamines, as well. Even where the therapist is not a physician, she or he must be accepted by anyone else involved in providing psychoactive substances to the alcoholic or to a member of the alcoholic's family as an authority with whom all psychoactive drug-giving decisions are reviewed. Ideally, a close collaboration will evolve between the family therapist and any or all nonpsychiatric physicians. Only then does it become impossible for alcoholic and family to perpetuate the problems associated with an altered state of consciousness through access to prescription psychoactive drugs. Many of the above clinical benefits of thinking about the family in treating alcoholism will be elaborated upon in Part Three of this book. They have been mentioned here because I believe that these benefits, in combination with the relevant theory and research also discussed in this chapter, provide a compelling reason to think "family" when dealing with alcoholism.

An Ethical Dilemma?

In the not-so-distant future, the alcoholism treatment field may be faced with an ethical dilemma over the question of whom to treat. Is it unethical to treat the alcoholic alone, without either involving other family members in treatment or addressing the alcohol-related problems of significant others? Is it irresponsible to prescribe medications to an alcoholic or member of the family without first conferring with the family therapist? Clinical experience and clinical research have pointed to these questions but have not provided answers to them.

Alcoholism surely affects all member of the family of an alcoholic. Research has not proven that families can cause alcoholism in a member, but there is strong clinical evidence that family interaction can contribute to the maintenance of alcohol abuse as well as to the resistance to sustaining newly achieved abstinence. The descendants of alcoholics have a greater-than-average risk of alcoholism themselves and perhaps of marrying alcoholics. At the same time, there is some evidence that family therapy can serve a prevention role, at least with the possibly related problem of delinquency.

Documented answers to our questions may be a long time in coming. In the meantime, it is likely that, more and more, therapists in the alcoholism field will be encouraging greater collaboration between physician and nonphysician therapists working with an alcoholic and also more family therapy approaches to the treatment of alcoholism.

References

1. Vaillant, G. F. A twelve-year follow-up of New York narcotics addicts: 1. The relation of treatment to outcome. *American Journal of Psychiatry, 122* (1966): 727–737.
2. Stanton, M. D. Appendix A: Review of reports on drug abusers' family living arrangements and frequency of family contact. In Stanton, M. D., & Todd, T. C. *The family therapy of drug abuse and addiction*. New York: Guilford, 1982.
3. Paolino, T. J., & McCrady, B. S. *The alcoholic marriage: Alternative perspectives*. New York: Grune & Stratton, 1977.
4. Ablon, J. Family structure and behavior in alcoholism: A review of the literature. In B. Kissin & H. Begleiter (Eds.), *The Biology of Alcoholism*: Vol. 4. New York: Plenum Press, 1976, pp. 205–242.
5. El-Guebaly, N., & Offord, D. R. The offspring of alcoholics: A critical review. *American Journal of Psychiatry, 134* (1977): 357–365.
6. Flynn, W., Davis, D. I., Foster, W., & Bast, D. The other victims of alcoholism. University Forum, Mutual Radio, WASH, August 17, 1978.
7. Cork, R. M. *The forgotten children: A study of children with alcoholic parents*. Toronto: Alcoholism & Drug Addiction Research Foundation, 1969.
8. Haberman, P. Childhood symptoms in children of alcoholic and comparison group patients. *Journal of Marriage and the Family, 28* (1966): 152–154.
9. Goodwin, D. *Is alcoholism hereditary*? New York: Oxford University Press, 1976.
10. Klagsbrun, M., & Davis, D. I. Substance abuse and family interaction. *Family Process 16*: 149–164, 1977.
11. Davis, D. I., Berenson, D., Steinglass, P., & Davis, S. The adaptive consequences of drinking. *Psychiatry, 37* (1974): 209–215.
12. Stanton, M. D. Fusion, compression, diverson and the workings of paradox: A theory of therapeutic/systemic change. *Family Process 23* (1984): 135–167.

13. Burton, G., & Kaplan, H. M. Marriage counseling with alcoholics and their spouses: The correlation of excessive drinking behavior with family pathology and social deterioration. *British Journal of Addiction, 63* (1968): 161–170.
14. Hore, B. D. Life events and alcoholics' relapse. *British Journal of Addiction, 66* (1971): 83–88.
15. Hore, B. D. Factors in alcoholic relapse. *British Journal of Addiction, 66* (1971): 89–96.
16. Pattison, E. M., Coe, R., & Rhodes, R. J. Evaluation of alcoholism treatment: A comparison of three facilities. *Archives of General Psychiatry, 20* (1969): 478–488.
17. Steinglass, P. Experimenting with family treatment approaches to alcoholism; 1950–1975: A review. *Family Process, 15* (1976): 97–123.
18. Janzen, C. Families in the treatment of alcoholism. *Journal of Studies on Alcohol, 38* (1977): 114–130.
19. Harwin, J. The excessive drinker and the family: Approaches to treatment. In Orford, J., & Harwin, J. (Eds.), *Alcohol and the family*. New York: St. Martin's, 1982.
20. Emrick, C. D. A review of psychologically oriented treatment of alcoholism: 2. The relative effectiveness of different treatment versus no treatment. *Journal of Studies on Alcohol, 36* (1975): 88–108.
21. Coleman, S. B., & Davis, D. I. Family therapy and drug abuse: A national survey. *Family Process, 17* (1978): 21–29.
22. Klein, N. C., Alexander, J. S., & Parson, B. V. Impact of family systems interventions on recidivism and sibling delinquency: A model of primary prevention and program evaluation. *Journal of Consulting and Clinical Psychology, 45* (1977): 469–474.
23. Weiss, R. L., Hops, H., & Patterson, G. R. A framework for conceptualizing marital conflict: A technology for altering it, some data for evaluating it. In L. A. Hamerlynch, L. C. Hardy, & E. J. Mash (Eds.), *Behavior Change: Methodology, Concepts and Practice*. Champaign, IL: Research Press, 1973.
24. Stuart, R. B. Operant interpersonal treatment for marital discord. *Journal of Consulting and Clinical Psychology, 33* (1969): 675–682.
25. Berenson, D. A family approach to alcoholism. *Psychiatric Opinion 13* (1976): 33–38.
26. Minuchin, S. *Families and family therapy*. Cambridge: Harvard University Press, 1974.
27. Haley, J. *Uncommon therapy: The psychiatric techniques of Milton Erickson, M. D.*. New York: Ballantine, 1973.
28. Watzlawick, P., Weakland, J. H., & Fisch, R. *Change: Prinicples of problem formation and problem resolution*. New York: Norton, 1974.
29. Bowen, M. The use of family theory in clinical practice. *Comprehensive Psychiatry, 7* (1966): 345–374.
30. Bowen, M. Alcoholism as viewed through family systems theory and family psychotherapy. *Annals of the New York Academy of Sciences, 233*: (1974): 115–122.
31. Haley, J. *Problem-solving therapy: New strategies for effective family therapy*. San Francisco: Jossey-Bass, 1976.

PART Two

Why Think About Alcohol?

CHAPTER 3

SOME FAMILY FUNCTIONS OF ALCOHOLISM: A THEORETICAL APPROACH

By Jeffrey Jay, Ph.D. and Donald I. Davis, M.D.

In this chapter we shall observe the nature of the interaction between alcoholism and other family problems and postulate certain mechanisms to explain these relationships. The goal is to enrich the clinician's understanding of the role of alcohol abuse in the family system and of the ways in which alcoholism can become an issue in family therapy.

No attempt will be made to establish cause-and-effect relationships between alcoholism and other family problems. At issue here is what factors may operate when problems (not necessarily alcohol-related) and alcohol abuse coexist, regardless of their separate or combined etiologies. As described in Chapter 1, once alcoholism is present in a family, it comes to serve whatever functions there are to be served. These we have termed the "Adaptive Consequences of Drinking." We noted that the "primary factors" maintaining the habit of drinking may differ from one family to the next. Bowen has emphasized that alcoholism should be considered "in the context of an imbalance in functioning in the total family system . . . (1)." The logical extension of this family-systems concept is that other family problems coexisting with alcoholism must share with the alcohol problem whatever stabilizing function they might have for the family.

In contrast to the individual (e.g., disease) model of alcoholism, within a family system's paradigm, alcoholism is seen as one component of the active life of the family. Since family life is an active, biological system responding to changing internal needs and changing external stress, alcoholic behavior will also change in a family's lifetime (2). For this reason, it is important in planning a therapy to relate the alcohol behavior to other changing aspects of family life.

Usually, investigating and treating the alcoholic characteristics of a family will lead the therapist to discover other aspects of family life that must be diagnosed and treated as part of the complete family therapy.

Pulling only at the thread of alcoholism can unravel the entire weave of family life. An understanding of the relationship between the various strands of family functioning, however, will enable the therapist to anticipate and avoid at least three potential roadblocks to successful treatment: the family's obstruction of the alcoholic's attempt at sobriety; the family's refusal to continue in therapy; and the family's collapse. Since each family will use alcoholic behavior to meet its individual needs, alcoholism must be understood in the context of each unique family. Examples of some of the ways in which alcoholism and other family functions interrelate are designed to suggest to the therapist the importance of looking for these connections and places to look.

Alcoholism and Physical and Psychiatric Illness

Family therapists sometimes allow the primacy of family dynamics to obscure those parts of a problem, such as alcoholism, that are inherent in the problem but operate independent of family dynamics. More will be said about this in later chapters regarding treatment for the individual. Here the focus will be kept on the interaction between the individual effects of alcohol and family function. The readily identified hazards of alcohol include psychological dependency (i.e., habituation), physical tolerance, impaired judgment, tissue damage, and psychotic reaction (3). With chronic drinking, the toxic effect of the drug will contribute its own debilitating impairment, so that whatever problems may coexist for the alcoholic, new injuries will be added to his physical, psychological, and social functioning. These impairments, in turn, add momentum to the continuation of the pathological drinking even though they increase the likelihood and advent of destruction and death. Even while new evidence, and critical reviews of Jellinek's early data, challenge the concept of an inexorable progression of alcohol problems proceeding through delineated phases (4), there is no doubt that the chronic use of alcohol generally creates increasingly adverse psychological, physical, and social effects (5). It would, therefore, be a mistake to reduce alcohol problems to the level of other family problems, just as it would be diagnostically and therapeutically incomplete, in family therapy, to ignore other problems and to focus solely on alcoholism.

Some Special Characteristics of Alcohol Use

There are at least four characteristics of alcohol use that are specific to alcohol and relevant to its abuse in families. First, there is the destructive potential of heavy chronic drinking already mentioned. Second, alcohol is a *depressant* (defined below). Third, society's response to intoxication has the effect of "permitting" the intoxicated person to act differently than a sober person. Fourth, alcohol use is *sanctioned* in our society.

To say that alcohol is a depressant means that, physiologically, it reduces nervous-system functioning, even though behaviorally it may have a disinhibiting effect; experientially its effect may be an increase or decrease in emotional reactivity (6, 7). Even though chronic use may lead to chronic dysphoria (8), the typical short-term response appears to be a dampening of the urgency and weight of personal problems (and therefore, also an escape).

Regarding special permission, the social consequences of intoxicated behavior often differ from the consequences of similar behavior conducted during sobriety; one behavior is seen as two different behaviors because of the mediation of intoxication. People often behave as if the alcohol were acting, not the person. Because of the shift in responsibility, from the person to the alcohol, a behavior conducted while the person is intoxicated is permitted, whereas similar behavior might not be tolerated when the person is sober (9). At the family level, in a strict and rigidly defined familial system, this permission during intoxication may serve to maintain the rigidity by facilitating the expression of certain behaviors that might otherwise force a confrontation or change.

The ambivalence of the American and many other Western societies towards alcohol use results in a curious form of sanction, which constitues a fourth special aspect of alcohol use. While alcoholic behavior is generally viewed as a disease, it is sanctioned and maintained in society. Alcohol is readily available, supported by a large industry, and typically associated with positive attributes, such as sexual sophistication and virility. For these reasons, among others, intoxication is a prevalent experience in adolescent and adult life. Thus, any detrimental or unpleasant personal experience with alcohol use is typically balanced by alcohol's purported positive attributes. Its use for facilitating a person's feeling attractive or powerful or relaxed is widely accepted, if not condoned.

Further, at the family level, patterns of alcohol use appear to be transmitted within cultural frameworks and through family lines (10), resulting in additional sanctions within specific families. Alcohol use is integrated into the identity and behaviors of many drinking families. If drinking is deviant, it is deviant in a paradoxical way; it often conforms to cultural and family expectations, and is thereby sanctioned, while at the same time being at odds with other personal and cultural constraints.

The Relationship of Alcoholism to Other Family Problems

The special characteristics of alcohol use described above largely determine the nature of the relationship between alcoholism and other family problems and determine how alcoholism functions in the family system. More specifically, three characteristics—(a) the depressant effect of the drug, (b) permission granted to exceed usual behaviors, and (c) the social sanctions for drinking—create their own types of relationship between alcoholism and other family problems. An overriding factor, the chronic nature of alcoholism, contributes an independent dimension to each of these types of relationships. The qualities contributed by the chronic nature of alcoholism will be discussed later.

Alcoholism cannot exist as an isolated dysfunction in a family system. It can become an attempt by the family to resolve other problems, that is, it can come to serve a function that is there to be served anyway; it can coexist with other dysfunctions; or it can cause other dysfunctions. The first two possibilities are logically distinct but in practice, or consequence, indistinguishable. The effect of the alcoholism will be an apparent reduction in the impact of the other problems, even though the other problems are neither resolved nor extricated from the family. Thus, ultimately it may come to be experienced by the family as *filling a void* in the amelioration of other problems.

Four types of relationships between alcoholism and other family problems that result from the special characteristics of alcoholism will be hypothesized here: masking, balancing, dampening and perpetuating.

Masking

The identification of family problems can be shielded by alcoholism. Individual pathology, psychotic behavior or psychopathic tendencies, for instance, can be felt as threatening the identity, control or organization of the family system. Alcohol converts the focus and force of the underlying problem to the more sanctioned and therefore more acceptable, albeit ambivalent, form of dealng with drunken behavior. Deviancy, if it is alcoholism, may be more acceptable than the specter of psychopathologies without the qualifications and sanctions of alcoholism. For instance, in some families it is better to argue about drunken behavior than to fantasize about strangling a spouse. If the masked problems are that dangerous, and the capacity for a constructive response unavailable, becoming drunk might seem a rational alternative. The fundamental issues generating conflict and unacceptable behavior can thus be deflected to the issues of alcoholism. But the arguments and attempts to rescue the alcoholic as well as the ambivalence and denial associated with alcoholism can leave the basic problem even further behind.

Clinically, the effects of masking may become apparent only after a successful major intervention for the treatment of the alcohol problem. For example, a man who periodically beat his mate and others, but only when drinking, was found to be extremely irritable periodically, after he had achieved abstinence from alcohol. Since he was in the hospital, his irritability could be assessed relatively calmly. He acknowledged racing thoughts at these times and admitted that drinking binges and subsequent fights had generally been preceded by irritability and racing thoughts throughout his adult life. He was treated with lithium carbonate, which had an almost immediate calming effect. He described being at peace for the first time in his adult memory, left the hospital, and was able to break off a by-then hostile relationship with someone, without fights or return to drinking. Both the Lithium-responsive irritability and the underlying impasse in the relationship had been masked for years by the serious consequences associated with this man's periodic excessive drinking.

Balancing

Inequities, or an imbalance, may exist in the distribution of power, roles, expression of affect, the personal development between spouses, and other components of a familial organization. (Identical functioning and roles among and between family members is unrealistic and unnecessary for the maintenance of the family. Its absence need not constitute an imbalance). "Imbalance" means that something threatens the functioning of the system. Because of the way in which alcohol *permits* behavior not usually present in a person's repertoire, basic family imbalances can be redressed under the umbrella of intoxication. The husband who is assertive only when intoxicated may temporarily right a system that is skewed in the sober state. Thus, his intoxication would be an essential part of balancing the distribution of power in the family. Similarly, imbalances in affective expression, which sometimes present as sexual difficulties, can be relieved through intoxicated episodes. Any relationship (or problem-solving) deficits that jeopardize the functioning of the family can be temporarily compensated during the disinhibited and permissive time of intoxication.

Dampening

The depressing and distancing experience resulting from alcohol use dulls involvement in conflict. It is likely that every family system has a limit to the stress and conflict it can tolerate. Alcohol temporarily decelerates the approach to the family's limit. In contrast to balancing, dampening does not lead to an apparent resolution of conflict; rather the impact of conflict is dulled by the *depressant* effect of the drug. For example, one alcoholic wife seen in family therapy tolerated and maintained sexual contact while intoxicated with a husband whom she, when sober, found repulsive.

At crisis points, this dulling may save the system from an uncontainable explosion. On the other hand, it may so soften the signal for action that the system fails to respond at all, as in Eugene O'Neill's play, *Long Day's Journey into Night*, in which the family drinks the pain of the son's tuberculosis into an unresponsive dullness.

Perpetuating: The Chronic Contribution

There is some evidence that families have stylistic, or typical ways of responding to problems (11). Alcoholism presents a family with immediate, obvious and severe pathology, yet, in alcoholic families, the maintenance of alcoholism is, almost by definition, the absence of a constructive response to the deviance. Alcoholism may become the paradigm of family problems, which, if tolerated, establishes a precedent for failing to resolve basic problems. It may, equally, be the manifestation of a family's tolerance for deviant behavior or their resignation to a less-than-optimal functioning without the expectation of true change. Thus we find, for example, numerous clinical examples of recalcitrant adolescents whose problems range from multiple drug abuse to school underachievement, who have in common an untreated or unacknowledged alcoholic parent. In addition to the obvious problems of poor modeling, these parents generally lack the fortitude necessary to effectively discipline an errant youth. The result is the perpetuation of self-destructive behavior patterns within the family, often, we suppose, even into the next generation.

The implication for treatment is that, unless a therapist can demonstrate an ability to help the family treat its alcoholism, it is unlikely that the family will believe the therapist strong enough to treat any other problem. It is also likely, then, that no other problem will be treated. It seems that too much of the family's energy is expended on the alcohol problem for the family to take on the work of change.

The progressive deterioration resulting from alcoholism presents a striking quality of its own. Over time, it will permeate the family system and will qualify the nature of the other relationships between alcoholism and other problems. The only relationship that may be maintained even with chronic deterioration is the *masking* relationship, since greater alcoholic problems will continue to divert attention and response from other primary conflicts or pathology. However, the facilitating role of alcohol in *balancing* dysfunctions, relations, power, etc., eventually wears down with chronicity. To carry out the balancing function requires active behavior, which becomes less and less possible with the deterioration consequent to chronic drinking. Similarly, the *dampening* of other problems does not outlive the problems because physiological tolerance acts against the effectiveness of alcohol, requiring more and more of the drug to get the same sedative effect. Eventually complications of the drug use itself crop up, which, in turn, ultimately alter the basic structure of the system, revealing the sharpest edges of whatever conflicts may be present. In the long run alcoholism is inadequate to the tasks of family life involving skills, social and emotional depth, and responsibility.

When a skilled family therapist helps in the achievement of a period of abstinence in an alcoholic family, a veil may be lifted from other ongoing family problems. Successful treatment will then require addressing the related dysfunctions. We have mentioned several ways in which chronic alcohol abuse can serve to maintain other family problems. A correlate of this maintenance function is that, in the presence of alcoholism, families fail to develop or at least to exercise the mechanisms necessary to resolve relationship conflicts. This puts a family at a disadvantage because all marriages and families experience conflicts in their relationships. Imagine how the disadvantage in the family with an alcoholic magnifies if we consider also the developmental phase that all families must go through and the challenge to the adaptability of a family brought by these phases.

The task here has been to convey the belief that alcohol abuse is inextricably tied in with other relationship problems and must be treated as a matter of first priority. It is hoped that by expanding the conceptual basis for seeing alcohol abuse and other family problems as inexorably related, it will become easier for therapists to think of the role of alcohol in their patient's problems. We would predict that when this occurs, and appropriate intervention is learned and used to alleviate the alcohol problems, therapy for other problems will proceed more efficiently than it has in the past with families with an alcohol-abusing member.

References

1. Bowen, M. Alcoholism as viewed through family systems theory and family psychotherapy. *Annals of the New York Academy of Sciences, 223* (1974): 115–122.
2. Steinglass, P. A life history model of the alcoholic family. *Family Process, 19* (1980): 211–226.
3. Whitfield, C. L., & Williams, K. *The patient with alcoholism and other drug problems*. Carbondale, IL: Southern Illinois University Press, 1976.
4. Pattison, E. M. Rehabilitation of the chronic alcoholic. In B. Kissin & H. Begleiter (Eds.), *The Biology of Alcoholism: Vol. 3. Clinical Pathology*. New York: Plenum Press, 1974.
5. Kissin, B. The pharmacodynamics and natural history of alcoholism. In *ibid*.
6. Garfield, Z. H., & McBrearty, J. F. Arousal level and stimulus in alcoholics after drinking, *Quarterly Journal of Studies on Alcohol, 31* (1970): 832–837.
7. Barry, H. Psychological factors in alcoholism, In B. Kissin & H. Begleiter, *op. cit*.
8. Tamerin, J. S., Weiner, S., Poppen, R., Steinglass, P., & Mendelson, J. H. Alcohol and memory: Amnesia and short-term memory function during experimentally induced intoxication. *American Journal of Psychiatry, 127* (1971): 1659–1664.
9. MacAndrew, C., & Edgerton, R. B. *Drunken comportment: A social explanation*. Chicago: Aldine, 1969.
10. Wolin, S., Bennett, L., & Noonan, D. Family rituals and the recurrence of alcoholism over generations. *American Journal of Psychiatry, 136* (1979): 589–593.
11. Reiss, D. *The family's construction of reality*. Cambridge: Harvard University Press, 1981.

CHAPTER 4

DEALING WITH THE SPECIAL PROBLEMS IN FAMILY THERAPY POSED BY ALCOHOL ABUSE

For many family therapists, there seems to be an inherent dilemma in treating alcoholism as a disease. It comes from the desire to treat family members equally yet still keep a family system's perspective. "How can I tell them they are all part of the problem and part of the solution and then tell one person he is an alcoholic and has to stop drinking?" That is the type of question often raised.

But the incompatibility is a false antithesis. I find analogies useful to allay these concerns. Let us take as an example a couple that is fighting at the top of the stairs. One pushes, the other falls downstairs and breaks a leg. If specific measures are not taken to treat the leg, it will heal poorly. There may be a chronic crippling effect. That effect in time will have its consequences, and the family will make adaptations to living with a crippled family member. The broken leg cannot be disregarded even though there are clearly relationship issues, in this case having to do at least with problem-solving, which precipitated this episode of physical injury. We must see to it that the broken leg is treated at the same time that we deal with both people and their fighting at the top of the stairs; and so it should be with the treatment of alcoholism in family therapy.

The dilemma is not that we treat both alcohol abuse and the family system, but how we approach doing it that may create troublesome inconsistencies. If the couple who fought at the top of the stairs were in family therapy, the therapist could tell them that each partner had the problem of living with somebody with an acute injury and rapidly evolving longer-lasting complications. It would be the responsibility of each to do their part in overcoming the problem. The one with the broken leg must seek the best available medical care, follow treatment instructions to the letter, and take on rehabilitation vigorously. The partner must facilitate the healing process in several ways, e.g., by helping with treatment-related transportation and with exercising procedures that call for assistance, and by practicing detachment to avoid overreactions to self pity or irritability. Both partners would be expected equally to take responsibility for attending therapy and doing assignments. Children might be called upon to be responsible for removing toys from tops of stairs or other hazardous zones and also to practice detachment.

Leg healing should be monitored frequently during our hypothetical family therapy. It does not take long, perhaps a few minutes each session if there are no problems. Is everyone doing their part well? How many fights were there in hazardous locations with toys underfoot last week? Last month? In what ways is the person with the healing leg still acting or being treated like a cripple? Poor healing or medical complications will perpetuate cripple behavior; therefore appropriate interventions must be made. Cripple behavior is incompatible with the new problem-solving behaviors between equals that the family is learning through therapy. If the cripple behaviors persist and the therapist ignores them, progress with the family will be surprisingly slow and erratic at best.

There are problems that reside in individuals, such as broken legs and alcoholism, that can and must be addressed for family treatment to be fully effective. There need be no dilemma for the therapist if it is made clear to the family that each member will be held responsible for his or her own efforts to deal with the problem and with the adaptation to it. More will be said in later chapters about specifics of how to address the individual alcoholic within a family-oriented treatment.

Treatment

Treatment of alcoholism within family therapy has three phases: (1) identifying the problem, (2) stopping drinking (abstinence is preferable over even greatly curtailing drinking), and (3) relinquishing the adaptations to alcohol misuse and learning alternative behaviors. All these can be accomplished in family therapy. In fact, having other family members present often makes the first and second phases easier and is usually essential to carry out the third phase.

Contrary to the opinion of some, identifying alcohol abuse is not difficult. A few detailed questions about quantity, frequency, timing, and consequences of use generally suffice. There are now some guidelines in the literature to make it easier. For example, there is the Michigan Alcoholism Screening Test (MAST) (1) and its brief version (2), which include a number of useful questions about the social consequences of drinking, such as "Have you ever neglected your family for two or more days in a row because you were drinking?", "Have friends or relatives ever raised any questions about your drinking?", "Have you ever lost friends or girlfriends/boyfriends because of drinking?" Our own survey questionaire, which includes questions from the Brief-MAST, is included in the Appendix. There is also the National Council on Alcoholism's Major and Minor Criteria for Alcoholism (3). It is extremely powerful for a therapist to be able to say with confidence in front of several family members, "From what you have told me about having blackouts and about drinking more than five or six drinks at a time more than twice a week, I should tell you that by the criteria set by the National Council on Alcoholism you would be considered an alcoholic." The therapist can then add, "In addition, we have seen that there are several areas of your life, e.g., marriage, driving, and your job, where you have already experienced the deleterious consequences of drinking; yet you have been unable to change your drinking habits; hence, also measuring strictly by social consequences you must be considered to have a problem of alcohol abuse." Alcohol abuse and alcoholism are used interchangeably here. This is not the time to fight over the presence or absence of an "ism." It is enough to establish that there is a serious problem that needs treatment. The drinker and family members can make up their own minds after some success with AA and family therapy as to whether they have been dealing with alcoholism.

The most productive time to ask question about alcohol use and its consequences is in relation to an interpersonal issue. For example, "Sometimes we can't seem to talk without arguing," would be the ideal cue for "Is alcohol in the picture at those times?" If the answer is, "Yes, always," or "Usually," detailed questions can follow about how much husband and wife have each had to drink, on each day of the past week, of wine, beer, and/or hard liquor (one drink of each is treated as equivalent in absolute ethanol content). Other questions about job, driving, and social problems associated with alcohol can follow quickly.

Half the job of identification is thus readily completed. The other half, equally important, involves confirming the diagnosis to both drinker and family members. It is not enough to ask the questions. In fact, if compelling answers are provided and yet the therapist fails to explicitly state a diagnostic opinion, and fails to insist on each family member also putting themselves on the line, the experience may be worse than if no questions had been asked. Hearing the evidence and failing to commit to dealing with alcohol abuse as a first priority is tantamount to sanctioning the alcoholic behavior or colluding with the idea that it is hopeless to discuss it and supporting whatever denial is being carried on by members of the family. However, taking a position that alcoholism is present and that drinking must stop in order to achieve success with any other issues in family therapy is a powerful positive step with the system as well as the disease. It may be a sensitive step to negotiate, but it cannot be neglected without risk of failing at both systems and symptom treatment. Timing does matter, but the novice therapist, where alcohol is concerned, will do better to err in the direction of addressing alcoholism too soon than to wait too long. Any risk of the former is balanced by the fact that the family will remember the therapist's diagnosis the next time they seek help; whereas, with the latter the family may continue to seek help that ignores the alcoholism and further to postpone effective change. Identification of and confrontation about alcoholism is dealt with in more detail in Part Three.

Stopping alcohol-abusing behavior is the next phase of alcoholism treatment. It is not enough to confirm that there is a drinking problem, even if done in front of the whole family. If the high volume and frequency of drinking persist, some of the most creative and energetic work with couples and families will be thwarted.

The collusive interaction of one person abusing alcohol and other family members denying the fact or complaining ineffectively seems to be a central factor in obstructing change. For example, a family was seen in therapy for a period of months with some benefit but less than might be expected. Oldest son was an underachiever in school, younger son was quite shy, and father was depressed and alcoholic. Early on, father's drinking was seen as the paramount problem. He refused to go to AA or to stop drinking but did enter into an agreement to greatly reduce his drinking "his own way" on a trial basis. Mother attended Al-anon and the boys attended Alateen. Father did curb his drinking substantially, and his depression lifted without medication. He continued to drink at times, though, and occasionally more than the two-drink limit he had set for himself. Father became an increasingly active participant in family therapy. He and his wife began to cooperate more around parenting issues, and it seemed that therapy would progress well.

After a while it became apparent that the shy son had blossomed socially; but the underachieving son simply continued not to do all his homework. Eventually a parallel was drawn between son's school behavior and father's drinking. Son admitted that he felt his lying about whether he had completed his homework was no different from other lying that went on in the family. By that he meant father's lying about whether he was truly an alcoholic and needed to stop drinking altogether, as well as mother's lying when she covered for father in many subtle ways. The family treatment came to a stalemate. This stalemate persisted until finally son was helped to express his concerns for father and offer to do his very best in school the coming year, provided father would accept his alcoholism and show it by stopping to drink altogether. Father did not immediately agree; nor did his son expect him to, for son appeared to have some stake in father's continued drinking as well, to keep the focus off the seriousness of his own difficulty with schoolwork. Hence, there remained much work to be done. Still, new lines had been drawn. It became clear that the drinking problem truly had to be stopped to adequately treat the family.

It should be acknowledged that there is an alternative family approach to the son's problems, one that would focus on helping the older son more effectively disengage and individuate from his parents so that he could deal with his school-work problem independently from his parent's progress. An approach that bypasses drinking may be easier than one that successfully stops father's drinking, but the results in treatment for the whole family are at risk of failure, as the above example demonstrates.

Stopping alcohol abuse by a family member requires both the conviction that it is crucial and also perseverance on the part of the therapist. Those are needed more than any one specific technique. Assigning visits to AA for the drinker, Al-anon for adult and young adult family members, and Alateen for teenage and pre-teen children is often a valuable starting point. In fact, not assigning them persistently may be experienced as showing less than total conviction or even timidity in insisting on necessary changes, even with reluctant clients. In assigning the AA self-help groups, each family member has his own personal responsibility for attending a self-help group; this responsibility is his, whether or not the drinker or another family member fails to go. Attendance serves multiple purposes that support and enhance family therapy. It provides a confirmatory experience, i.e., that others who have experience agree alcohol is a problem. It eventually provides 24-hour crisis support in the form of a sponsor. It helps teach family members how to detach themselves from the alcohol-abusing behavior and go on with their own lives rather than contribute to perpetuating the problem. And it emphasizes that one is responsible, primarily to oneself.

I advise people to go to more than one meeting before deciding if they like it, and to shop around. There are hundreds of groups in most urban areas. People should find one that is socially compatible and geographically accessible. I check frequently if they have gone to the AA self-help group meetings and what they have learned from them, just as I check about drinking behavior. I also let people know that they may find others at the AA meetings who are bitterly opposed to any psychotherapy because of bad experiences of their own with therapy that they feel delayed their alcoholism recovery process. When we have prepared them for these attacks, people usually are comfortable saying simply that their therapy and AA are compatible. The compatibility of AA and family therapy are discussed further in Chapter 9.

Predicting in front of the whole family what is likely to happen in therapy if drinking does not stop is also helpful, at least in the long run. For example, I might say to a couple, "If the drinking does not stop, I would predict the following: You will seem to be working on the right things in therapy but you will not resolve your differences. After a while you (the spouse) will get fed up and have an affair or leave. You (the drinker), if you survive without a car accident or don't run over somebody else or get some alcohol-related illness, will gradually do less well in your job and do less and less with other people except a few drinking companions, and you will continue to lose the respect of your children." I say this in a matter-of-fact way, tailoring the details to the particular people. I let them know it is their choice, but that I have a responsibility as an expert to share with them my evaluation and recommendation. The effect of this kind of approach is to foster a "no-lose" situation for the therapist and therapy. Hopefully, the family will be persuaded to commit to a plan for achieving abstinence as a first priority. If they have some members who are not ready to do that, however, it is then possible to proceed without hypocrisy. As the predictions come true and the family is in therapy, the therapist then has the leverage of an ongoing relationship and enhanced credibility. As with confirming the diagnosis, making such relevant predictions is more powerful because they have been made in front of other family members. Everyone knows what the authority has actually said first-hand, and each person knows that the others know. This process also models alternatives to the usual subtle protective cover-ups of alcohol abuse within many families.

Resistance to working on overcoming alcohol abuse, then, is best handled by persistent open reassessment of the current family consequences of drinking and by predictions of what will follow with and without stopping drinking. In addition, one can blatantly disregard the drinker in the family sessions when alcohol is in his system and recognize the drinker attentively on a dry day. If someone cannot stop drinking or is in imminent danger because of the level of drinking or the behavior associated with it, hospitalization or detoxification (withdrawal from alcohol) should be recommended. Most alcohol abusers can stop drinking without hospitalization, and hospital detoxification in itself is often a stop-gap measure without lasting value; but when hospital detoxification is used as one component of an ongoing family treatment strategy, it can be invaluable.

Once abstinence is achieved, there are new alcoholism-related issues that must be addressed as part of family therapy. This third phase of treating alcoholism focuses on teaching the family how to substitute for the adaptations they have made to living with alcohol-abusing behavior. Families are inclined to have the same expectations of the newly abstinent member as they had of that person drinking. For example, if the drinker is an adult, he or she may continue to be feared at the first hint of anger, yet disregarded in family decision-making and viewed contemptuously as a parent.

Let us use a case to illustrate. A family of five began family therapy when father was discharged from the medical service of a general hospital. He had been a daily drinker for more than ten years until the day he was hospitalized as a medical emergency for complications of his drinking. Having narrowly survived, he began attending AA from the hospital and remained abstinent post-discharge. In the early stages of once-a-week therapy, he and his wife were frankly bewildered. They were encouraged to talk about family matters that previously had not been subject to joint discussion. Husband did not want to be bothered with thinking about such family matters as chores, vacation or social plans, home repair costs, etc., while wife openly resented even his reluctant contributions as intrusions into her affairs. They had no verbal mechanism for joint problem-solving, and she expected him to silently tolerate whatever she decided. When these roles were acknowledged and attributed benignly to a healthy adaptation to active alcoholism, the couple gradually came to try out more equal roles in decision-making on everyday matters.

About that time, a twenty-year-old prodigal returned home to live. He had been accustomed to getting his way in virtually all matters. He had done this through seeking a form of protection from his mother from verbal lashings and other emotional wrongdoings on the part of his father, and the pattern resumed immediately even though his father was both abstinent and more approachable. If father objected to son's drug use and noisy parties, son would complain that father was his old heartless self. Initially, mother would then automatically criticize father for his insensitivity toward this son; and the drugs, noise, etc., persisted. In therapy, much work was done with mother and father in jointly setting limits with this son and on supporting one another as parents. Through this process, son was required to attend family therapy as a condition of living at home. Then it was possible to start the process of father and son talking with one another on a more open and respectful basis. This included giving the son a chance to vent his anger and disappointment toward father for his many drinking years marked by erratic and unapproachable behavior. That was followed by father being helped to tell his son of his genuine concerns for the son's drug experimentation and lack of work discipline. He also shared his views on his own mistakes and what he must now do to change. As it became clear that mother now supported father's mandates and that father and mother consulted one another before committing themselves, there were fewer and fewer incidents caused by this son.

Summary

It is important and often crucial to identify and to treat alcoholism when it exists in a family in therapy. Relationship problems rarely go away while the drinking problem continues. Individual behavioral disturbances often do poorly as well. Disregarding alcohol abuse perpetuates a hopelessness in family members. Couples or parents and children fail to practice new problem-solving skills. Non-alcohol-related social activities continue to diminish, further reducing support systems that should increase with effective family therapy. Furthermore, drinking problems are not likely to stop through treatment of other behavioral disorders in a family. The converse, however, is not so true. Marital relationships and symptoms, at least in the identified alcoholic, do tend to improve from the treatment of alcoholism. Still, there is much "alcoholism treatment" to do in families even after abstinence is achieved, in order to generate alternatives to some of the adaptations the family has made to alcohol abuse that are no longer appropriate.

There is a wide range of indirect cues that should trigger inquiries about patterns of alcohol use. They range from obvious statements, such as that a person only does a certain undesirable behavior when he or she drinks, to the presence of any inexplicably treatment resistant symptom in any family member.

Effective intervention begins with gathering detailed information about quantity, frequency, timing, and setting of alcohol use, by clinical interview or with a standard screening test. This must be followed by the therapist's explicit assertion of the presence and nature of an alcohol problem. Demonstrating an association between alcohol use and identified relationship issues can be useful in this process. Making treatment of the alcohol problem a first priority in the family therapy should then follow.

A treatment plan should require an equal commitment from all family members toward working on their family's alcoholism problem. Each member attending AA, Al-anon, and Alateen—as appropriate—is an excellent way to reinforce this commitment. Frequent checks on the progress of each family member in carrying out their part of the alcoholism treatment facilitates this process. Once active drinking is no longer a problem, using family therapy techniques to foster changes in expectations of one another will complete the alcoholism treatment phase of family therapy.

References

1. Selzer, M. L. The Michigan Alcoholism Screening Test (M.A.S.T.): The quest for a new diagnostic instrument. *American Journal of Psychiatry, 127* (1971): 89–94.
2. Pokorny, A. D., Miller, B. A., & Kaplan, H. B. The Brief M.A.S.T.: A shortened version of the Michigan Alcoholism Screening Test. *American Journal of Psychiatry, 129* (1972): 342–345.
3. Criteria Committee, National Council on Alcoholism. Criteria for the diagnosis of alcoholism. *American Journal of Psychiatry, 129* (1972): 127–135.

PART Three
Treatment Techniques

CHAPTER 5

IDENTIFYING AND CONFRONTING: SUGGESTIONS FOR IDENTIFYING A DRINKING PROBLEM AND CONFRONTING ALCOHOLIC AND FAMILY

Think alcohol (and other drugs). How many times my colleagues or I have slapped a hand against a forehead in dismay when someone has said about a case, "Is one of them a heavy drinker?" "Of course," we say. "Why didn't we think of that sooner?" And that shock serves as a reminder for the next several months to think about alcohol with every new couple or family. When something just doesn't add up, when therapy is not progressing well for no apparent reason, think alcohol. Under the same circumstances, one should also think of an affair, of physical or sexual abuse, of an unresolved death in the family. But above all think of excess alcohol use. It is ubiquitous in a therapy or counseling population and, besides, it often underlies a failure to resolve the other hidden issues.

"How do I broach the subject?" That is an ever recurring question, even from colleagues who know a great deal about alcohol's effects on the family. It seems to come from one of two sources. Some therapists have not gotten over a sense of impropriety in raising such a personal question as, "How much do you drink?" and "When?" and "Where?" Others have a tendency to be so heavy-handed in confronting people about their drinking that experience tells them they will drive away their patients. I find that the best answer is to broach the subject early and when there is any suspicion, but in a way that paces well the content families are ready to discuss. Explore the relevance of alcohol use to the problems they present. A prime example is any discussion of fights, whether mere verbal spats or down-and-out brawls. The question, "Does it make any difference whether alcohol is present or not?", asked at the right moment will open the floodgates to an enormous amount of relevant information about the relationship between alcohol use and the presenting problems. If any one member of the family so much as flinches in response to that question, it legitimizes a torrent of questions that might otherwise have been fended off as intrusive, silly, or inappropriate. With the slightest opening, the therapist can (and should because the moment might quickly be lost) rapidly move from the fight or argument context to a brief but thorough alcohol-use history. For example, "I noticed some response to my question. Yes, it makes some difference whether alcohol is present or not. What kind of difference does it make? How, specifically, does it make a difference when you fight?" Notice that these are also leading questions. They form the beginning steps of planting the suggestion or reframing in such a way that alcohol use becomes clearly related to the family's fights. The family members must now disprove the presupposition that alcohol plays a role in their problem.

One of the most common reasons for teenage referrals for therapy is for oppositional behavior, usually combined with either mixed drug experimentation or underachievement in school or both. So often, the parents' major complaint concerns near-constant arguing between the teenager and one parent in particular. He/she "shows no respect" is the usual refrain. Allowing everyone in the family to describe what typically happens (I prefer framing this in terms of how they would like things to be different), and then simply being curious as to whether "anyone is having anything to drink" when some of these family encounters occur, will reveal, with an incredible frequency, in my experience, that one or even both parents has been regularly drinking at these times. Commiserating with how challenging it is to have a teenager, combined with pointing out both the need for keeping cool and the disinhibiting effects of "even a few drinks," can sometimes lead very rapidly to an agreement to "find out what things are like without alcohol" for several weeks. The truly chemically dependent will either refuse, insist on cutting down but not stopping, or agree and then fail. The steady drinkers who are not dependent, some of whom may only be in the two-to-four-drink-per-evening range but who still act less effectively with their children because of alcohol, will test out the hypothesis. Getting to any agreement with the truly alcohol-abusing parent will usually require all of the additional documentation of the alcohol problem as outlined below. Once such an agreement is reached, almost invariably there is a major calming effect when the drinking is eliminated; and the teenager's behavior either straightens out on its own or the teenager becomes much more amenable to working in therapy.

Don't worry about false positives in the identification of alcohol abuse. It occurs but is more manageable and far less frequent than false negatives. Go for highly specific details about how alcohol use by one or more members of the family becomes associated with behaviors that family members have already indicated they would like to change. The present example involves arguing or fighting, but it could just as easily have to do with sexual encounters or other parent-child interactions. "What happens differently in sex when she's been drinking?" "Do you mean that you tend to take the initiative less when your wife has been drinking even though you otherwise enjoy sex with her?" This kind of comment that is made to a couple who has just admitted that sex is less frequent and less enjoyable than it used to be, and has just responded with a qualified but discernible yes to a first probe about any difference in sex when alcohol is present, gives a therapist substantial leverage in all future discussions of alcohol abuse that might otherwise never have been gained through months of therapy.

Once partners have successfully fended off more straightforward questions about the extent of alcohol use, they frequently shore up their already well-developed defenses against further inquiry into their alcohol habits, leaving the therapist with little leverage or inclination to force the issue of drinking as a factor in their relationship. If, however, the therapist can establish a solid link between presenting relationship problems and drinking with an unsuspecting couple or family, then she can override all future denial of drinking as a problem with a "That may be true, but [or "Even if that were true] we still have all agreed that, when you fight [make love, etc.], there is a definite difference when alcohol is present versus when it is not." "In fact," we might go on, "the intensity of the fights, which is the main thing you want to change, is only present when one of you has had something to drink. Isn't that right?"... "Wouldn't you agree, then, that at least one of you believes that drinking is central to what you came in here for help with?" Remembering to pace well, one might empty both barrels and say, "I am aware that stopping drinking alone will not necessarily bring about all of the changes each of you want. However, as the professional to whom you have come for help, I should let you know that it is unlikely that you can make the changes you want unless the drinking is stopped or unless there is at least a substantial period of time-out from drinking long enough to enable you to learn the new behaviors you are seeking with one another without all the old cues associated with alcohol to set off the old behaviors." (If your patients go into a trance when you say all of this, so much the better! The length and complexity of the above type of statement is likely to induce a light hypnotic response, i.e., turning one's thoughts inward. Those familiar with Ericksonian hypnotherapy will recognize the many embedded, positive suggestions to which patients will be most open when conscious reasoning is bypassed.)

Some family members will seem impressed with the connections being made between drinking and their unresolved relationship issues, yet they remain wedded to their belief that alcoholism is not their problem. That is a good moment (as are many moments) to be curious about what alcoholism means to them. "When you think of an alcoholic, what comes to your mind?" "Well, you know, someone who is drunk all the time." You respond, "Not necessarily. I find it's different to different people depending on whom they've known who drank a lot. Some people think the only alcoholics are those who live on skid row, even though statistics tell us that less than five percent of alcoholics end up there; and most alcoholics still have jobs and live with their families."

The education process begins while the family members are thinking out their answers so that by the time the questioning is finished, the answers they give are what they used to think or believe, and now they are not so sure. Frequently they will admit to believing that alcoholism is only the degree of drinking or drunkenness that their father or mother or brothers do or did, or that those few people who drank a lot in college but couldn't hold it well and made fools of themselves did. One woman who had been married thirteen years, and whose husband was severely dependent on cocaine and alcohol, said, "He always had a drink in his hand even when I met him, but he never acted drunk. He could hold so much! I guess I should have known then, but he was so different from my father who acted so loud and violent when he got drunk."

Continuing in a low-key educational format, the therapist is now in a position to say that lots of people think alcoholism is only present when people frequently act drunk. They don't realize that holding a lot of alcohol is likely to be a developed talent, that there is such a thing as *tolerance*, which means that the cells of the body adapt to alcohol in such a way that, after enough use, it takes more alcohol to get the same psychoactive effects that used to occur with less. In our culture we are fooled because often in high school or college we are admired for holding our liquor well. At this point the therapist can punctuate this part of the discussion with, "I always worry when somebody can hold a lot because it means they've been drinking long enough and hard enough to build up a tolerance."

People will admit to all sorts of notions of when there is a problem with alcohol. For some, only seeing is believing. For example, there were the parents of a 19-year-old boy who rarely drank in front of them. His bedroom was strewn with beer cans and his car trunk filled with still more, but they were never sure he had a problem. Then there was the husband whose wife bought a half gallon of whiskey each week, who found the levels in wine bottles steadily declining, but who never saw her drink more than one, so he wasn't sure either.

At some point, one must take a drinking and drug-use history. The very best time is within a relevant context. But earlier in therapy rather than later is always advisable, whether or not the relationship concequences of drinking have been established. Without prior relevance documented, a good lead-in is simply, "I always ask about the use of alcohol, caffeine, sugar, cigarettes, marijuana and other drugs and prescription medicines." With the connection to drinking already made, one need only say, "This would be a good time for me to find out more about your drinking habits." Either way, it only takes three to five minutes with most people for a rapid but thorough sequence of questions. It takes longer with the obviously problem drinkers who are denying, but then it would be inappropriate not to allot the better part of a session early in therapy when so indicated. Consider what message a family is left with if a therapist, under these circumstances, brushes over drinking. The covert message to patients, as reported over and over again by families who had been in prior therapy when problem drinking was hinted at but not picked-up on as a major issue, is that the therapist is prepared to collude in the family's denial to themselves and to the outside world.

How does one ask how much someone drinks? Global questions generally beget global answers. For example, "How much do you drink?" is likely to yield something on the order of "Not much," especially for the still-denying heavy drinker. Of course, one can pick up the pieces here by saying, "How much is 'not much' for you?", and then take the same detailed history we are about to describe. I recommend more specific questions from the outset which contain the presupposition that drinking occurs. "In the past week what have you had to drink, on the average, each day?" "Yesterday, what did you have to drink from the time you came home from work until bedtime?" And then never settle for the first answer, or the second or the third.

Let's say the first answer is, "I probably had a martini when I came home, just before dinner." This answer is often presented in a tone and a manner usually intended to convey that the person just has one before-dinner drink, that most people do the same, and that this whole topic is rather silly. At this point it is quite useful to act obtuse, using the television role of Columbo as a model. From that position, like Columbo, the therapist can unleash a deluge of petty, detailed questions without regard for the usual amenities such as staying away from topics upon which a nonverbal blanket has been thrown. "You said one drink before dinner—is that a measured drink from a jigger or just poured and estimated?" If poured directly, "Would you guess that that is equivalent to one shot from a shot glass, or two, or three?" If the answer is about two, "Okay, so we will call that a double which equals two drinks for our purposes." "What time before dinner do you have this drink? Is it just before or when you just get home from work? Would you have had another drink earlier (or later)?" Let's say the answer is, "Well, yes, I sometimes have one when I first walk in." "Is that also a double?" "Yes." "Now that's two doubles when you come home. How about during dinner?" Let's say this answer is, "Well I may have some wine with dinner," said with an intonation to suggest that wine is just wine and not hard liquor. A quick eductional reply is in order. "Since a five-ounce glass of wine and a twelve-ounce can of beer and a shot of whiskey each have about the same amount of ethyl alcohol, we just count each as a drink. How much wine do you have with dinner?" Remember to attend to nonverbal as well as verbal responses from the other family members present at the same time. A sigh or an askance look from a spouse, child, or sibling, when commented upon immediately, can change the admitted count from two doubles to two triples. Remember also to ask who else is drinking at these times. It will provide a very rapid inroad to most of the drinking behavior—of the problem drinker's spouse particularly. One spouse, whose husband drank heavily from the time he came home from work, seemed to have only one alcoholic drink until I asked about late-evening drinking. It turned out that she regularly retired to her separate bedroom with a gallon jug of wine.

Returning to our hypothetical case, let's say the heavy drinker's answers have totaled two doubles before dinner and three glasses of wine with dinner. By now—it takes about two minutes to get here—the count is uncomfortable. Look at the floor, look at the walls, act confused and mumble something about "Let's see, did I ask you about after-dinner drinks?" Usually a brandy. "Oh, and how about later in the evening? How about at bedtime?" "Maybe one drink if I'm tense and I want to go right to sleep." "All right, so what you're saying is that, by my way of counting, you have seven to nine drinks most days after work until you go to bed. Is that right?" "Yes, I guess so, but—" Here, I interrupt. (We're not finished.) "How about at lunch time? And before lunch? What's the earliest you ever have a drink? Now this is what is typical of your drinking on a weekday. How is it different on a weekend? Do you sometimes start earlier or drink more? Is this past week typical or do you drink more or less most weeks?"

By this point our hypothetical drinker may have acknowledged seven to twelve or more drinks most days—a good time for more education. "I should tell you that, just on the basis of the quantity and frequency of your drinking some people would feel you have a problem with alcohol. By the National Council on Alcoholism's criteria (1), just having more than, say, six to eight drinks in a day more than once a week is cause to go looking for other evidence of early alcoholism." In addition, I often add that I conducted a study of some 5,000 patients of all sorts at a large urban medical school and should tell them that the level of drinking we identified in our session placed this person well into the upper five percent of all drinkers in that study. All it takes to get into that lofty percentile group, as determined by a self-report on a questionnaire (the Substance Use and Abuse Survey, or SUAS, is presented in its entirety in the Appendix) is averaging more than three drinks of any sort per day. Saying that usually provides the opportunity for further education about how it is possible for them to know so many people who drink more than that and still have them all be in the upper five percent. I explain that heavy drinkers tend to gravitate to other drinkers, and that eventually one's social circle becomes limited largely to others who drink heavily too. I ask if they have noticed that in their lives, and inquire if they can think of anyone they know socially who is a light drinker or doesn't drink at all—who, if they drink, can stop at one or two under any circumstances. I point out that they might want to start looking for such people because they aren't going to like to just stop drinking if that means they don't have any social life anymore. And I warn them that some of their friends who do drink heavily won't be happy with them around if they aren't drinking alcohol. They might lose some friends. In addition to locating non-problem drinking friends, there is a readily available source for new formerly problem drinking friends in AA.

Now that we have established a drinking (and other drug use) history and family relevance of drinking, and a little education about what constitutes heavy use, it is a good time to document other consequences of drinking. Has drinking ever affected work in any way: caused them to show up late for work on Monday or miss work for sickness, or decreased their efficiency at work whether or not others have noticed? Have there been times when someone was concerned about the safety of driving because of drinking, or have their been any DWI's (Driving While Intoxicated) or other legal mishaps related to drinking? Has a doctor ever said that a particular medical problem was in any way related to drinking or that drinking should be stopped?

Some therapists prefer to use one of the structured-assessment questionnaires to get at the answers to these questions and to provide some outside, objective verification of the presence of alcoholism based on the drinker's own judgments. A widely used questionnaire, as mentioned in Chapter 4, is the brief verson of the Michigan Alcoholism Screening Test (or the MAST) (2,3). The SUAS questionaire is made up of sections that are modifications of other widely used substance-use surveys and contains a section on consequences of use, the alcohol part of which is borrowed directly from the Brief-MAST. It can be used either as a self-assessment questionnaire or as a reminder to the therapist of useful questions to ask. Clinically, many therapists have found that the most useful definition of alcoholism is the presence of any detrimental consequence of drinking, whether to the medical, legal, social, vocational, or family and marital aspects of one's life, while the pattern of drinking remains unchanged (4). These simple questions, and this definition, allow the therapist to readily make the diagnosis of alcoholism, then to turn around and educate the family to this diagnosis and finally confront each with the now compelling question, "Do you personally now believe that anyone in your family has an alcohol problem or is an alcoholic by the definitions we have been using?" In my experience, everybody who I think qualifies will acknowledge *problem-drinking* at this point. Quite a few will still hedge on the presence of the "ism". It goes against their beliefs. They can acknowledge that you, their therapist, might well conclude that *alcoholism* is the issue; but they aren't ready. I'll settle. As long as we can proceed to do everything I would want to do to treat alcoholism, I will not insist at this early phase, and may never, on acceptance of the "ism."

References

1. Criteria Committee, National Council on Alcoholism. Criteria for the diagnosis of alcoholism. *American Journal of Psychiatry, 129* (1972): 127–135.
2. Selzer, M. L. The Michigan Alcoholism Screening Test: The quest for a new diagnostic instrument. *American Journal of Psychiatry, 127* (1971): 89–94.

3. Pokorny, A. D., Miller, B. A., & Kaplan, H. B. The Brief MAST: A shortened version of the Michigan Alcoholism Screening Test. *American Journal of Psychiatry, 129* (1972): 342–345.
4. Whitfield, C., & Williams, K. *The patient with alocholism and other drug problems*. Carbondale, IL: Southern Illinois University Press, 1976.

CHAPTER 6

IDENTIFYING AND CONFRONTING: AN INTERVIEW WITH CHILDREN ALONE

Some families cover up or smooth over a parent's drinking problem so well that only a therapist's firm conviction that drinking could be a problem combined with artful interviewing will elicit the truth. Often this requires splitting family members up, at least separating parents and children for separate interviews of ten to twenty or thirty minutes or more. It may be necessary to see each individual in a large family, but usually it is not. Typically there is one person who is closer to spilling the beans about the alcohol being a problem in the family and one or more others who are prepared to be indignant at the very thought. The therapist must be prepared to support rapidly the one whom others view or hear as the family snitch. If one person confesses to a drinking problem and another denies it, to reframe these as legitimate attempts to do what is best for the the family is often essential. Be prepared also to accept that one or more persons truly may not feel their lives are made more difficult by another's drinking, yet someone else might. Then document how the drinking impinges on the life of the person who identifies it as a problem, all the while educating as to possible ways alcohol use can impinge on relationships and individuals. These are useful strategies in enabling children, for example, to begin to admit that a parent's drinking is a concern.

To illustrate, a transcript of a portion of an actual first session with a family follows. This was a case of a family of five that presented with the chief complaint that the oldest child, Teddy, 14, was not doing as well as he could and as he used to do in school and was arguing at home too much, in a family that was otherwise doing quite well. The only hint of alcoholism was the smell of alcohol that seemed to be emanating from father. The first half hour or so of the session was spent with the whole family together. The therapist, a social worker seeing this family as part of postgraduate family therapy training under live supervision, began by asking each family member in turn what he or she would like different. In the course of doing this, first with parents and then with Teddy, daughter Patty, age 13, and son Bobby, age 9—in that order—several leading questions about alcohol use were asked. For example, when Teddy said he'd like less arguing with his father, the therapist asked if there was any difference in their arguing when someone was drinking. The answers were equivocal, and nobody either congruently denied or confirmed any role of drinking in their family's issues. This was a subtle case. It would have been much more comfortable to drop the issue of drinking. Only the firm conviction that, when there is any suspicion, alcohol use should be probed further, kept the subject alive long enough to later get the confirming, and essential, information that father's drinking was central to their chief complaint and to all other issues that were elicited.

The family was told it was customary for the therapist to spend some time with parents alone and some time with children alone in getting to know them, and that the children would be first. They agreed to that format, and the parents were sent outside to a waiting area while the therapist met with all three children together. The choice of first meeting with the children was made on two grounds. First, the family came in with a child-focused complaint, and it was felt wise to respect that, as there had already been a bit of chafing in the parents at the extent to which parental issues had been exposed at the outset. Pushing parental issues at that time would not have been useful if it had led to no further therapy sessions. Second, it is often easier to elicit drinking information and to rapidly gain leverage over an alcoholic parent through a private dialogue with chilren before parents have had time to send signals to children about what and how to respond to the therapists. The transcript picks up at the point that the parents have exited and the therapist has sat back down with the children.

The Interview

Teddy: Ha, ha, ha, now the truth will come out. We hate them. Ha, ha, ha.

Therapist: (*inaudible*)

Patty: I want to be an orphan.

Teddy: That we hate them?

Therapist: Um-hum.

Teddy: It's not true. It's just that my father is a conservative, my mother is a liberal— (*laughing*).

Therapist: And you?

Teddy: —and I'm cynical and my sister's cynical. My brother is—

Patty: —is perfect.

Teddy: —is a liberal. My parents won't nag him about, Well, he'll say he's liberal— They'll blame it on me and Patty, and my brother will get perhaps away "stark free."

Patty: Scot.

Teddy: Scot-free. Got it.

Patty: It's not "stark free."

Teddy: "Stark free." Hey!

Patty: With what crowd do you hang out? It's a mistake. Say it.

(TELEPHONE INTERCOM RINGS.)

Bobby: Telephone. Telephone. Telephone.

(THERAPIST GETS UP AND CROSSES ROOM TO PHONE.)

Teddy: A microphone.

Patty: Teddy, haven't you noticed that? God, you'd be a terrible spy.

(*All three kids wave to people behind the mirror.*)

Patty: Hi. Hi.

Bobby: (*Stands up and waves jacket.*)

The supervisor calls on intercom from room behind observation mirror. The therapist has to leave her chair to go to the phone, and the children cannot hear the conversation. Suggestions are made to help the therapist get out from under the rapid-fire banter of three highly verbal siblings by creating

Patty: Doing a little dance there? Was that the man behind the mirror?

Therapist: Yes.

(*THERAPIST RETURNS TO SEAT*)

Patty: That's what I call perceptive.

Therapist: Yes. It takes a lot of people a long time to figure that out. You did very well. So, how does their being a conservative and a liberal affect how they raise you?

Patty: Nothing. Nothing.

Teddy: It does too, Patty. My father has certain points of view. His father ran his life since he was one day old 'til he was 18. In fact, it hasn't stopped. He hasn't really told me. He just told me that his life was run and therefore, even though he hated it, that's the way my life should be run. I think that I live in a totally different day and age and—and—I-I mean—I know that lots of things are the same, but I think that the way people—I mean—lots of problems have been begun by this, but lots of — The way that people think is different, and you should raise your children not in the past, but now and—

Therapist: Okay, but how did— how did it affect you that one is conservative and the other is liberal? That they don't agree on political issues?

Teddy: Okay. Well—well—

Therapist: Political issues.

Teddy: Okay. My mother and

an opening to get back to issues of family conflict (and eventually to the role of drinking in their family conflicts). To this end, soon after returning to her seat, she raises again the conservative versus liberal issues conveniently provided earlier.

father will yell at each other, but not so successfully, and we try to put in our point of view. They'll yell at us and then we try to get out of it, but they keep us in it, also keep me in it and make me argue my point. All of them gang up on me—

Patty: Make you?

Teddy: Yes. Make me.

Therapist: So when they don't agree—

Teddy: Aunt Nell. Remember that, Patty?

Patty: No.

Teddy: Well, you weren't even there. You were upstairs asleep.

Patty: Maybe that's why.

Teddy: Kept her 'til 11 o'clock arguing.

Patty: You had a dumb argument.

Therapist: Okay. So when they disagree on what to do with you, they bring you into it.

Teddy: Yeah. Not—Not always.

Patty: No. He gets himself into it.

Teddy: Patty, shut up.

Therapist: Okay. Let's have each person speak for himself. Okay. So not necessarily, but sometimes.

Teddy: That was silly, but sometimes—

Therapist: Okay.

Teddy: Yeah. That would—it would— They would probably bring me in when it was totally stalemate and if they had to let it out on someone else.

Therapist: Okay. When they

get into a fight and they can't come to an agreement, they may bring you into it.

Teddy: Yeah.

(*Therapist*: Okay.
INTERCOM RINGS: THERAPIST GETS UP AND CROSSES ROOM TO PHONE.)

Patty: Hi, mirror man. (*Waves at video camera.*) We know it's you. (*Kids breathe into microphone, giggling.*)
THERAPIST RETURNS TO SEAT

Patty: A very lively crew.

Therapist: So this is—this is very nice of you, then to— to do this work for your brother and sister—

Teddy: It's not nice of me.

Therapist: —because if you didn't put yourself there between your parents, then one of the other two would have to do it.

Bobby: No. They wouldn't have to do it. They have— The idea is that they never brought anyone home with them.

Therapist: No. Because you do—

Bobby: No. I brought myself home, once.

Therapist: It's very nice of you to help your brother and sister out of that.

Bobby: It was (*inaudible*) against Teddy, and I defended Teddy.

Teddy: He—he does defend me sometimes. It gets my parents—especially my father—my father.

Therapist: Bobby, when your

A reframe of Teddy's behavior is introduced, one that incorporates a positive intent and seems rather paradoxical to Teddy—and that is, that when he steps into an argument with his parents (and it has just been established that it is often really first between his parents), he is actually being protective of his father's drinking, could you—do they—do your mom and dad fight more?

Bobby: No. They fight more when they're not drinking.

Patty: When they're sober.

Bobby: But my dad drinks all the time. So you can't really tell.

Therapist: What is "all the time?" When he comes home from work?

Bobby: Well, when he does, he drinks one glass, at least, a day, or three or four. Et cetera, et cetera.

Therapist: And then what does he do?

Patty: He's pacified.

Bobby: And whenever anybody disagrees—

Therapist: What does your father do when he's not drinking?

Bobby: —he screams his head off.

Therapist: Even when he's drinking?

Teddy: Yeah. If we disagree with him.

Therapist: Okay.

Patty: But if he's not drinking, he's very, very edgy. Plus if he goes on a diet when he drinks he's really grumpy, and anything you say can set him off. So if he is drinking, it—like—pacifies him—

Therapist: —for a while, until he screams and you argue.

Patty: When you argue with him—I mean—he's just temperamental. If you argue with him,

brother and sister. This approach soon has the desired effect of uniting the siblings more, when Bobby and Teddy start talking about how Bobby does sometimes defend Teddy. This mutually supportive attitude is important to establish because the therapist is about to go for confirmation from one or more of the children of parental drinking as a problem, which calls upon the child (ren) to take a big risk.

Out of the blue, in a matter-of-fact way, the therapist has asked a question that links drinking with parental fighting; and she does so using a presupposition that father drinks rather than a question whether he drinks, which might be more easily defended against with a flat no answer. She has also asked the youngest sibling, who is least prepared to sidestep the question. In fact, he gives an answer which is both a no and a yes. No, they don't fight more. Yes, drinking changes their behavior.

The therapist simply disregards the no part of the answer and persists with probing about alcohol use in the family.

he's just going to argue with you. He'll do it with anybody, even if he's not drinking, but—I mean—he's more prone to do it if he's not drinking.

Therapist: To be argumentative. And he's more prone to be violent, to get more excited, to yell louder.

Patty: When he's drinking? No. Just does it.

Therapist: Okay.

Patty: Drinking has nothing to do with it.

Therapist: Does he fall asleep in the evening?

Teddy: Sometimes.

Patty: Well, yes, but—I mean—

Therapist: Not at night. I'm talking about after dinner and for a greater part of the evening?

Patty: He goes to bed pretty early. I mean— He gets in bed, doesn't go to sleep. He —Either he's playing on the computer—I mean the times that he doesn't go to bed early is when he's playing on the computer or he's in an argument. That's—I mean— Usually he goes to bed—

Therapist: Who's he usually in an arugument with?

Patty: Either my Mom or Teddy.

Therapist: What kind of time does he spend with you?

Patty: Whatever time I want to spend with him.

Therapist: He will give it to you?

Patty: Well, I guess.

Therapist: What time have you spent with him?

Patty: Well, sometimes we just sit down and talk. It's not like I'm dying for his company. It's not like I feel deprived, the way you see it.

INTERCOM RINGS: THERAPIST GETS UP AND CROSSES ROOM TO PHONE.

Bobby: Here he is again.

Teddy: Probing questions.

Patty: I don't feel deprived of time.

Teddy: You're deprived of time. You just don't know it.

Patty: You're always blaming it on Mom and me. I didn't blame anything.

Teddy: It's just that I get really angry at Mom. She doesn't nag you as much.

Patty: Oh sure. She doesn't nag me as much. Ha, ha, ha.

Teddy: She doesn't nag you as much.

Patty: You get it all, Teddy. Oh, she doesn't take me to Bloomingdale's, poor me. I'm just a poor orphan, a pathetic, little orphan.

Bobby: And you're also rich, and if Mom doesn't get you polo pants, you take us back [to the store].

Patty: And Mom doesn't what?

Bobby: And Mom doesn't get you polo pants and then she gets Teddy polo pants.

Patty: That's a (*inaudible*) argument.

Teddy: Polo pants.

Bobby: Polo pants.

Patty: You don't even ask for them. You just get them.

Bobby: A polo tie and polo *wear.*

Teddy: I don't get polo ties. I don't think polo ties are effective in a blue tie.

Patty: Yeah, well, I do. I happen to think they are, still.

Teddy: Because they're more expensive.

Patty: Yes, why? Does status and all that bother you?

THERAPIST RETURNS TO SEAT.

Therapist: I appreciate your concern for your Dad. I don't know if you're aware that when somebody drinks a lot at different times of the day and then they stop drinking they get irritable because they would like to drink some more. I gather that you are concerned about your Dad's drinking. Is that right?

Teddy: Well, I don't really think about it anymore. I used to once a day. It hurts your mind. It hurts your vision, but I stopped because he'll get mad at me; and I don't think it will make much of a difference anyway. He won't stop now, no matter what you do, so—

Therapist: You know—sometimes parents need help. Would you be willing to work with me to help your parents?

Teddy: Depends on what.

Therapist: It would be some-

The supervisor has noticed that the children are successfully taking the subject away from drinking, before a correlation between drinking and interpersonal conflict (the chief complaint for this family) has been either confirmed or disproved. As much time as necessary has been taken over the phone to consult with the therapist sufficiently for her to feel confident of having an acceptable way to reintroduce the drinking topic. When she returns, she simply disregards intervening subjects and makes a statement that presupposes they are all still talking about drinking. She then stays with drinking (out of blind faith at first) until the issue is fully developed, at least one child has acknowledged he is concerned about father's drinking, and then the children's support is solicited by the therapist in assisting her to help father to overcome his drinking problem.

thing different from what you've been doing. I think you have been trying to help, but I'm not sure it's been effective; and I think we can talk about it next week, ways in which you could help.

Patty: It's not a problem.

Therapist: He thinks it's a problem.

Patty: You do?

Teddy: Patty, you're such a—

Patty: You think it's a problem?

Therapist: That's okay. If you think it is, then it is.

Teddy: The problem. I'm not exactly sure what you think is a problem. I'm not very sure. You mean his drinking? Or the way he acts toward the whole family? The way he acts towards me? The way he acts to my Mom—

Therapist: I'm not sure that those are all separate.

Teddy Well, they're all interrelated.

Therapist: That's right.

Teddy: But some are more important to me especially than others.

Therapist: That's right, and you would be willing to work on the way in which you could help your Dad be different, at least towards you.

Teddy: Yes. I know I'm very out—want to get my point across. I want to be right, and he gets mad at me because I introduce my point of view. I say it right to him, and I don't see what's wrong with that. He gets very angry , and recently he had gotten angry because I introduced my point of view. If I'm right, then it will take a lot for me to change my mind, but he has changed my mind several times. Then my sister yells at me because—she gets mad at me because she thinks that's wrong. Abraham Lincoln—whether he was a good president or not was a big thing. My parents—Me and my father talk probably about more important stuff than me and my Mother.

Therapist: But you are concerned about him. You do think that drinking affects the brain. We know that it affects the disposition, affects how calm he is and how violent he is and how able he is to handle your differences of opinion, and you would be willing to help him—

Teddy: —stop.

Therapist: —find another way—yeah—stop, and find another way of relating to you.

Teddy: Yes, that's as long as I don't have to give up stating my own point of view.

Therapist: And I'm sure that they would be interested in hearing your point of view, and we need to find a way in which you can say it where it doesn't upset them too much.

INTERCOM RINGS.

Therapist: Excuse me.

(*THERAPIST GETS UP AND CROSSES ROOM TO PHONE*).

Bobby: Probably don't know nothing, the guy behind the mirror, there.

Patty: It's not a problem.

Teddy: To you it isn't, Patty.

Patty: In what way is it a problem? You tell me. What way is it a problem?

Teddy: What, drinking?

Patty: Yeah.

Teddy: It changes—it changes the way he acts.

Patty: It pacifies him.

Teddy: It pacifies him sometimes, Patty.

Patty: It just makes him better.

Teddy: No, it doesn't.

Bobby: (*into microphone*) Will you stop calling up? (*laughter*)

Patty: (*into microphone*) I don't want to talk with you. It's not a problem. Get it? Get the message?

(*THERAPIST RETURNS TO SEAT*).

Therapist: Another thing. I'm sure you guys have friends whose parents have separated or divorced. When you hear your parents arguing or fighting, does that ever occur to you? Do you ever worry about it?

Patty: No.

Bobby: She thinks it's better because she gets more things.

Patty: No, just because they'll probably be happier if they were divorced.

Therapist: You think that they would be happier, separate.

Patty: Well, it depends, if they—if they—if they fight as much as they do—if they continue fighting as much as they do, then I think they'll be

The supervisor has suggested, over the phone, for the sake of time, now that drinking as an issue is confirmed, that the therapist probe for the other likely sensitive issues that the family may have avoided when all were together. Since so many children think at times about their parent's possibly separating, and since marital discord is usually associated with at least some type of transient behavioral disturbance in children, raising the issue early and pointedly is helpful. Relief may occur for the children either through mere sharing of their concerns or through subsequent reassurance they get from learning their fears are excessive.

happier being divorced, but my Mom doesn't want a divorce and my Dad doesn't either, so—

Therapist: —So neither one of them wants a divorce but you're not sure what that fighting means.

Patty: It means that they disagree with each other.

Therapist: But does that mean that they don't get along or don't love each other or don't want to be with each other?

Patty: I think they don't like each other.

Therapist: You think that their fighting means that they—

Patty: Not that they don't love each other, but that they don't like each other.

Therapist: You think that their fighting means that they don't like each other.

Teddy: Is there a difference?

Therapist: There is a difference.

Teddy: Sometimes I think about it—you know—in my room with the door locked, and I think that if they get divorced my life will get screwy.

Patty: That's exactly what I thought you were going to say.

Therapist: So you worry about that.

Teddy: Yeah, because I can't just handle one of them all by myself. It's just totally impossible. Walking around with one of them—I'm going to get in an argument with him for one reason—I think that my Mother is going to nag too much, and I'm going to get really angry and—I wasn't going to say this, but I'm becoming stronger than she is. She can—she can't—she can physically hit—she slapped me a few times, but that doesn't really hurt me, and I knew if I actually fought back like I fight back with my Father, I might win. So I don't for that reason.

Therapist: That's hard.

Teddy: And then my Father—I know that if I get in a fight with him and he gets violent, physically violent, there's not going to be anyone to protect me.

Therapist: Um-hum. Your Mother comes to protect you?

Teddy: My Mother comes to protect me?

Patty: Tries.

Teddy: She tries to protect me, but I think that's a trick of my Father's—just—

Therapist: I think you're probably right.

Teddy: I think that it deters him from hitting me. He hits me less. He hasn't hit me in a while now.

Therapist: How long?

Teddy: Four months, about. I mean—he's slapped around with me a few times, but not like really hitting me.

Therapist: How much did he used to hit you?

Teddy: Once every four weeks—three weeks? I mean—really get after me. And when he got—when he got this game called "Wizardry" and I was better in it, he—Somehow I think he has to be better than me in everything, and I was better in computers than him, and he didn't like that, and he doesn't like it and he's trying to get it. He's reaching for it. He's going crazy with computer books, computer magazines, learning things, trying to catch up with me in languages; and I don't really care if he was better than me or not. That just means I can just go to him and ask him a question about the computer instead of having to look it up and read a whole book. So, I think he strives to be better than me. He has to be better than me.

Therapist: What would happen to you if you had straight A's in school?

Teddy: I think they would leave me alone more.

Therapist: You do?

Teddy: And I—I—I know they would leave me alone more, and I know that if I started doing badly again that I would get back even more and that— I would hate that so much. I can't handle it. I mean—it's just something I can't handle. There are certain people—I mean—if I'm not interested in the subject and I don't—Then the teaching—that they teach me in a non-traditional way. It takes me a long time to adapt. They're teaching me about the brain, but I did well in art. In history they're teaching me about anthropology without even a book. So, it's really hard to—and I have to adapt to that, and I had to adapt to the seventh grade, and I have real problems, and Patty was just doing well in the seventh grade, and so they started stopping nagging her and started nagging me.

Patty: I was doing really bad—really bad in seventh grade.

Teddy: Yeah, but in sixth grade you were improving.

Patty: I was getting—like—almost straight A's.

Therapist: I want to wrap up for this week, and I want to say that I think you're remarkable children. You're all really very close and very concerned, and I think that we can just give it what you want. Okay? I'll meet with them next week.

Patty: Can we see ourselves? Did you use the two videotapes? Do we get to see ourselves? (*asked as all leave the room*).

The time interval between this first and the second session was longer than expected. The parents decided to cancel one appointment because of children's school conflicts and were ready to cancel another appointment, during what would have been the regular weekly time. Mother also had reported on the phone, while discussing the second schedule conflict, that things were much better. The therapist had responded that there is often a honeymoon phase early in therapy and surprised mother with a very accommodating last-minute time change just for the second appointment, which was accepted. Most of the ensuing session was spent with the therapist and parents talking while the children stayed in the waiting room.

The parents were given feedback at the outset that at least two of their children were concerned with two significant issues. First, they worried that their parents might get a divorce. Second, they were concerned about their father's drinking. The therapist felt comfortable sharing what the children had confided to her, because she believed that she, in fact, now had their explicit agreement to support her in her efforts to help the parents. Armed with this knowledge, framed as positively as possible in terms of the children's concern for their parents, she confronted the parents without being accusing, yet with considerable leverage to prevent their minimizing the issues raised. From that leveraged position, the parents were then asked their own opinions on each issue. They dispensed with the divorce issue in short order. Each affirmed their commitment to the relationship, their pleasure with an active sex life, and their readiness to reassure the children that, while they argue frequently and loudly, divorce was not a consideration. That was accepted by the therapist, who then pursued the drinking issue much more persistently.

Using the style presented in Chaper 5, she teased out, little by little, all the information necessary to document father's chronic, daily, heavy drinking from the time he got home until early bedtime. Mother's drinking was also found to be problematic but in a different way. She felt quite dependent on—truly—only a drink or two "to relax" after work and also feared that stopping drinking would jeopardize the couple's social life, which was comprised largely of heavy drinkers. Father admitted concern over his own drinking behavior and its consequences, while his wife first contested the veracity of the therapist's report of her children's concerns, then of her son's especially. Next she challenged the therapist's judgment and knowledge regarding alcoholism, for example, by describing others she knew who drank more than her husband and pointing out that he rarely acted drunk. It was only after the therapist carefully explored the ecological effect on the couple and family if her husband were to experiment with several weeks' or months' of abstinence that her fears of his stopping to drink came to the fore. An agreement was negotiated between husband, wife and therapist that he would attempt an extended period of abstinence, during which she was free to drink as she wished, with their proviso that they would not tell the children of this change; rather they would do it and wait to see if it were noticed. The therapist went along with this; and toward the end of that second session, the children joined in and were told convincingly by each parent that their parents were not going to get a divorce and that they would be making another change which they would just do, without further discussion.

The ensuing therapy consisted of 13 more sessions over about five months. Initially parents and children came in together. As Teddy was doing better in school and arguments had decreased to acceptable levels, the parents came in for the last few sessions without their children and began to address certain relationship issues. Within a week after the agreement to make certain changes, the children were fully informed by the parents at home of father's determination to alter his drinking habits. Whether or not he drank between sessions and the extent to which he drank, if he had at all, were inquired about routinely in subsequent sessions. As his drinking frequency and quantity lessened over a period of weeks, the time spent on the subject in sessions also decreased, eventually to simply a moment's check. The family's summer plans dictated a time-out from therapy. By the Fall, the family did not feel the need for resuming, and their therapist concurred.

CHAPTER 7

BICKER, BICKER, BICKER: A SESSION WITH A DIFFICULT COUPLE

Sometimes a couple walks in and you wonder how you're even going to get a word in edgewise. They seem to be continuously arguing, talk right over one another, and, in general, act like they have very limited interpersonal communication skills. On top of all that, you suspect alcoholism. At about this time you're thinking of Ordeal Therapy (1) and deciding that it applies more to what certain couples put the therapist through than vice versa. In this chapter, a transcript is presented of a session of the author's with a such a couple. There had been one prior session, only with the wife, Mabel. In that session she had made the case that she thought her husband, George, had a drinking problem and that she had wanted to alert a therapist privately to this before coming in as a couple, because George did not acknowledge drinking as a problem. This transcript then, is of the first session with the couple, shortly after one session with the wife. George and Mabel were in their early fifties.

The Interview

Brief conversation before videotape is turned on.

George: There are other problems.

Therapist: Let's go back to—for example, let's go back to a couple of things that you were mentioning. What are some examples of things where you feel— you feel she's—that Mabel's bossing you, telling you what to do and she—maybe she isn't.

George: All right. Let me—when we were first married, I knew that the house she was living in was her house; and I knew that her husband and her had bought it, and when I moved in May of 1978 I moved in with the feeling that we can share. Not that I was going to get anything out of it in the future, because I didn't want anything. You know—Well, so I cleaned the house up. I really did everything to it. Painted, I got storm windows on it now, I pulled out most of the rug except the living room. Then I was paying—My kids don't fool with us. My kids don't even come to see us because I feel I don't want them to bother us. I want to live the rest of my life just with her, not—. Things were going good. Her son had his own house on Leary Drive. Well, all of a sudden here, I got boats in the front yard, had to clean the garage out for her car to go into, see my—

Mabel: Don't you wish you had that boat now. You said you were going to use it. You sold it.

George: Now, honey, let me tell—I mean—

Mabel: Okay. Well—

George: Well, anyway, I come home and I'm real tired—I went down one time to go into the garage, here he's got another old car, piece of junk that's way in the—I can't even get to my tools.

Mabel: It's a Porsche and it cost $24,000.00.

George: It's an old car, let me tell you something. When it was new, it was expensive, but right now you could probably sell it for a hundred dollars.

Mabel: George, he—paid a lot for that car, so you—you—

George: All right. He has no place to put it, so she has him—He drives it in the garage, right up against everything. Now all of a sudden I look in front of the house and there's another car in front of the house.

Therapist: Am I correct to understand that your point is that you've asked your kids not to come around—

(*The session begins with the therapist making both non-verbal and content attempts to establish rapport with George, to hear his issues and his side of things, since he knows the therapist has talked with Mabel already.*)

George:—Because I don't want them to interfere in our lives, but she can't do that with her son.

Therapist: You want her to do the same thing with her son? Is that what you want?

George: Well, I want him to have—He's 35 years old. He has no place to live.

Mabel: He has a house, George.

George: —but it's rented. It's rented out.

Mabel: But the people are moving out this week and he's going to move in. He doesn't live with us.

George: Well, then he might take his two cars.

Mabel: He has never stayed with us and he never will and he's not dependent on us and I—

George: I commented on her car one time. Well, we don't drive her car. Any place we go, it's my car or—Well, she says that's her car—or our car.

Mabel: I bought it before we were married. I pay the insurance, I pay the personal property—

George: Well, I do all mine. I do all mine the same way but that's all right. That's okay.

Therapist: Are you saying you'd like to—to feel that sometimes—

George: I'd like for us to be a pair. We are not a pair, Doctor, and I can sit here and talk to you for five hours and she can not convince me we are man and wife. We are two different people separated right at this time by many little problems in existence. Money for one. If I bring up money, right away she comes back at me and she says, "Well, I can't help you out on my salary because I have to pay $400 every three months on added income." Well, that's income that has nothing to do with me. That's all right, but she should take her $400 from her added income to pay the taxes and help me when I need help out of her salary. She don't help me nowhere.

Mabel: When I ask you to help me pay half the taxes you say, "It's your house, you pay the taxes," When I wanted a bedroom set—

George: I'm talking about you—

Mabel: Listen, when I wanted a bedroom set [it was] "This is your house, you buy the furniture."

George: Honey, everything in the house is mine now except that little bedroom set.

Mabel: George, it was all furnished. I had lived there three years when you moved in.

George: Yeah, but I brought in good stuff, honey.

Mabel: You had an old bedroom set—

George: That's immaterial. I can move out and leave it all here—

Mabel: You had an old bedroom set and an old dining room set. You had nowhere to put it, so I gave my bedroom set away and my dining room set—

George: You didn't give it away.

Mabel: —so you could move it in there. You had—were going to have to give it away.

George: Well, I could have sold it.

Mabel: Well, you didn't have anywhere to put it so I made a place for you to put it. Now don't tell me nothing was there.

Therapist: So you're saying that the two of you haven't yet come up with ways to work out your differences so that they're done with, is that correct?

George: We can't resolve them. No.

Mabel: You sold my son your lawnmower. I bought a new lawnmower after you moved in. I bought furniture for the rec room—

George: We bought a new lawnmower—

Mabel: I bought the lawnmower myself—

George: That's the lawnmower we bought at Sears and Robuck—Montgomery Ward.

Mabel: —no, on my credit card my husband gave me.

Therapist: What would be something—like when you come home from work and you say you've been listening to a lot of things at the office—

Mabel: So have I.

Therapist: And you have, too. What would be your request that you take—that you hear as a demand. Okay? What would be one thing?

George: Oh my God. That is hard.

Mabel: I had his dinner ready for him when he comes home—

Therapist: Just mention one.

George: She—she comes at me. It may be that I didn't make the bed up or something or I didn't have my breakfast when I went to work. She'll tear in on me on that or—

Mabel: I just say, "Honey, you didn't eat breakfast at home."

George: —or it might be that I'm running—I'm rushing to get to batting practice.

Therapist: Let me—let me hear that. Could you say that again?

Mabel: I said, "Honey, you didn't have breakfast at home. What did you have for breakfast?"

Therapist: Okay. Now how did you hear that?

George: And I said, "Well, I didn't eat any breakfast." And you just can't accept it.

Mabel: I'm very concerned about his weight.

George: You know where my weight's from.

Mabel: He won't get on the scale.

Therapist: Where is your weight from?

George: Well, I just love—I eat and I drink and all and I don't exercise. I sit in an office by a desk all day.

Therapist: Okay. What—what do you drink?

George: Whenever I want.

Therapist: What do you drink?

(*The therapist's experience of the session is that it moved from his letting them hassle irrelevantly to suddenly focusing in on alcohol use and holding on to the alcohol issue like glue as its expanding role in their lives is developed. As soon as, but only when, a relevant opportunity arises, the therapist asks about drinking, and immediately, once the door is open, he leaps through without stopping to say the amenities. In this case the opening is Mabel's statement, "I'm very concerned about his weight." Soon the therapist asks George, "Where is your weight from?" George obliges by admitting, "Well, I just love—I eat and drink and all and I don't exercise. . . . " There follows a steady barrage of questions directed either at eliciting the specific amount George drinks or the ways in which his drinking has come to have negative consequences in his relationship with Mabel.*)

George: All of it, really.

Therapist: Like what? I mean—

George: Well, if I want—I drink beer when it's warm. I love beer.

Therapist: How much—typically how much beer would you have?

George: I don't have no certain amount. Sometimes I can drink six bottles. Sometimes I can drink one bottle. I don't know. It differs.

Therapist: Well, let's say, in the past few days. What would have been typical each day?

George: All right. I went through—over a weekend, I guess, I could drink about 18 bottles in three days. Now during the week I don't drink that much.

Therapist: These are what-size bottles?

George: Twelve ounces. Regular bottle. I sweat it out, though, because I'll be down at the beach and I move around a lot. Not a lot, but I move around some. It's something that I can stop if I want to. I have enough will power.

Therapist: Do you have days when you drink more than six or seven?

George: No, no. Not more than six or seven. Not in a day. In the three days' time, sometimes, I'll drink—in the three day—period I can buy four, six packs. That's 24 bottles, but I give some of them away if I'm at the beach. On weekends. I would say over the three-day period I could drink 15 bottles. Maybe drink eight one day, and the next day I won't drink five. She's on me all the time for that.

Therapist: For what?

George: For drinking beer. Even at the beach she's cutting down on me. Even at home. I will bring beer home and as soon as she sees it, she gives it to her son.

Therapist: Do you know what—

Mabel: George—

George: Or you give it to somebody. I can't find it.

Therapist: Do you know what about it she's down on you for?

George: She don't want me to drink it.

Therapist: Why? What about your drinking bothers her? Do you know?

George: Because of my weight.

Therapist: Is it? Is that the reason? Weight?

George: Yeah.

Mabel: Calories, too.

Therapist: Can you check that out? See if that's her reason?

George: I know that's the reason. She'll tell you that's the reason.

Therapist: Ask her right now.

(*George begins to minimize his drinking early on, but that is simply ignored. An early opportunity is found, through direct interaction, to facilitate Mabel's affirmation of the concerns she has about his drinking. As other issues are developed, the role alcohol plays is woven into them.*)

George: Is that the reason you don't want me to drink, honey?

Mabel: That's partly the reason—

George: What's the other part?

Mabel: —and part of the reason is you drink too much and it's embarrassing to me when you keep drinking.

Therapist: Do you know what part of that is embarrassing? What about?

George: She just don't want me to drink cause of my weight, that's all.

Therapist: Can you find out from her what she means by that?

George: All right. When does it embarrass you, honey? She's not—she wasn't brought up this way.

Therapist: You're answering. Let her answer.

Mabel: It's embarrassing to me when I went to the Al-anon meeting; and you were fussing and ranting and raving and cussing the whole time because you drove me down there, and I didn't like to go where it was. It was raining and bad and you said, "I'm going to be drinking in the bar the whole time you're in there." And he did, so I went there and cried, knowing that you're not trying to work with me, to try to drink less, and you hide your drinking from me, and I'm worried about your drinking problem.

George: And that's embarrassing you.

Mabel: Yes, and it bothers me.

Therapist: Are you—are you worried for him? What will happen?

George: I know that.

Mabel: When he was operated on a couple of years ago, the doctor—

George: —four years ago.

Mabel: —told me he found that he has a —has liver damage and the way he drinks is not doing him any good.

Therapist: So you're worried for his health when he drinks—

Mabel: Yes, his health.

Therapist: —and not just his weight.

Mabel: Both.

George: Well, you have to appreciate it and I do.

Therapist: Were you aware of that? That she was worried about liver damage?

George: Sure. Yeah. Yeah. Oh, yeah. The other problems are if I could sit down, if I could ever sit down and talk with her, but when you're at the dining table we can't discuss things, she—she—she—if I was to bring up something—

Mabel: You're the one who blows up, George. You have a very short fuse. You told me when we were married that you didn't have any patience.

George: Well, I still don't have any.

Mabel: And you blow up, you can't—I can't talk with you because you're not reasonable.

George: Honey, you won't sit down and reason things out.

Mabel: You're the one. I can—I would love to sit down and talk, but—

George: Have you ever gone through my checkbook, honey, like I asked you to, to find out where the money is going? Like I've asked you many, many times. I says, "Honey, just sit down with me and let's work it out." I says, "I cannot continue the way I'm going. I am broke. I am spending $1,800 and my income is $1,500—and that's even having the kids' money, and I'm spending $3,000 more a year than I'm making. I cannot do this.

Mabel: All right, George, you made more than I did. You make more than I do.

George: Where do I stop? How much more do I make than you do? How much do you make a year? I'll ask you. I don't know. I couldn't tell her.

Mabel: You know, I make 16.

George: All right. So I make 18.

Mabel: All right, so you can afford to pay $180 a month rent.

George: I'm paying you when I make it.

Mabel: You can afford it. Every month I ask you, You say, "I'm broke."

George: Mabel—

Mabel: You know exactly when the first of the month comes and you never—you always will draw out $100 cash or do something so—

George: For the house. It's not for me.

Mabel: No. No. No.

George: Oh, okay.

Mabel: You told me that you're not spending a nickel on that house and you weren't going to do that.

George: Honey, I just spent $27 for paint.

Mabel: All right. I spent $36.

George: For what?

Mabel: For the living room and the hall and the dining room. You said—

George: Okay. Okay.

Therapist: I'm also hearing you say that something goes on at home that makes it hard even to talk. The talking that you're doing right now, is this better than it goes at home?

George: Same thing. The same thing goes on at home that's going on right now.

Therapist: Same thing.

George: You cannot reason with her.

Therapist: Does it make a difference whether alcohol is in the picture, as far as how you can talk and chat?

George: No, because I'm not even drinking when we were trying to talk.

Therapist: That's what I am trying to—I want to understand if Mabel feels it makes a difference whether alcohol is around.

(*At a moment's pause in the therapist's vigilance, this couple diverts to new and often tangential subjects. After a while, whenever resolving any difference comes up, or any specific issue is raised such as money, the therapist redirects the issue to drinking as a contributor to prolonging whatever other issue is at hand.*)

Mabel: I think so too. I think he's more belligerent, more arrogant when he's—

Therapist: Is—is alcohol in the picture right now?

Mabel: I don't know. I haven't been home with him.

George: No. I haven't had anything to drink. Didn't have a drink yesterday.

Mabel: When I went to a meeting Monday night it was (*inaudible*)— Yes. And I know if I leave him at home, and it's happened, when I went to my meetings at the clubs, every time I would come home he couldn't focus his eyes good. He drinks by himself.

George: When was this? Monday night or are you talking about Tuesday?

Mabel: I'm talking about all those years that I was in the club, and it happened every night. You did that, George.

George: One drink. I can come home from work, my eyes are this way because of the way I have to do close work.

Mabel: No, honey, I'm talking about you—you would drink to excess. I know you would tell me you didn't have anything in your drink, and one night I drank it just to prove to him that he was lying to me, and I got so drugged that I couldn't go to bed unless I crawled. This is one drink in a 16-ounce glass. And he still insisted that there was nothing in it, and I was seeing double. I had never been like that in my life.

Therapist: Are some of the beers—Is there—

Mabel: This is alcohol.

Therapist: —hard liquor?

George: This is when I have a drink. I have a bar full of drinks if I want—

Mabel: And he told me, he insisted, there was nothing in it and he still—

George: —If I want a drink I'll have it, don't worry. Everything you could drink I've got in my bar. But I don't drink this much of liquor, hard liquor, but sometimes when I come home I am so down and so—I've had a lot of problems at the office. I had two weeks laid off for something I didn't do. Suspended without pay for two weeks and I tried to explain this to her in March. I said, "Now honey, I can't give you the $180 the first of March because I have only drawn $300 for the month. Now, out of that I have to pay for all the food and all the bills.

Therapist: I don't think that's quite the issue, though.

George: Oh. You mean the drinking now?

Therapist: Well, yeah. Drinking is one of the issues now and, of course, having just—

George: I'm from a drinking family. I've always been a man from—My father was from—my father—even my grandfather—My grandfather made alcohol. He made bootleg whiskey.

Mabel: So your brother died from alcoholism.

George: I have a brother that died. Well, that was one of the causes, alcohol.

Therapist: Your brother is alcoholic.

George: Now, my brother that's younger than I am is—you might consider an alcoholic.

Mabel: So, that's all the more reason why you should tell—

George: The only one who seems to be away from the alcohol is the oldest.

Therapist: So part of what you're telling me is that you saw so much drinking going on as you were growing up and you were aware of so much with two of your brothers, by comparison you're not—

George: No, I drink because of her.

Therapist: Okay. Now hold on.

Mabel: What, George?

Therapist: Wait. The reason doesn't matter.

George: Oh.

Therapist: If you use alcohol like a medicine, for example, if you come home and you had a bad day, so you drink or you had a fight, so you drink, that's using it like a medicine. That doesn't—that doesn't make any difference as to whether there's an alcohol problem or not. In fact, when you use it as a medicine you're at a higher risk for developing alcoholism. An alcohol problem. We've demonstrated that statistically

George: That's true.

Therapist: And what I'm interested in is that in your family, though, the people were such heavy drinkers that, by comparison, you're not as heavy a drinker.

George: No way.

Therapist: Okay. And that may be misleading for you.

Mabel: Because you have a damaged liver from it.

Therapist: See, your standard, your threshold for seeing a problem as alcoholism might be awfully high compared to someone who didn't grow up in a family with heavy drinkers.

(*A strong family history of alcoholism is easily elicited. Often, when that is the case, the information is offered by way of justifying one's own behavior. That is presupposed here, and the therapist adjusts by shifting into an educational mode to which he returns frequently therafter. For example, he teaches (reframes) that when one has so much heavy drinking in his background, his threshold for recognizing his own drinking as excessive may be quite high. Also, George is told that why he drinks is not important here, that the use of alcohol like a medicine creates higher risks of alcoholism, and that the most useful definition of problem drinkers is simply having "problems relating to alcohol in their lives and yet they haven't changed their drinking habits."*)

George: See, that's it. She had no drinkers.

Therapist: Okay. So that—that in some ways you're at a disadvantage, George, when it comes to alcohol, because your measure of the problem is so high that you may not have realized that you could get into problems with alcohol on a lower level. In fact, most people who are problem drinkers in this country drink at a lower level than your brothers.

George: Probably, yeah.

Therapist: They still have—They're still problem drinkers. They still have problems relating to alcohol in their lives and yet they haven't changed their drinking habits. That's—that's a drinking problem. That's probably as useful a way to define alcoholism as any—Is that if you've had problems and maybe they're in a marriage, maybe they're in the liver or whatever, but if you've had problems related to a certain level of drinking and yet that level of drinking doesn't go down or isn't eliminated, then you've got a drinking problem. People in Alcoholics Anonymous would say, "Well, you're an alcoholic." Why call it anything else because it needs the same approach to get help. Sure, there are people who are futher along and are a lot sicker than you. It's just a difference of degree, though. You know.

So I hear your [Mabel's] concern. I hear it as a genuine one, and you may start from a much different point than George does. You may start from a background that didn't include much alcohol, much exposure to it. So, for you, his drinking must be very large, but for him, and I think you can see, for him it's really not so much. It's a lot—He's really much more moderate in his use than people he grew up with, or maybe even some of your friends now.

George: They live off of whiskey where I come from.

Therapist: Yeah, Now they also died of it, but they didn't know it too much. I mean—they just—

George: I wouldn't doubt it. My father died of a heart attack but—could have been from whiskey. I don't know.

Therapist: It could have been related. See, because if you drink enough whiskey for long enough the heart muscle also wears down, gets a disease from the alcohol itself.

George: I don't drink this much.

Therapist: Okay. You don't drink as much as they did.

George: No. I don't drink as much. I think she thinks I do. It looks—I drink in spots, Doctor.

Therapist: Okay. But what I'm getting at is, you can drink in spots or you can drink six beers a day and—

George: It'll never faze me—

Therapist: —knowing that the doctor already said that you had liver problems related to alcohol. What we are saying is—

George: I was once a heavy drinker. I'm all right now. When I married her I was a very heavy drinker.

Therapist: Okay, so you really—

George: I would down a gallon of whiskey a week, and I won't lie.

Mabel: I didn't know that because—

Therapist: Okay. So, you're drinking a lot less now. Is that right?

George: Oh, hell. A third less.

Mabel: That's why he drinks when I'm gone because he doesn't want to hear me worry about it.

George: I drink lots less because I don't want—I stopped drinking right after I met her. This was my way—of going home at night, watching TV. I was alone, by myself, watching ballgames. Well, I could sit down and drink Canadian Club and 7-up—you know—until the game is over.

Mabel: A whole fifth.

George: And all of a sudden a half gallon of Canadian Club was gone, so I'd go get another one. And I drank heavy at that time. This was after my wife died. I didn't drink this much while she was living because I was in the trucking business and I was gone a lot, but then I met her [Mabel] and her and I were dating. We fell in love. We're still in love. It ain't a matter of being in love. We—I—I love her more than anything in the world; but I can only be dominated to a certain point—then I break.

Therapist: Okay. So I—I—I've got a better understanding.

George: But, now, like when I'm mowing the grass, I'll get out, I'm real hot in the yard, well, I want a cold beer. I don't care what happens. Hell can freeze over. I'm going to have a beer. If it's not in the house, I'm going to go get it.

Mabel: All right, when I came here the last time—excuse me—when I came here the last time and I was all worried and I wanted you to come and you wouldn't come and I—there was a pint of whiskey on the cabinet, and I just marked it with a felt pen and—

George: Good whiskey, too.

Mabel: —the next night I looked at it and it was down to a third so you had drank a half a pint of whiskey while you were cutting the grass. And I looked—then I looked at it again that night and—

George: No. I drank it watching TV.

Mabel: Well, it was down to a third and when I looked at it to show you, it was down to a fourth, and you had a drink you had just poured out, and you were hiding it by the refrigerator—

Therapist: That was the third drink.

Mabel: Yes. You were hiding it by the—You told me. "Well, I just got some"—

Therapist: That's whiskey, right?

Mabel: Yes.

Therapist: And that would have been in addition to beer that day?

George: I didn't have no beer that day.

Mabel: But he hides it from me.

George: I didn't have no beer that day.

Mabel: He evidently feels—

George: That's one thing. I won't mix the two.

Mabel: Honey—honey, you must feel guilty because you hide it from me. You don't want me to know that you have that drink. You'll say there's nothing in it. You said that so many times.

George: Only because you cannot accept me as I am. If I want a drink, I'm going to have it, but if I said, "Yeah, there's a drink in it, you'd grab it like a wild woman, and you'd thrown it into the sink or—"

Mabel: Well, honey, when you drank a whole pint, I think that's time to say something.

George: This is one of your problems, you won't listen.

Therapist: Now—now one thing that's—that Mabel, you—clearly you feel that alcohol is a problem in your relationship, okay? And you have begun to do something about it. You guys—I understand you did go to an Al-anon meeting.

Mabel: I went one time and—

Therapist: Would you be prepared to go some more?

Mabel: Oh, God, it was so depressing, and then when he's not helping me and he's out drinking beer and I know it, I'm just wasting my time. (*Crying.*)

Therapist: Well, actually, Al-anon is for people who feel they're living with someone who's drinking too much. See, Al-anon is for the spouse, the family members.

Mabel: (*Crying.*) I know it is, but I felt like just chucking it all. Why do I have to put up with this and why live the rest of my life like this, if he's not going to try to help me?

Therapist: I think going there, as we've talked about, is something independent of whether the person who's doing the drinking is ready to do something more about it. Right? See if—if—one of you feels that alcohol is a problem in your life—

George: I don't feel it is.

Therapist: —and the drinking is not changing—

Mabel: You're the last one to admit it.

Therapist: —you see, then it is.

Mabel: That's the way it goes.

Therapist: Clearly, for Mabel it's a problem in your lives. Right? Are you agreeing with that? Would you agree with that?

George: Well, it has been since we were married. I'd have one drink, since we were married, and she would raise hell.

Mabel: No, no, no. I can have one drink.

Therapist: But—but the reality is that in your relationship, alcohol is an issue, a constant issue.

George: One of the issues.

Therapist: Yeah. It's not the only issue, and I think if—

George: No.

Therapist: —if—like—What I'd love to know is, what issues would be left over if you went six months without having a drink. Now, because over the period that you're not drinking, we could really do some effective work on some of the other things that you're trying to deal with. Where so often while people are focused just on the drinking that—

George: But we're not.

Therapist: —that they really don't make—Well, one of you is—that they really don't make good use—as good use as they could—of the work we can do on the other issues that you have to deal with, 'cause alcohol sort of takes over the situation. You've seen that, haven't you?

George: Many times.

Therapist: And whether it's—whether it's the effect of the person doing the drinking or the effect on the people around him, it still takes over, and I—

George: I haven't drank a pint of whiskey for a whole year. I mean, since the first of the year.

Therapist: I am not saying you are. Now—

George: Now I haven't, 'cause we haven't been any place.

Therapist: But—but—but still your wife is conditioned to react to that alcohol. Right? She's been around you an occasional time [. . . inaudible . . .] even when you've known her.

George: We can go to dances, if I drink more than one I catch hell when we come home.

Mabel: Honey, don't say that because I'll drink at least two myself.

George: Well, she does in her own way give me hell for it.

Mabel: All right. New Year's Eve you'll drink and drink and then after we have breakfast then you keep drinking and drinking and drinking and you take one to drive you home and when you get home you have another. Just like the other night at the Holiday Inn—

Therapist: Do you feel there are times when he drives unsafely?

Mabel: Yes. A lot of times, and I have driven some, but when we went to the Holiday Inn you drank for two—

George: Honey, I haven't gotten drunk in ages.

Mabel: —let me talk—for two solid hours. I know you can drink a lot. I couldn't begin to drink—

George: No you couldn't.

Mabel: —what you drink. If I did, I'd be laying on the floor.

George: That's right.

Therapist: See, George, when somebody says, as you have,"I don't get drunk"—

George: I don't.

Therapist: See? I get worried.

George: I don't get drunk.

Therapist: I get worried when somebody says they don't get drunk, because you know what not getting drunk means. It means—it means that your body—the cells in your body have adjusted to the point where you have the tolerance to more alcohol—

George: I've always been this way, though.

Therapist: Well, you've always been—You've always been a heavy drinker.

George: No, sir. I didn't drink heavy until my wife died.

Therapist: Okay, perhaps—

Mabel: Oh, George, you told me you came home and she was laying on the floor. She was drunk.

George: Only the once—once in all the years we'd been married.

Mabel: Well, I know you drink—you have always—

George: She had only had a couple of drinks. She didn't drink that much.

Therapist: Again, heavy by whose terms, George?

George: Hmm?

Theapist: Heavy by whose terms? In other words even while you were married to her, what—could you have four of five drinks in the evening and not show it?

George: No, because I didn't have time for that.

Therapist: But if you did, would you show it?

George: No. It wouldn't bother me.

Therapist: Would or would not?

George: Would not.

Therapist: Okay. What I'm saying is—

George: I could drink a fifth of whiskey a night, it wouldn't bother me that much.

Therapist:What I'm saying is that you already had a tolerance to it, and you didn't realize that.

George: When I signed up for World War II, I didn't drink very much. I drank very little when I was in my teenage years.

Mabel: But you said that you could drink a fifth of whiskey and it wouldn't bother you.

George: Mixed, right now or over a period of time and it wouldn't bother me. I could drink it all day and it wouldn't bother me.

Mabel: Well, that's just what he's saying. That's a case of—That's serious, honey. That's serious.

George: Well, honey, I know that, but I don't drink—To you, I can have two or three beers and it's a lot to you. To me, I can drink eight beers and it's not a lot to me. It don't bother me.

Mabel: No. Let the doctor talk.

Therapist: Eight beers is not a lot for you—

George: I could stop drinking, Doc, and it still wouldn't stop her problem with me.

Mabel: Let the doctor talk.

Therapist: I'm not—I'm not disagreeing with that. I'm saying two things. One is, if you can drink eight and it won't affect you, that you have a tolerance to it. It means your body had made an adjustment to it—

George: I know that.

Therapist: —which is not good for you. It's actually not a good sign.

George: I know that, too.

Therapist: Okay. The other is that even if you deal with the alcohol—even if you were to stop drinking entirely, I know that there would be issues for the two of you to work out.

George: Many of them.

Therapist: You've told me that, but I'm saying still a third thing, and that is that if you really wanted to get the kind of help that I hear you seeking in your relationship, because I hear you care about the relationship, you really want it to work out, but you may have to get some help on stopping the drinking.

George: I can walk out of here and not touch another drop ever, and it wouldn't bother me. I can do that. I have enough will power, if I wanted to do it.

Therapist: For our purposes, if the two of you really want to go a lot further in working things out so that you can be happier with one another, and I think you have the potential, would you be prepared to go ahead and, let's say—just taking it week by week—to go ahead and stop the drinking?

George: I'm not going to stop but—

Mabel: Hallelujah. I wish you would—

Therapist: Wait. Wait. Wait—

George: Now, the reason I say that—I just want her to accept—sometimes I can drink one beer and not want no more for two or three days.

Therapist: Yeah. I understand, but not with any guarantees and I'm just saying—you're saying you can't do it—

George: Oh, I can do it if you want to.

Therapist: I'm saying—I'm saying that you can only get what you want with Mabel, and my work with you, as well as you want it, if alcohol goes out of the picture. And there are a lot of reasons for that, and some of it has to do with how she reacts to alcohol. But I'm saying, why disregard that, and take that into account if you really want to see how she—

George: If she would take other problems into account. I wouldn't mind taking one of my major problems in account, if she takes one of hers.

Therapist: For example. For example, what would you like her to take into account?

George: To settle her money issues and to settle her issues with her son. Now, I told her one time I says, "Honey, tell your son, "Get your damn cars out of here and keep them out." He sells cars and old junks, and he brings them to the house where I live and I know, being in my work, what happens.

Therapist: How about—how about if Mabel told him she wants the cars out tomorrow?

George: She can't tell him this.

Therapist: Let's say that she did—

George: She won't.

Therapist: Let's say she did. Would you—would you go along with our part of starting out the working together without drinking this week? We could then meet and talk about—

George: I won't drink no more until Saturday. Then I'll have a few beers when I'm on the fishing boat. I'll drink three or four beers when I go fishing. I won't—I told her, I won't drink all week. I cannot touch it—

Mabel: He told me that, but he did it.

George: —and I can do this.

Mabel: George, you lied to me, though, and I have to say that.

George I say, honey, I can do it.

Therapist: Let's say 100 percent. You're saying you can do it, you've got the will power and I'm prepared to find that out.

Mabel: Well, he's—he's—he will always—

George: Like I tell you, I won't drink it during the week, but when I go to the beach I want a few beers.

Mabel: George, you told me that last week, but you did.

George: Why did I do that?

Therapist: How about—well, we didn't have any other kind of agreements, so how about at all times when you're together—

George: I don't drink around her—with her.

Therapist: Well, I mean—I mean, even when you're going to be together, because if you've been drinking, it's the same thing for her as if you're drinking in front of her. You know. She can tell.

Mabel: I can smell it. That's why we've had arguments at night.

Therapist: She has her defense. See? Alcohol is in the picture in your lives together any time that she is *aware* that it's been around. Isn't that right? She reacts to you as though you're drinking. Right?

George: One drink and she reacts.

Therapist: That's right.

Mabel: No, I wouldn't say that. I wouldn't go that far.

Therapist: But, I think—I would. I would say very likely just alcohol being around—

Mabel: Because I can't trust him.

Therapist: Smelling it—seeing it—doesn't matter. It's a signal for you two to start acting certain ways together that you might not without alcohol; and I'm saying that if you want to get the things in here you want, in terms of your relationship with one another, I can help you with those things, but I can help you a lot better if alcohol is out of the picture, because it's a—it's just a—it's a constant stimulus.

George: Well, well, I—

Therapist: You know what I'm saying, now?

George: I can go all week while I'm working and coming home without it.

Mabel: That's what you told me last week—

George: Well, I'm telling you here now. That's last week. Who cares? Let's start in the future.

Therapist: Are you saying that you could not go a week and a weekend?

George: I probably could, but then again, I don't know. It's a round gem and I enjoy sitting in the sun having a cold beer or—

Therapist: See, George, the problem is- the people in AA will tell you this: If you can't imagine enjoying a period of time without alcohol, then you've got a problem with alcohol.

George: I wouldn't disagree with anybody that it turns out that I have a problem with alcohol, but at the same token I'm not saying that it's something that I can't do without, but at the same token if I'm sitting on the beach—

Mabel: Well, he asked you a question. Could you do without it one week?

George: If I wanted to, I probably could.

Mabel: When you go fishing, they ask you to bring all the beer, and these are the low-class people that I don't like.

George: She thinks these people—she thinks they're low-class. I don't think they're low class. She does.

Mabel: I know, honey. That's what everybody in the campground said. I hate to go down there—

George: I don't hate nobody. I don't know them that well.

Mabel: They all have a beer in a hand all day long, and that's who you associate with.

Therapist: Well, it sounds like they're problem drinkers.

Mabel: They are.

Therapist: Okay.

Mabel: They are and that's why they have brawls and—

George: How can you judge people? I don't know.

Therapist: It doesn't mean anything except that they're problem drinkers. You know—we've got congressmen and other people who are problem drinkers too.

Mabel: That's why I hate for him to associate with them because he does the same thing just like when we were—

Therapist: So you're not really saying that it's low-grade. You're saying that you don't like it because you're concerned that he's going to do more drinking with them.

Mabel: Yes, he does.

Therapist: Okay.

Mabel: I know, I shouldn't—

Therapist: —and afterwards—

Mabel: I know, he drinks when I don't see him, but what I don't see I can't—

Therapist: Okay. Now, I want to know if you're prepared, whether or not George is prepared to do anything with alcohol? Do you recognize it as your problem in life sufficiently where you're prepared to go to Al-anon because I can be more helpful with the two of you also if you're going to Al-anon, no? That's independent of what he does. It's your own personal responsibility.

(*The therapist raises the topic of Al-anon, confirms that Mabel has gone as she was directed in her individual session, and educates a bit more about what and who Al-anon is for. He also teaches, while ostensibly agreeing with the still ardently resisting George, that alcohol comes to serve as a conditioned stimulus for co-alcoholic behavior by a spouse, so that even one drink can set off alcoholic-type interactions. Note: "Co-alcoholic" refers to a significant other person whose behavior has the effect, on balance, of perpetuating the drinking behavior of the alcoholic, presumably quite unwittingly, through behavioral conditioning.*)

Mabel: That's awfully hard.

Therapist: I know.

Mabel: From what I heard of them, not to say anything when their husbands go on a binge or— That's not helping them—

George: I don't go on a binge.

Mabel: —because—different degrees, honey. It gets progressively worse and you're drinking more and more.

Therapist: Okay. It is—I think you're describing a reason for going to Al-anon, aren't you? Because you really feel the problems are there whether or not George does, and you're constantly trying to deal with it in your own way. And I would need that kind of evidence and commitment from you if I'm going to go ahead and work with both of you. I need to know that you're working on those parts of the problems that have to do with this constant issue of alcohol because you need to be certain things outside of these sessions too really make these sessions helpful.

George: Can I say something, Doctor? There's only two places I drink. I don't go to bars or anything like that to drink. I don't drink out. I do not drink in a bar, or I don't go into restaurants and drink or anything like that unless I'm with her.

Mabel: Honey—honey, he's already heard that.

Therapist: Do you notice how it doesn't seem to make a difference what the conditions are, what the situations are? In terms of your relationship with one another, alcohol is the problem, isn't it? You're agreeing with that—with me on that, aren't you?

George: No. I can't see why it should be, cause I don't drink that much.

Mabel: Why do you hide it? Then why do you hide it?

Therapist: I didn't say whether it should be, I'm saying it is.

George: If she could accept when I come home at night—I'm very tired, weary, very downhearted—I could have a drink, sit down, watch TV awhile and relax—

Therapist: George, she doesn't accept it.

George: She don't. That's right and it makes it very hard on me.

Therapist: In fact, every time she sees the alcohol, she's worried about you. She's worried about what it will do to you. She's also worried that the two of you won't be able to talk anything out that you need to talk out because she's worried about how you act when you drink, even if it's just a little bit of drinking and— So it's a constant problem in your lives, isn't it? I mean—you both are telling me that.

George: Used to not be. Only lately it's become a problem.

Mabel: Honey don't you feel guilty hiding it?

Therapist: Nobody's questioning that either.

George: I don't hide it. It's open.

Mabel: You always hide it. I asked you—

George: She takes it out.

Therapist: I don't think you're saying you'd feel any better whether he drank this much hiding it or in secret. You're concerned about this much drinking, aren't you?

Mabel: That's right.

Therapist: So it really doesn't matter whether it's hidden or not.

George: You weren't concerned about your first husband. He drank every day.

Mabel: George, he had one little "toddy" he called it—very small—before dinner, and that was it. You drink before dinner, after dinner—

George: I take one drink and you give me hell.

Mabel: Honey, you drink until you go to bed, and then you're just knocked out.

Therapist: See. You're both right. She could have—You could have one drink only and she'd give you hell. That's right, too, but that's because alcohol has been around so much now and is associated with so many unhappy things in your relationship, that one drink triggers everything that eight or ten would trigger. So you're right in what you're observing, but it doesn't mean that it's not a problem, does it?

George: Never bothered me too much. You're right.

Therapist: But I understood that you cared about working things better in this relationship.

(*The focus is brought back to George's relationship goals as a reason for stopping the drinking. The therapist reaffirms that there are other issues in the relationship than alcohol use alone but that they cannot be dealt with without also stopping the use of alcohol.*)

George: If I knew that quitting would solve the problem, I would quit today and never drink again, but I know it won't solve the problem—

Therapist: Have you ever done anything—

George: —because she's going to come back with something else to—to—and then it will be something else, and she's always going to have something to come at me with.

Therapist: George, what I'm saying—what I'm saying is you can—you can get help, I can help you both with those things that would be left over after the alcohol. I agree with you that there are going to be other things, in fact (*inaudible*); but I'm saying that, until this alcohol issue is dealt with in your marriage, you're not really going to get very far with those other issues. It doesn't matter who helps you. Have you ever had a time when you went ahead with something not because you already knew what the result was, but because you thought you had a pretty good chance? Have you ever had a time like that? Was there something where you didn't have a job or—

George: No. Worked all my—Never was without a job in my life.

Therapist: Have you—have you ever had a time, though, when you went ahead and you did something not because you knew for sure, but because—it was just a chance.

George: No. Not that I know of.

Therapist: So—so you like sure things, right?

George: Hmm?

Therapist: You like sure things.

George: More or less. I don't like to gamble.

Mabel: How about when you went to the racetrack?

George: I haven't been to the races very much.

Therapist: How do you convince yourself that something is a sure thing? What's something recently that you've convinced yourself of?

George: Cause I'll check it out.

Therapist: How do you check it out?

George: Well, even at work I will sit there for a while and review it and go over it before I make a decision. I do the same thing anywhere.

Therapist: Okay. Today we've been reviewing and going over the various ways in which alcohol plays a role in the problems that you have as a couple, and we've also been reviewing and going over how alcohol—dealing with alcohol—can help in the kind of work that I can offer with you as a couple. The relationship issues, you want to deal with; and so what I'm saying to you is—is that in reviewing all these things, that I believe that what it comes down to is that—that far and away the best chance for getting the kinds of changes you want in your relationship—

George: Well, I'll try anything, but I can't guarantee you anything. I will try.

Therapist: No guarantees are necessary.

George: I will try. If I have a beer, though. I don't want her to come down on me, but I will try.

Therapist: See, she's—I want you—I want you—

George: She's got to try to understand that—She's got to realize that at times I don't have no money. There are times when I want her son to get that damn stuff out of the house.

Therapist: There are no guarantees.

George: Things I throwed away he picks up and puts back in the garage.

Therapist: The money issues are important, and how you handle one another's kids are important, and these are issues that we can talk some more about. It's very important to me that you [Mabel] keep going to Al-anon. If you went to a group and you weren't crazy about that group, then you go to another group, because you'll find a group that you can be comfortable with. There are people—

George: I don't know why she should have to go.

Therapist: Because—

George: I don't know why she should have to go herself.

Therapist: Because if she doesn't go, then she's not really making a commitment to what she thinks is true.

George: Hmm?

Therapist: You feel you're dealing with an alcohol problem and—and, in addition to you coming and working with me, that's the best resource around to help you with that. If you don't go then, you're only doing it halfway because of your own—

Mabel: Honey, how about when you kept drinking after we got home from the Holiday Inn and you had another drink and it was two o'clock in the morning. You just don't know when to stop whenever you start. There's no line that you draw. You don't need another drink, but somehow I got mad and I took a newspaper and hit you over the back of the head with it, and you scared me then. You said, "You do it again and I'll"—

George: Nobody hits me on my head. No matter where they hit me. I kill people for that.

Mabel: —"slam you through that wall." And that was threatening—

George: Honey, don't ever hit me on my head, because you know my head was fractured real bad during the war.

Mabel: Well, I just tapped you with the newspaper. That didn't hurt.

George: I don't want nobody hitting me, though.

Therapist: But perhaps you might react to it differently if you're drinking or not drinking.

George: No. No. I'm at work that way. You touch my head at work and I'll come at you. I had a very, very severe fractured skull—

Mabel: Honey, that was a newspaper that I just tapped you—

George Oh, honey, I don't want people hitting me on my head.

Therapist: Well, that's an important thing to keep in mind, then.

George: You get your son and get those damn cars away from the house. Get them damned mattresses out of the garage, get that surf board out of the garage. I can't even get to my own stuff.

Mabel: Honey, I keep my car in the garage. You have never kept your car in the garage. You didn't even know it was down there.

Therapist: Okay, this is an issue—

George: Why should I be responsible for his stuff?

Therapist: —that you're not going to resolve.

Mabel: You're not responsible for his stuff.

Therapist: Clearly there are some things that you'd like one another to do differently. You were just saying something about—you were saying something to George just now, weren't you about something you'd like him to do differently. What was it?

George: Well, I can't—(*inaudible*)

Mabel: I would like you not to keep drinking. You drank for two solid hours and I kept saying "Let's go," and you had somebody bringing you another drink and another drink and then you took a drink on the way out and then—

George: Well, that was bad, I agree with you. I shouldn't have done that.

Mabel: And then after we go home you fix another drink.

George: Did I?

Mabel: That's over two hours of solid drinking, and the drinks you drink are a whole glass.

George: Well, I'll agree with you. That was too much. I shouldn't drink that much. I'll agree with that.

Mabel: Every time we go out you drink more than anbody else.

Therapist: How about—Would you say some of the same things right now, but I want you to say them soft. Okay? Just repeat what you just said to him. Okay?

Mabel: Repeat what I said?

Therapist: Yeah, about the Holiday Inn. Would you just—Right now. Just repeat what you just said to him. Same words, but just say them soft. I just want him to experience—

Mabel: (*More softly*) Honey, you drank for two hours and you took one drink home, and then when you got home you had another drink and it was after 2 o'clock and I thought that you had had enough and I was afraid to ride home with you and it made me angry.

Therapist: Okay.

George: Tell him what actually happened that night. You hit me and knocked the drink out of my hand onto the floor.

Mabel: I tapped you and the drink fell.

Therapist: How did you react just now, George, to her saying that?

George: I agree with her.

Therapist: Okay. Was there any difference—

George: That night was different. She hit it and knocked it out of my hand.

Therapist: Was there any difference in how you reacted—

George: Well, if she had just said—asked me like that, I would have just thrown the drink away.

(*The transcript ends shortly before the actual end of the session. The content of the last part of the session is deliberately shifted away from alcohol to give the couple an experience with some positive change of the type that can occur in the course of marital therapy. The method the therapist chooses, asking Mabel to soften her tone of voice as she repeats a request, is deliberately directed at putting some of the pressure to change back onto Mabel, in this case by showing that George can respond more generously to her requests when she says them differently. Once the centrality of his drinking has been made quite clear, it is assumed he needs to know through demonstrated behavior that the issues he has in their relationship have not been discounted, only delayed in their resolution by the presense of alcohol.*)

Therapist: If she had said something to you like that—

George Oh, yeah. It would have been a lot different, I think.

Therapist: Okay—

Mabel: I'm trying to do that when we're out and—

Therapist: Just—just a second. Come on back here before we finish up, 'cause I want to just—I've got the TV back here. Come on back here.

(*Therapist motions to couple, and all three leave the room to view videotape replay of the preceding several minutes to illustrate the more receptive response Mabel elicited from George when she repeated similar content in a softer tone of voice. Session ends soon after.*)

Reference

1. Haley, J. *Ordeal therapy: Unusual ways to change behavior*: San Francisco: Jossey-Bass, 1984.

CHAPTER 8

CONTRACTING WITH A COUPLE (WHEN SHE WANTS MARITAL THERAPY AND HE WANTS ALCOHOLISM TREATMENT)

A couple in their forties, Jeff and Linda, with three teenage children were referred to the Family Therapy Institute by the husband's employee-counselor. He had sought the counselor's advice on how to deal with his wife's drinking. The counselor had met once with him and his wife and then strongly recommended alcoholism treatment for her immediately. I was consulted by the counselor. The wife had adamantly refused hospital-based alcoholism treatment, and I was asked to meet with the couple in the hopes that I could convince her to seek help for her drinking problem. I met with them once as a consultant and then offered to see them as a supervisor (consultant) behind the one-way mirror while they met directly with a social worker who was an advanced family therapy trainee. They agreed to be seen together in that format. The therapist called them back to confirm and asked them to bring with them their two younger children still living at home.

In the first two sessions, the therapist met with several combinations of family members: the whole family, the two children, the two parents, and each parent alone—while others waited outside the office. By the end of that time she had accomplished several short-term goals well and several others partially. First, she established at least a modicum of rapport with everybody and had elicited a thorough history of the drinking behavior of each family member. She had gotten the children to confirm in front of both parents the extent and nature of their concerns over not only mother's increased excessive daytime and evening drinking over the past two years but also father's periodic excessive drinking, especially on weekends, for many years. Further, she had elicited from mother alone and in front of the others, mother's goals of improved school performance from all the children and greater support from her husband on setting limits on the children and on helping out at home now that she had begun working outside the home. By the end of the second session, the therapist had been able to take the position with everybody present that mother and father each presented with their own forms of alcoholism, and that the drinking patterns of each were associated with both the marital and parenting issues that also were legitimate problems deserving of attention through therapy. Both parents were advised to pursue abstinence immediately for their own welfare and to enable successful resolution of their family issues.

The children returned for another session and then were indefinitely excused from therapy with the understanding that they would come back whenever requested and would begin attending either Al-anon or Alateen meetings regularly for their own benefit and as a confirmation that they did indeed feel they were living with alcoholism in the family. Attendance at AA was urged for both parents, and the couple was asked to come back together for the fourth session.

After the third session, the husband stopped drinking entirely and began attending Al-anon sessions regularly, usually with his son. The wife attempted to reduce her drinking and failed. She did attend an AA meeting, though she did not accept the label of alcoholic for herself. It turned out that she had long believed her husband to be alcoholic and had attended Al-anon meetings occasionally over several years, without telling anybody in the family.

At the fifth session, it was clear everybody had a different agenda. The wife's energies were put to making a convincing argument that she had tried for years to get her husband to treat her more as an equal without success, and she doubted that stopping drinking or anything else would change that. For his part, he said that there might be some changes he should still make but that there was no point in coming to therapy while she was still falling asleep on the living room floor in the afternoon from drinking. The therapist's agenda had been to utilize each of their resistances to gain a mutual commitment to a therapy that simultaneously addressed both of their concerns. It seemed touch-and-go as to whether therapy would abort or enter a new phase no longer held hostage to the mood of the moment. The consultant came out from behind the one-way mirror for the last 20 minutes or so of the session to emphasize the importance of coming to a working agreement at that session and to confirm what the therapist had already been saying.

The transcript of that 20 minutes follows and is offered as a (not atypical) example of contracting for marital therapy with a couple in which alcoholism is an issue. With only slight modification, the transcript would also be typical of similar contracting for family therapy where the presenting problem was a symptom in a child, e.g., underachievement in school, as was, in fact, the case in this family. It is also applicable to families in which there is excessive drinking and family consequences to the drinking, yet no other blatant manifestation of alcoholism. Finally, I would point out that it is as relevant to cases that present first as a case for marriage counseling as to a case such as this, that presents as probable alcoholism.

The Interview

Consultant: Since time is so short, may I come in and make a few comments?

Therapist: Please.

Consultant: We've been talking on the phone a lot today, so I know where you are. Ruth [the therapist] and I have come to a conclusion—a number of conclusions. One of them is that—an absolutely crucial issue is that Linda doesn't think you can handle her changes and—umm—Isn't that right?

Consultant (C) is reframing the issue. Instead of bickering over whether alcohol treatment or marital therapy should be the primary agenda, Jeff's ability to handle certain positive changes in Linda, of which achieving abstinence is simply to be one but only one, is questioned.

Linda: I have been changing.

Consultant: Right. And you don't feel that he's been handling it.

Linda: He hasn't. No.

Consultant: Okay, and—and—

Linda: Not—

Consultant: So as far as you're concerned—

Linda: I don't mean—

Consultant: —the marriage is intolerable unless you drink, right?

A function alcohol has come to serve is presupposed by C.

Linda: It has been a lot easier.

Consultant: Okay. So, unless Jeff can adapt to your changing in ways which—by the way—we support completely. She's been changing in some terrific ways. She's also gotten into trouble with alcohol.

Linda has been under attack as the alcoholic who is still drinking. While the pressure on her to stop drinking is maintained, her growth in other ways is highlighted. C then will go on to put equal pressure on Jeff to catch up with his wife in "certain kinds of development," so each has some catching up to do.

Jeff: I agree.

Consultant: Those are two separate things and alcohol has come to serve an interesting kind of function. It's allowed her to put down, dampen her feelings about her observation that you're not changing with her, you're not keeping up with her. She's ahead of you, which is not unusual—I mean—couples go at different speeds and, in terms of certain kinds of development, she's ahead of you. She's worried that you're not going to be able to come along. She wants you to come along, but she's worried you're not going to be able to.

Jeff: I only have one criterion—I only have one requirement to do that. I—I agree with you. I have gone to Al-anon for ten meetings now and I agree that there are some things that I need to work on, but I don't see any need for me to come here for anything else until Linda isn't ill with her drinking—

Consultant: Okay. Another side—

Jeff: —and I cannot—I cannot do anything.

Consultant: —another side of saying that, you see, is what Ruth already said to both of you, and that is that Linda should not stop drinking unless and until she has a commitment from you to stay with the therapy, and we've said, sort of arbitrarily, for at least five months after she stops drinking. I don't think she should make any commitment to stop drinking unless she knows she has got that commitment from you and unless both of you have a commitment to do this kind of work. Otherwise she's going to be absolutely miserable and she would rather drink. She feels better drinking—right?—

A modest paradox is used to gain leverage for a future commitment to post-abstinence marital therapy. Linda, the couple is told, "should not stop drinking unless . . . " C says this, even though Ruth has insisted all along, and C will repeat, that Linda is an alcoholic and needs to stop drinking for herself. It is assumed that drinking is serving a function for Linda in their relationship. Hence, linking a commitment to the couple's therapy (and therefore to finding ways to eliminate the need for the function served by drinking) should provide additional motivation for Linda to seek abstinence.

Linda: Um-hum.

Consultant: —than the way things are, if you don't make these changes together. That's the reality as we see it right now. That—that could change. You're not the first couple to be in that kind of a situation, and it's possible for each of you to learn some things you didn't know before without giving up your personality. Nobody loses what they already can do, they just become more flexible if they choose to do the work. And it's work. The issue of when you come? Hey, life's not fair. If you want to do this kind of work and you want to—and you want to

When couples feel they're being asked to change, it is useful to frame change as an "addition," a stretching of oneself without giving up any of one's personality.

do it here and you think we've got something to offer you—umm—this is when we can do it. We don't have another late-in-the-day kind of time that also doesn't conflict with something else. Leaving one's—resigning from one's job in order to make some fine adjustments in appointment time seems a bit extreme. I would think that's a bit—bit too much. So either one goes to the effort to work in the time as most people do, who come to a therapist, or not. The real issue is, is the commitment there and if it is, can you make it work? No guarantees at the end except that any choices you make at that time will be for good reasons and you won't regret them. That is, you will know the best you can have in your relationship and you will either choose that positively because you like it or you will reject it because it's not for you, but you'll know why. Those are reasonable goals. Right now you're not in a position to choose either one. You're stuck.

Earlier the couple had raised objections to continuing therapy at the same time (already a prime, late-afternoon time). Jeff had offered that Linda could quit her work if the therapist could not be more flexible. C supports Linda's new job (role) and forces the issue of commitment to therapy.

C, shifting to an educational mode, defines the goal of the marital therapy phase for which they are contracting as "knowing the best you can have in your relationship," rather than as a prior commitment to stay married no matter what.

Jeff: I will be glad to come to therapy only if Linda stops drinking. I'm not interested in any therapy if there's not—

Consultant: Okay. And we're telling her, "Don't stop drinking unless you get a commitment from him to come to therapy."

Jeff: I've made that commitment.

Consultant: Okay. He's made that commitment. Do you believe him?

Linda: I don't know.

Consultant: What would it take to believe him short of already doing it for five months? What would it take to believe him? (*pause*) Now, this is very important because—I don't care what anybody says—you are giving up something that has served a very positive function for you over the last six months, at least, and that is the drinking. There is no question about it and that you are losing something in the short run and so you should not give that up lightly. So, at a minimum you need to believe that he's really prepared to make this commitment and that no matter what happens during that period of time, that as long as there is a session scheduled, you'll both attend and regardless of what happens during that session there will be no major decisions made and no one is going to get physically hurt and the process will continue. You have to believe that that's actually going to happen now or there's no way you're going to give up the drinking. What would he need to do right now to convince you that he really means it?

It is not enough for one partner to say "I'm committed" or "I agree." The spouse must believe it.

C says "six months, at least." It is not useful at this initial contracting stage to push Linda to accept that her alcoholism has been around two years, as her family claims.

Linda: He really means that he will come?

Consultant: He will come,

and it won't be a week-to-week kind of thing, and he won't bring up the schedule no matter how hard it is or—you know—or say, "this isn't useful" and use that as a reason not to come anymore—

Jeff: I'll even go one step further. I won't only agree to come, I will agree to participate to the best of my ability.

Consultant: Now, do you believe what he's saying or not? It doesn't matter whether I believe it or not. What matters is whether you believe it.

Linda: Well, as Jeff always tells me, "The proof is in the pudding."

Consultant: Okay, but you don't have five months to see. What would it take for you to believe now that looking back on it next Fall you'll be able to say, "He meant it. The proof is that he did it." Can you imagine doing that?

C utilizes (drawing upon Neuro-Linguistic Programming (NLP)) what Linda has indicated is her strategy for convincing herself. That is, she has said (and shown with the upward eye movements associated with her words) that she must see Jeff doing over time what he promises, before believing him. Therefore, C leads her nonverbally to look up and at the same time to imagine herself five months hence looking back at him, having done what he, congruently, had just said he would do. She does this mental exercise and is convinced.

Linda: Okay.

Consultant: Okay. Now that's what he's saying will happen and he's prepared—he's saying he's prepared to make that commitment. Do you believe that?

Linda: Yes.

Consultant: Okay, now your side of it, initally, is harder. I think, after that, his side of it is harder 'cause I said I genuinely think, in certain ways you're ahead of him, but initially your side of it is harder. Are you prepared to make your com-

C immediately returns to the neces-

mitment, which is to do whatever it takes to stop drinking and then also to commit to that same period of time coming regularly to therapy?

Linda: Yeah, I could come here.

Consultant: There are two parts to that because I don't think it's worthwhile for the two of you to do this without alcohol out of the scene 'cause it's—it's—it plays a part in your relationship which is not going to allow you to do this work. In effect, the presence of the alcohol now undermines the whole value of the changes you've made over the past 10, 20 meetings, so that I—umm-it takes away any motivation for him to make the adaptations that he nonetheless needs to make. From a pragmatic standpoint there is no point in your doing this together at this time, that is, the result would not, under those circumstances be any different than what they have been in recent years. We've said that's unacceptable. It's going to—for you to stop drinking it's going to make it harder for Jeff, but for good reasons and he's—we now all believe he's prepared to take that on. Your side of it is—your commitment includes doing whatever is necessary, to stop, which might be stopping cold, it might be saying, "I need help." Help could be a variety of things. You could say, "Okay, I made this commitment, I find—

sity of abstinence, once Linda has been supported to the extent that she feels she has a commitment from her husband to marital therapy.

C refers to future meetings as if they were in the past since this was a useful strategy with Linda before.

C returns to educational frame and reiterates optional ways to get help achieving abstinence.

I find I can't do it myself, I want to take Antabuse because it will give me a little something extra to think about if we're acting on impulse, because, after all, it's just a habit we're talking about; or I want to take three weeks off and dry out somewhere. It doesn't matter how—how it's done or, "I'm going to go to AA meetings four nights a week—going to attend your alcohol group here in addition to coming to therapy. I'm going to come one night a week and attend your alcohol group. Whatever it takes, "What I'm saying—your part of the commitment is, "Whatever it takes, I'll do, to stop drinking and commit myself to at least five months of working together in therapy—here—right here working on that point." Are you prepared to make that commitment?

Linda: What is your feeling on —umm—social drinking?

Consultant: My feeling is that there is no place for it in this commitment, at all.

C takes an unequivocal abstinence position in the face of Linda's lingering denial of her alcohol dependence.

Linda: Why?

Consultant: Because it will completely detract from what you're trying to accomplish in your relationship.

In response to Linda's challenge to an abstinence approach, C uses the leverage of the already well-documented relationship consequences of her drinking rather than a discourse on the nature of alcoholism, which she does not yet accept as her problem. Then C moves back into the educational mode, since part of Linda's resistance may still be that she

Linda: Why?

Consultant: Because of the nature of the role that alcohol has played in your relationship up till now. See, there's nothing fair in this at all. I don't claim it to be in any way fair. What I'm saying is, what would be okay for someone else would not be okay for you because of what you want. Certain things that need to happen in order for new habits and interactional patterns to develop in people, a certain amount of time is necessary. So, I really am saying, yeah, it's a commitment when among friends and others who are drinking of saying, "I'll take a club soda with a lime in it," or "Give me a ginger ale." It really does mean that. That's tough, too.

Linda: Yeah, I've been thinking about that.

Consultant: As you'll discover that in every social situation you're in, there will be some people doing that, even though you never noticed it, but it is tough initially to learn to do that and to feel okay about one's self and to deal with the occasional comments of, "What's the matter, why aren't you drinking?" You have to learn how to say, "I prefer to have this," or to somebody closer to you, saying, "Well, I decided that I was getting into too heavy drinking and so I stopped." It takes a little while to learn how to do that and to feel okay about oneself. So, that is part of it. See, we here have a responsibility to the two of you to give you feedback, and you've been working here long enough for us to have an opinion, to give you feedback on what it would take in order for

cannot yet imagine how, under certain conditions, she will act without alcohol.

the two of you to have a worthwhile experience here, and this is that feedback; and Ruth and I have said it, each of you have an independent choice to make.

C reincludes the therapist, Ruth, as the session draws to a close.

Linda: Okay. Can we—can I have some time?

Consultant: That's your choice. You don't have to ask. Either you're ready or you're not ready. If you don't feel ready right at this moment to make a decison, then it falls to you and nobody else to do what it would take to get to the point where you can make a decision, and I think that's something for you privately. I would not discuss that with Jeff. If you would like to discuss that with Ruth, maybe you could set up something where you could talk with her, or if you have not decided before next week you might come in alone and talk with Ruth at that time, 'cause that's a good reason to use that kind of time, because there isn't anything else more important at this point than each of you making that kind of decision for yourself. Because of time, I know you need to make a decision.

Linda: Yeah. I—

Consultant: How would it be—Ruth, would it—Would you feel okay about leaving it that either one or two of them would come in next week?

Therapist: I won't be here for two weeks.

Consultant: You won't be here for two weeks, so we're really talking about three weeks from now—that either one or two of them would come in, in three weeks.

Therapist: Right.

Linda: In three weeks?

Therapist: Right.

Linda: So we're not coming in for three weeks?

Therapist: Two weeks, Two Mondays.

Consultant: The next two weeks. We've forgotten that Ruth, you're going to be out of the country. So we're really talking about three Mondays from now that either you would use that time to talk further—you alone would use that time to talk further with Ruth about making this kind of decision or the two of you would come in together and say, "We've both decided that we're prepared to make this commitment and we want to go to work."

Linda: Okay. So, today is the 9th. You won't be here the 16th or the 23rd.

Therapist: Right.

Linda: Okay. You'll be here the 3rd of April.

Therapist: Right.

Linda: Okay.

Consultant: —to be left up to you to decide whether it's one or two?

Linda: Yes. I have to go.

Therapist: Okay.

Subsequently, Linda came in alone for several sessions over close to three months. The focus was on her stopping drinking while being supported in her goals for personal growth and marital enhancement. Her attempts to limit or control her own drinking failed, and she eventually requested a prescription for Antabuse. The first week she stopped Antabuse three days before a planned drinking episode and then drank to excess. The second week, she took Antabuse daily, did not drink at all, and came in for therapy with a greatly relieved Jeff. At that point, all agreed that a new phase, the previously contracted five-month trial period of marital therapy had just begun.

There were further slips for Linda; and when she drank, she usually drank heavily. Automatically, Jeff would refuse to come in. She would then come in alone. After several months, the position was taken with her that no more progress could be made (in what she was seeking) until she could resume therapy with Jeff. Intellectually, she agreed, though this, of course presupposed her stopping drinking. A brief crisis of heavy drinking ensued, after which she finally accepted hospitalization in an alcohol treatment program for several weeks. She used that time well, and she and Jeff both attended a follow-up outpatient couples' group and rapidly made excellent progress in their marriage. At a follow-up phone call about one year after their initial contact, Linda reported that their two younger children were doing much better in school and that she and Jeff were finally beginning to jointly set some more effective limits on their oldest child, whom they had come to admit had been abusing alcohol and other drugs himself.

A note of caution is in order here. There are couples for whom the approach in the transcript in this chapter either should not be taken; or, if it has been tried, should be dropped. As soon as it becomes evident that a couple is locked into a power struggle within which maintaining one's own personal integrity of choice is paramount, and the non-drinking spouse is, or is perceived as, still taking responsibility for whether or not the drinking spouse attempts to abstain, then the exchange part of the approach in this chapter should be scrapped. Many of the reframing and educational statements may still be useful, but a different type of agreement should be structured, one that in no way links the abstinence efforts of one to any initiative taken by the other.

CHAPTER 9

ALCOHOLICS ANONYMOUS AND FAMILY THERAPY

Among some members of Alcoholics Anonymous (AA), memories are still strong of well-intentioned, individual psychotherapy techniques and particularly psychoanalysis apparently causing long delays in getting help (from AA) in achieving abstinence. These delays were widely presumed to be the result of ignorance of alcoholism, combined with an overzealous conviction in the power of the therapeutic method used. It is naive to assume that these negative factors would not come into play again in the application of any new psychotherapeutic approach, including that of family therapy, to the treatment of alcoholism. Yet, in recent years, there have been some advances in therapeutic approaches and in the education of professionals about alcoholism that it would be a shame to ignore because of past fears.

This chapter deals with ways in which advances in the treatment of alcoholism contributed by family therapy have been used in a manner that complements rather than detracts from the contributions of AA, Al-anon and Alateen. Some cautions are included on the possible misuses of family therapy.

Historical Review

Most of the major developments in family therapy have occurred only within the last 20 years. During that time, there was a parallel but independent development growing out of AA involving self-help groups for mates of alcoholics (Al-anon) and for teenage children of alcoholics (Alateen). In fact, 20 years ago the development of Al-anon and Alateen was probably at a more advanced stage than the corresponding development of therapeutic approaches to the family of an identified patient. This was particularly true of the application of family therapy theory and practice to the field of alcoholism (1).

As noted early in this book, though, there is now a considerable basis for the application of family therapy to the alcoholism field, both pragmatic and theoretical. Harwin has demonstrated this rather recently in a scholarly review (2). Even Janzen's review of the developing literature through the mid-1970s concluded that family therapy, in and of itself, does help in the treatment of alcoholism (3). As we also mentioned earlier, the results of a national survey of over 2,000 drug treatment programs, including treatment for alcoholism as the primary abused substance, which Sandra Coleman and I reported on in 1978, strongly suggested that therapists in these settings were already beginning, in significant numbers, to experiment with family approaches to treatment (4). Attitudes within the self-help movement toward the benefits of family involvement in the alcoholism recovery process have been correspondingly positive. Though unsubstantiated as yet, it is widely accepted that recovery from alcoholism is facilitated when mates seek help for themselves through Al-anon.

Case Illustration: Bob B.

The following is a case illustrative of the complementary relationship between family therapy and AA self-help groups. At the onset of therapy Bob was a 38-year-old alcoholic, with a record of 15 years of chronic, daily, heavy drinking, often to the point of passing out, with numerous blackouts. He usually held no job, and had a long-standing seperation but no divorce from his alcoholic wife. During all those years, his heavy daily drinking pattern was interrupted only by multiple two- to three-day hospitalizations for alcohol detoxification. Over the years he went to one or another AA group, one or two times, each, and then stopped. Prior to becoming an alcoholic, he had been adddicted to heroin for several years. After a stay at a heroin addiction treatment facility, he switched to alcohol exclusively. Bob's family is middle class, and Bob himself attended two years of college, dropping out permanently when substance abuse became too problematic. In recent years, Bob had returned to live with his family of origin (parents and siblings) most of the time. Although prior to that he was often in close contact with them, as seems to be true of the great majority of young adult male drug abusers, at no time until the present were his family of origin or his wife included in the various attempts at his therapy, nor did they attend Al-anon.

Bob and his family came to us for therapy because Bob's 12-year-old brother, Bart, had recently been doing less well in school and had begun acting disrespectful toward his parents. The family's initial telephone contact led to our strong recommendation that the entire family then living together—which included father, mother, Bob, a 30-year-old sister temporarily back at home, and Bart—come in for an evaluation. An early part of the initial family contact involved asking each member of the family to express his/her own opinion on the nature of the problems that they would like to see dealt with in therapy. Mother described Bart's recent behavior changes as her primary concern. Father agreed that that was why they had come in but added he could not restrain himself from saying that he felt Bob's drinking problem was the worst problem for the entire family. Bart and Bob each acknowledged their own problems, but Bart also indicated that his parents had a problem involving their difficulty in agreeing with each other about what they wished him to do. The sister concurred with everything, including the latter statement, which she felt also applied to her parent's dealings with Bob.

The family was given the feedback that Bob's alcoholism was seen as the most serious and top-priority problem for the family to work on and that the best way for the therapy to be effective would be for the entire family to work with the therapists (initially there were co-therapists, later one therapist) in order to find new ways to deal with Bob's drinking problem. The family was assured that Bart's problems would not be disregarded.

Over a 3½ month period, about ten one-hour family therapy sessions were held. Hospitalization was not considered an option at the time because Bob had worn out his welcome at public facilities in the area and lacked private or Medicaid insurance for alternative hospitalization. Once the primacy of the alcohol problem was established, the focus of the therapy was rapidly shifted to helping mother and father explore their differences over what to expect from and how to deal with Bob.

An essential part of keeping track of the objective was for the therapist to repeatedly state how relevant it would be for the parents to attend Al-anon in view of their deep concern for their son's drinking problem and of their long frustration in getting help to deal with it. Within a few weeks they did begin to attend Al-anon intermittently, after being encouraged to actually phone for information during a family therapy session and making plans to go to their first session accompanied by the therapists. While a similar procedure was used with Bob about attending AA, it was not until much later that he began to get involved.

After several weeks of therapy, the parents, with help from the therapists, had come to agree on certain rules for Bob's behavior if he were to continue living with them. At about the point that his parents were prepared to present these rules to him, Bob managed to fall down a flight of stairs at home while only mildly intoxicated and to break a leg. It took several weeks to fully restore the parents' resolve. During that time the parents demanded and got more acceptable behavior from Bob at home, there were fewer fights, and mother and father agreed on a plan. They would no longer respond to calls to come pick up Bob from a street corner or bar, and allow him into the house only if he were not actively drinking or acting intoxicated. At about this time, Bob fell in the street and cracked his skull, not too severely but enough to require a few stiches and to miss what the family viewed as a crucial session. Fortunately, the therapist had predicted a setback, warning the family early that there could be high risks attached to producing a significant change in a chronic pattern of disturbed behavior. They also advised the family that these risks were justified by the clearly *life-threatening consequences of doing nothing* to bring about change and by a reasonable likelihood of success in overcoming the drinking problem.

Not long after this time, the family took a moratorium of several months from therapy, an action precipitated by the therapist's moving away. By then, mother and father were attending Al-anon, family fighting had significantly decreased, and Bob's drinking-to-stupor had become uncommon. In addition, Bart's school work and behavior had fully returned to their previous high level. A new therapist was not immediately sought, because it seemed to all concerned not unreasonable to give the family time-out to see how far they could continue to improve on their own.

A three-month follow-up revealed that mother and father were attending Al-anon regularly, while sister, with parental encouragement, had moved into her own apartment, taking Bart with her. Bob rarely attended AA. Under pressure from his parents, Bob was exhibiting less public drunkenness and generally trying to be much more cooperative at home. His level of daily alcohol consumption, though, had gradually inched up to its previous high level. Apparently as a result of dealing with his parents' changed behavior toward him, combined with his inability to reduce his alcohol intake, he had managed to get himself covered by Medicaid insurance and thereby became eligible for community treatment not previously available to him.

By the time the family was recontacted, it was clear that Bob would be unable to achieve abstinence and would physically deteriorate outside of a hospital or similar setting. Thus, a strong recommendation for hospitalization was made. Bob was contacted by phone each week for three weeks. After the last call, he entered the hospital. The family was able to act in a consistently supportive way and accompanied Bob to the hospital. They signed their part of the contract, which obligated them to continue family therapy as one condition of his admission.

There followed five hospital admissions for Bob, each one more successful than the former (as is often the case with alcoholics). The third lasted more than a month and represented the first period in Bob's adult life of a month-plus of abstinence. Bob's satisfaction with himself during this period was marred only by the discovery that lengthy alcohol abuse had left him with permanent cerebrellar impairment affecting his gait and speech. His parents were pleased with Bob's abstinence, but they also felt guilty at the thought that they had not viewed it as likely. As part of Bob's contract, he attended AA during these hospitalizations. He and his parents worked together in therapy on a trial plan for Bob to live nearby but out of his parent's home.

After his third hospitalization, Bob had a month of sobriety out of the hospital as well. Then he resumed drinking. He did so at first in binges. Each binge was followed by a brief detoxification on his own and then another binge. In addition, he became disenchanted with the new living situation, and his parents were unable to feel good about his being out of the home. They had mutually agreed to again have him live at home for a temporary but indefinite period. Unfortunately, his planned vocational rehabilitation program had also been slow in developing during this period. He went back to the hospital. The primary issue in the treatment of his severe chronic situation shifted. The elimination of drinking was now seen as achievable and would be facilitated by Antabuse. His parents were getting more support from one another and from Al-anon, which would keep them from providing the familiar cues that might stimulate another drinking episode. But mother, father and adult alcoholic son needed more help than ever to accomplish what was not completed during Bob's adolescence; that is, the parents still needed to develop a mature adult marital relationship, one that did not have as the focus of most of their energy their problems with their drunken son (2), while Bob needed support to withstand this same transition and gradually to give up his dependence on his parents.

Briefly, let us summarize the complementary ways in this case in which family therapy and AA and Al-anon were used at different phases of therapy. First of all, none was sufficient in itself. Clearly, AA in the past had never captured Bob's involvement for long enough to matter. Individual approaches involving hospitalization for detoxification had similarly failed. Other family members had never attempted to get help through Al-anon, though they knew it existed.

Hence, the first positive interaction between the two approaches was when family therapy led promptly to involvement in self-help groups, an involvement that previously had failed, over many years, to develop. However, once family work had begun, the self-help groups were then needed to reinforce and sustain the whole family in the face of the great risks inherent in the pursuit of change, especially change in the role of a family member with a well-established drinking problem. Al-anon seemed to provide just enough extra support to keep the parents coming to family therapy when the going got rough (e.g., when Bob broke his leg). Later on, when abstinence and moving out of his parents' home became possibilities, Bob could then turn to AA for vital support while making these moves towards greater independence. The family had known before that AA represented an alternative source of support for Bob; but his parents' interpretation of the disease model of alcoholism promoted in AA had only confirmed them in their resolution to take care of him in their home regardless of the consequences. Family therapy helped his parents overcome this obstacle to change that grew out of their own perception of the message in AA. They became able to reconcile, finally, the illness concept of Bob's problem with the value of fostering increasing responsibility in Bob for his own well-being.

There is a sad postscript to this case, but one that does not detract from its basic instructiveness. Bob died some months into his apparently abstinent phase of vocational rehabilitation in a flash fire, that may have been set off by cigarette ashes smoldering in a flammable mattress while he was sleeping. There was no indication he had been drinking. The family knew that videotapes had been made of a number of their family sessions, felt therapy had been helpful and, on their own initiative, urged that their son's case be used freely for teaching purposes so that what was accomplished might be used to help others like Bob.

Self-Help vs Family Therapy

The case above was provided to help readers keep their feet on the ground before being lead through more theoretical territory. Hopefully, it has imbued them with a sense of the practical side of the current discussion. The often halting and clumsy way in which we therapists must proceed with therapy can make us lose sight of the fine points or underlying theoretical notions; and nice, neat theories can leave us frustrated if we try with too great expectations to put them into practice. This case gives us a kind of tangible example that can be helpful in considering the similarities and differences between the AA self-help groups and family therapy as well as their compatibilities.

Commonalities

Let us look at what there is in common between these self-help groups and family therapy:

1. Both approaches do not readily subscribe to will power as an essential motivation for change.
2. Both recognize that others in the family besides the identified alcoholic are also suffering from the problems of alcoholism in one member of the family. Sometimes this statement is questioned by critics of family therapy. Family members have been exposed to considerable blaming as a part of psychotherapy; but this is more often the result of an individual approach to psychotherapy, in which it is more difficult for the therapist to avoid taking sides emotionally with the identified patient. Family therapy, properly conducted, operates from a premise of relative equality among family members, both in difficulties and in rights to seek assistance.
3. Both family therapy and self-help groups make use of contact with significant others to facilitate change in the drinking behavior of the identified alcoholic.
4. Finally, among fundamental considerations, both approaches contain the implicit assumption that family members can be a source of resistance to change on the part of an alcoholic. This is particularly true in the approach to the more chronic drinking problem. The often explicit message to the mate or child of an alcoholic in Al-anon or Alateen and in family therapy is to watch out because they are or may be doing certain things that foster more excuses and trigger more drinking. Within the context of either approach, it is common to counsel family members as to how to gain appropriate ends without offering ammunition or cues for further problem drinking.

Differences

While there is much in common, there are also important differences between family therapy and AA self-help groups. We shall examine these differences here.

1.) The primary medium for focusing on the addiction differs. In family therapy, the family is treated as the primary medium in which change occurs; the focus is on generating within therapy an impact on the relationships between family members. In the self-help groups, the primary medium for change is the group, and the focus is on each individual within the family; the emphasis is placed on bringing about change for each individual in him or herself and in relation to others in the family, rather than on changing the quality of the relationships within the family. Often the effects are similar. Often, too, they are not.

2.) Direct work with relationships differs. In Al-anon a mate learns greater detachment. He or she is helped to delay or eliminate what had become frequent, extreme responses to the alcoholic's drinking behavior. At the same time, a priority is placed on the identification of his or her own wishes and the pursuit of them. There is support from others in a similar role to foster these gains. But there is no direct work with relationships, either between alcoholic and mate, or alcoholic and children, or parents and children; and there is certainly no direct work involving alcoholic and family of origin (unless, by chance, an alcoholic parent of an alcoholic attends the same AA group).

On the other hand, *bona fide* family therapy that makes use of recent advances in techniques rarely goes on entirely as separate activities involving either identified patient alone or other family members alone. An only apparent exception to this is family work done with one individual where the constant focus is still on family relationships, such as planning for cross-generational work to be done with members of the family of origin. In that case one might say that, relative to self-help groups, the medium is still much more the family. Another exception, discussed later in this book, is the use of certain highly specific individual techniques, generally for one or only a few sessions, at which spouses or other family members may be present but need not be. I am referring here to the use of Neuro-Linguistic Programming techniques to anchor in or install in a family member a more resourceful, detached state as a substitute for the previously automatic conditioned negative internal state and the associated overreactive behavior that the alcoholic family member so often uses to justify further drinking.

3.) The supportive agent differs (family *vs.* peers). A mate's learning to recognize alternatives to extreme responses to drinking and to identify his/her own wishes and pursue them can be as much a part of family therapy as we have said it is of self-help groups. In family therapy, though, the therapist facilitates the individual's actually acting differently in family relationships during the therapy session. Since this occurs live and under direct supervision, family therapy allows for strategic interruption and intervention. A disadvantage of family therapy is the lack of the shared support available in self-help groups for making changes. This is, of course, less true of marital group therapy or multiple family group therapy; though it should not necessarily be concluded that family group work always combines the best of both approaches. There is often much that is diluted or forgotten, as well as something gained, in sharing therapy with others outside the family.

4.) Observation of relationships provides the potential for a different range of problem identification and solution. Being able to directly observe a relationship at work allows the family therapist to learn and to guide family members along several dimensions largely unavailable in self-help groups. It becomes possible to identify and substitute for functions that a problem drinker's behavior may have come to serve within a family. Being guided, then, through trial experiences of dealing in new and more satisfactory ways with the decision-making process around issues that are specific to each couple—whether these issues turn out to involve sex, parenting or vacation planning—is a unique benefit of family therapy that can have major and self-sustaining effects.

Discussion

I have not mentioned the treatment philosophies underlying self-help approaches, of which AA is just one, or those of family therapy (or, more broadly, of psychotherapies). I am aware that there are readers who will believe and feel strongly that there is inherent in any psychotherapy a different notion from self-help approaches about the nature of the human being and his/her capacities for change or growth. To develop these issues would require going beyond the scope of this book. Suffice it to say that I do not hold that there need be fundamental differences. As a therapist, I operate according to the same presuppositions that operate in self-help groups: that every patient/client already has the resources or the capacity to develop the resources needed, that experts don't have all the answers, and that we are ultimately responsible for our own behaviors. And I can hold these presuppositions even though, as a therapist, I take full responsibility for the success or failure of each particular clinical intervention. My patients' responsibility is to stay with me until we succeed in achieving the stated goals or reject me and find someone with whose help they can succeed, so that ultimately they remain responsible for their own outcome and I remain responsible for the success of our particular mutual therapeutic endeavors.

By now, it should be clear that family therapy and self-help approaches to alcoholism contribute much that is mutually reinforcing. The objective of generating less destructive and more mutually satisfying behavior in relationships in a family with an alcoholic member is one that these approaches have in common. At the same time, they offer supplementary goals that naturally grow out of the different contexts in which help is offered.

The ways in which they are, at times, in conflict are largely attitudinal. For example, while it is true that an emphasis on the self-actualization of a mate can be incompatible with an emphasis on learning, with the mate, new ways to show and be shown caring, the incompatibility is usually the outgrowth of an attitude that one either cannot do both or must do one first and take chances with the other. That view has probably led to a sizable number of "successful operations" to achieve abstinence after which the relationship, unfortunately, died!

Another, more subtle yet equally undermining problem may arise when family therapy and self-help work are combined. Family members may use the presence of one approach to allay their anxieties generated within the other approach. As the going gets rough, the tension rises, as it will, inevitably, with a significant change of behavior within a relationship; and the family or some of its members will suddenly find the other approach more to their liking and insist that the other approach will be sufficient. This is not an incompatibility; this is a pitfall, which wise family therapists and members of self-help groups will be careful to help alcoholics and their families avoid.

The strength of family therapy as a medium for change to occur in alcoholism treatment is potentially also its drawback. This is true when family therapy is used without proper attention to the drinking problem itself. The case at the beginning of the Introduction provides an illustration of this.

In that case, a working-class family was referred for family therapy because individual therapy and brief hospitalization had only partially relieved father's mixed anxiety and depression. In the course of a partially successful family therapy, family members commented from time to time about father's occasional drinking as a way of dealing with depression. The question raised by the consultees had to do with what might be done to deal with or do away with these diversionary concerns about alcohol that seemed to pop up at times when something important or stressful was happening in the therapy. Daughter's comments about too much drinking were (wrongly) ignored by therapist and family, and the therapist managed to bring the family back to the original topic.

The family therapist chose to pursue the issue of timing of depressed affect and its relationship to marital conflicts. Father was an alcoholic, but neither his family nor his therapist were acknowledging it. In this otherwise effectively conducted therapy, he likely would continue to show promise of improvement but never quite seem to get better, just as had happened before in individual therapy. On the other hand, if the drinking-related problems were explicitly addressed and confirmed, especially within the context of the family therapy—then the chances would be good for a recovery relatively unhampered by the need to fight denial in other family members as well as in the problem drinker.

Shifting the focus away from the identified alcoholic patient to shared problems and to relationships should not be done unless there is an implicit and an explicit understanding that eliminating the problem drinking has top priority. Without the explicit commitment, family therapy could take alcoholic and family through an endless series of frustrations. With it, family therapy has a great deal to contribute.

When and How to Refer Clients to AA, Al-anon and Alateen

Timing the referral to AA self-help groups is best left to the judgment of the experienced therapist, provided his or her experience has included dealing with alcoholism. For the uninitiated, a good rule would be to err on the early side. It is better to drive away a family but leave them with a clear message that alcoholism is a top-priority problem, than to keep a family but serve the function of confirming their denial of alcoholism by failing to explicitly address the problem. Documenting the patterns of substance use in a family and the family, social, legal, medical and vocational consequences associated with heavy use has been demonstrated to be a relatively easy and not greatly resisted task, at least among people designated as in- or outpatients in a medical center, as we have documented from our own experience, (see Appendix). The therapist should remember to encourage Al-anon for the spouse and Alateen for adolescents as much as one would AA for the alcoholic. (Pre-teen may also be available in some areas for pre-adolescents, as well as Adult Children of Alcoholics-ACOA-groups within Al-anon.) Often family members will badger the alcoholic to do something while doing nothing to change themselves. Major changes occur in individual rights, responsibilities, boundaries, and role expectations when the nonalcoholics (often referred to as "co-alcoholics" by people in the alcoholism field because of the enabling role they unwittingly play in perpetuating drinking and the centrality of alcohol to their own life issues) are helped to take a clear stand on the issue of alcoholism, as exemplified by their participation in Al-anon or Alateen. Which family member attends first is not important. When one or more begin to attend, redefinitions within the family can be accelerated.

From a practical standpoint, referral to self-help groups may "take" through persistent suggestion and frequent checking up; but it is much more effective to have people actually call AA or Al-anon during the treatment session. They should be advised that there are many different types of AA groups and that they may need to shop around for one that is socially compatible as well as geographically accessible. If the therapist has specific contacts in AA, it will facilitate attendance. Going with people to their first AA meeting is also a uniquely successful tact that unfortunately is practiced by very few therapists.

Conclusion

Self-help groups and family therapy each provide some of what may be needed to effectively maintain the abuser's abstinence. AA, for example, may help him or her to achieve sufficient humility to truly participate in therapy. It may disengage the family sufficiently (from unhealthy interactions with the drinker) that they will be more open to therapeutic changes in dealing with the alcoholic family member. On the other hand, used appropriately, family therapy can effectively enhance the process of achieving and/or sustaining abstinence. It can be used to further identify the cues from the family that have come to engender more drinking, and then to teach alternative behaviors. It can be used to identify the role of excessive drinking in the family's problem-solving and to help the family find substitute mechanisms for conflict resolution. Family therapy can support family members through periods of role confusion and through periods of unexpected confrontation, such as greater anger or assertiveness from a sober alcoholic spouse who previously was assertive only when drunk. A spouse's psychological problems that often become prominent after a mate has sustained a period of abstinence can be either prevented or aided by family therapy. In these ways and more, family therapy can ease the pressures on the alcoholic who is successfully recovering through AA. Ultimately, what family therapy offers this person that cannot be provided as well through any other forum is relief from the many inevitable and unintentional family pressures to return to drink, and an easing of the disillusionment that often arises at the discovery that major relationship problems have not gone away.

If family therapy is applied to multiple problems within the family of an alcoholic, without a commitment from all concerned to work toward eliminating the problem-drinking behavior as a *first priority*, an error is being made. It is inappropriate, just as it was with individual therapy in the past, to blindly hope that improving the communication, the problem-solving or the expression of affect among family members will in and of itself stop a chronic alcoholic from drinking. Setting erroneous priorities is what has been traditionally incompatible between the psychotherapy (family or individual) approach and the self-help approach to alcoholism. When the alcoholic is in treatment with a skilled family therapist who is also knowledgeable about alcoholism, there is no incompatibility. On the contrary,the benefits self-help groups offer will, in all likelihood, be enhanced.

References

1. Steinglass, P. Family therapy with alcoholics: A review. In E. Kaufman & P. Kaufmann (Eds.) *Family therapy of Drug and Alcohol Abuse*. New York: Gardner Press, 1979.
2. Harwin, J. The excessive drinker and the family: Approaches to treatment. In J. Orford & J. Harwin (Eds.), *Alcohol and the Family*. New York: St. Martin's, 1982.
3. Janzen, C. Families in the treatment of alcoholism. *Journal of Studies on Alcohol 38*: (1977) 114–130.
4. Coleman, S., & Davis, D. I. Family therapy and drug abuse: A national survey. *Family Process 17* (1978) 21–31.

CHAPTER 10

TREATING THE INDIVIDUAL: GENERAL PSYCHIATRIC CONSIDERATIONS

In self-help and professional circles, there is, at times, controversy over whether alcoholism is often secondary to some underlying emotional disturbances or should always be treated as a primary problem. A useful guideline is that there is roughly the same prevalence of psychiatric disorders in an alcoholic population as in the general non-alcoholic population. Fifteen to twenty percent or so of alcoholics are going to have some psychological disorder either preexisting or coexisting with their drinking problem that is not likely to go away solely because the drinking stops. For the other eighty percent or so, alcoholism is the primary problem. They may also have behavioral symptoms of psychiatric disturbance. For example, most people who drink long enough and hard enough eventually manifest some symptoms of clinical depression, but when they are off alcohol for two or three weeks or more, their symptoms disappear without other specific medication or psychotherapy. There is no evidence that the great majority of alcoholics have had any psychiatric or personality disorder prior to their excessive drinking. Unfortunately, this has led to the belief, particularly within some AA circles, that one should never treat an alcoholic as though he or she were suffering from an additional condition, and, more particularly, that non-hypocritical members of AA should never use psychoative medications or be in a psychotherapy that is not solely directed at achieving or maintaining abstinence. That attitude is an injustice to perhaps one fifth of all alcoholics. Since AA is valuable and worth encouraging all alcoholics to participate in, it falls to the therapist to forewarn patients of this attitude and rehearse them on non-defensive, assertive ways to fend it off themselves, such as "I know that's true in many cases, but my therapy is not incompatible with AA; and this is what I believe is best for me." We can explain to patients that the attitude they must counter is quite understandable, because over the years prescription drugs and psychotherapy have, more often than not, truly been the villain in dealing with alcoholism. The topic of combining AA and family therapy was taken up at greater length in Chapter 9. What follows is a discussion of other individual needs in treating alcoholism.

Violence, Mania and Depression

Certain individuals who have a marked tendency to act explosively when they drink respond uniquely well to drug treatment with the naturally occurring salt, lithium carbonate. Not to use lithium with these people is not to treat them. This is statistically a very small proportion of alcoholics. I first learned of this special subgroup from Kenneth Williams in the late 1970s. Then director of an alcoholism treatment program at the University of Pittsburgh, Dr. Williams had noticed that certain alcoholics who had a history of severe violent or destructive behavior when drinking, such as burning buildings down or beating people, had a pattern of experiencing their thoughts racing ahead of their ability to act on them, which in turn was followed by drinking and then by violence. Patients generally do not volunteer that information and may not even recognize the pattern until asked specifically if they have a time before they begin a period of heavy or binge drinking during which their thoughts are racing along so fast it is hard to keep up with them. A definite "yes" to that question combined with a history of repeated violent outbursts when drinking, which may be limited to verbal output but more often has been frankly physical or destructive, is a strong indication for prescribing lithium. If it works, the effects can be dramatic and swift. I have seen several men who responded to only one or two 300-mg. lithium carbonate tablets a day for only one or two days with a calming or mellowing of affect, which was visible and audible to everyone around and which was accompanied by the self-report of an obvious and unique internal calming. These cases did not have clear-cut personal or family histories of manic-depressive disorder.

It is well known that some people with obvious manic histories, who are actively manic and alcoholic, have an easier time abstaining if they respond well to lithium treatment for mania. A man whom I had followed up on for several years provided his own control study by stopping and starting the lithium several times for extended periods of weeks or months. On lithium, he acted calmer and had little difficulty stopping his drinking entirely. He was both episodically violent and, I believe, suffered from true mania in the form of nearly perpetual racing thoughts, high energy, little sleep without fatigue, hypersexuality, expansive plans and deeds which could only be overseen in a highly revved-up state. He felt the need for heavy use of alcohol to put a damper on his highly charged internal state, but physically abused his wife if they disagreed while he drank or if she denied sex, even though they had already had intercourse that day and on many preceding days. His violence diminished through the use of certain hypnotic-style interventions, borrowed from Neuro-Linguistic Programming, to help instill in him alternative behaviors, when previously he would have struck out automatically. His drinking decreased with help from AA, and lithium calmed him sufficiently so he could practice what he was learning in marital therapy about problem-solving. Further individual therapy was necessary to help him adapt to having lower energy and less sex drive. No two approaches to his treatment were sufficient. Sometimes we therapists must use drugs and individual therapy and marital therapy and AA and more.

A severe depressive disorder persisting four to eight weeks or more beyond the start of abstinence should also be treated—by whatever the most appropriate means available, were that person's depression uncomplicated by alcoholism. The same is true for severe persisting thought disorders or psychosomatic symptoms. I am reluctant to use antidepressant medication or other potent psychoactive drugs while someone who is an alcoholic is actively drinking, even if by history there is a very good likelihood of a primary depressive disorder. Exceptions are made on an individual basis if a problem drinker with a likely primary depression has reduced alcohol intake for several weeks or more to one to three drinks a day or so without any binges. An antidepressant drug used judiciously may improve sleep and mood, and thereby enable abstinence, which might otherwise remain elusive. Judicious use includes an explicit warning by the therapist about the possible potentiated central nervous system sedating effects of combining alcohol with antidepressants, a warning which I have usually found to be taken quite seriously by properly selected patients. In this regard, an antidepressant has sometimes served the same function as Antabuse in providing that one extra reason to delay the next drink. Since these drugs are not without side effects, they should not be substituted for a more benign drug that can be used as an aversive stimulus, such as Antabuse, unless there are clinical indications. Intractable insomnia and, to a lesser extent, anxiety—besides depressive mood and behavior—may be other legitimate reasons to use an antidepressant rather than Antabuse or no drug. Because of their addictive potential and cross-tolerance with ethyl alcohol, there is very little reason to consider tranquilizers or sedative hypnotics with an alcoholic for other than clear-cut major withdrawal symptoms, which usually occur only from the second to fifth days of acute alcohol withdrawal.

Alcoholics, of course, are subject to a myriad of medical complications (1). Numerous books have been written on this subject. Suffice it to say here that any alcoholic patient who has not had a recent thorough physical examination and routine laboratory screening for specific organ system complications or chronic infections should have them. A therapist should take the initiative for seeing to it that the patient either visits his or her family physician or is referred successfully to an appropriate family practitioner, internist or medical clinic.

Hospitalization, Group Therapy, and Antabuse

Certain other treatment options that uniquely pertain to the individual cannot be disregarded by the family-oriented therapist, although, because of the nature of this book, they will not be discussed at length. One is hospitalization for detoxification; another, group therapy; and a third, the use of Antabuse. For many years, until rather recently, these three comprised the major and often entire treatment armamentarium for alcoholism.

Not every alcoholic can stop drinking without the removal from alcohol and/or the protective environment provided by a full-time residential treatment setting. Most alcoholics can, with well-managed guidance; the estimates I have seen and heard range from less than 50 to over 90 percent. The variation seems to be based on the speaker's commitment to and experience with either outpatient or residential treatment. In my own experience, perhaps 80 percent or more of alcoholics who stay engaged, however tenuously, in some process of therapy beyond a first contact can eventually stop drinking outside a residential facility. Recently there has been a significant development of day hospital or part-time residential options as well. It is too soon to comment on the added benefit they offer; but I think they will come to serve a distinct subgroup of the alcoholic population well, especially those programs that incorporate a substantial family component.

I describe residential care as an option frequently,usually emphasizing the 21- to 28-day treatment programs in hospital based, chemical dependency units, which are reasonably close by and which offer some post-discharge follow-up and include the family in most phases of care, although few programs, as yet, deal with the family well. Since I urge or insist on residential care infrequently, it has been fairly easy to identify my reasons for doing so. The easiest criterion is a failure to stop severe, life-endangering heavy drinking even with reasonably good therapeutic rapport and support from family and friends. An inability to locate any family or friends who can be prepared well by the therapist to put into abeyance for a week or two any old grudge and simply be available and encouraging is a poor prognostic indicator for successful detoxification (which is simply a term for the first few days, especially, of stopping heavy drinking). Similarly, since detoxification and treatment for alcoholism are not synonymous, the absence of any supportive social or work network after initial detoxification may be a reason for choosing a residential setting that requires several weeks' stay to deal well with the early post-detoxification phase of therapy. Another reason for residential treatment is the evidence of organic mental disorder, generally alcohol-related, that consists of sufficient recent memory impairment and disorientation to time and place so that the alcoholic cannot reasonably be expected to meet any commitments made in therapy, or in his work, for that matter. These people may need several weeks off alcohol just to return to sufficient mental acuity to benefit from therapy.

Group therapy is invariably a part of a residential treatment setting, but may also be used concomitantly with outpatient family therapy. Our own Family Therapy Institute usually has an ongoing group into which can come any alcoholics (or mixed substance abusers) in family or marital therapy with one of us. It is not routine; it is an option. There are patients who I find are in need of the added confirmation of their alcoholism by others with drinking problems. They either have totally rejected AA or attended AA with little or no impact. Some reject an abstinence approach within the context of family therapy and become more open to abstinence as a choice for themselves through the group process. Our group policy on abstinence is that members may attend up to six sessions without a commitment to an abstinence approach, after which they must choose to pursue abstinence (not necessarily immediately) or leave the group. The group also offers an essential support system for those alcoholics, in AA and especially those rejecting AA, whose spouses have already decided to leave them prior to their coming to therapy.

Regarding Antabuse (disulfiram), it has only one use: that is, to make someone feel sick (generally to their stomach, though more serious shock-like reactions can occur with high levels of alcohol) when they drink, with the intent to make them stop and think an extra bit when the impulse to drink comes on, so they will be less likely to indulge. I almost always mention it as an option, and rarely use it. I have found it highly successful with an occasional individual who definitely has decided to abstain but slips and wants help. A case example of such use is provided in Chapter 13. Antabuse, of course, is of little value to the person who chooses to stop it a day or two in advance of a potential drinking occasion.

Sexual Dysfunction

A different type of general consideration I will mention here is the coexistence, with alcoholism, of sexual dysfunctions. Heavy alcohol use causes sexual dysfunctions in two ways: It operates directly on the genital organs; and it alters behavioral interaction between couples who are sexually intimate. A preexisting sexual dysfunction may have exacerbated a drinking problem, just as a preexisting depression might. Unlike depression, however, some specific sexual dysfunctions that did not pre-date problem drinking may nonetheless persist as conditioned responses, long after drinking ceases. Non-specific sexual dysfunctions, such as low interest or a conditioned avoidance to the sexual advances of a formerly heavily drinking spouse, usually abate with a general improvement in a couple's relationship post-abstinence, with or without the help of therapy, but also may not, without specific intervention to deal with the sexual inhibition. Some form of diminished sexual satisfaction is more the norm than the exception, in my experience among couples with an alcoholic partner. It is beyond the scope of this book to enumerate the range of sexual problems that can occur as part of alcoholism and its treatment, except to say that between the depressant effect on organ responsivity (for both men and women) and the interactional effect on intimate behavior, few if any sexual dysfunctions are not seen in couples dealing with alcoholism. A truly integrative approach to alcoholism requires an exploration of sexual function pre- and post-abstinence; and whatever specific interventions are usually indicated for the identified sexual dysfunction should be implemented, especially when the problem persists weeks or months into the post-abstinence phase of treatment.

Adolescence

A final general consideration I will raise only briefly is dealing with alcohol issues specific to adolescence. All of the general psychiatric considerations mentioned above for adults apply to adolescent problem drinkers as well. And most of the recommendations for identifying alcoholism, for confronting the alcoholic and family about drinking and its consequences, and for intervening at the family level and/or the individual level apply also.

One difference, however, is that the therapist—in working with the parents of, and sometimes the siblings or surrogate parents of, the adolescent (or young adult)—has potentially enormously greater leverage, through indirect systems interventions, to bring about change in the young alcoholic's drinking behavior than is available in treating most adults. Hence, with adult alcoholics, we might emphasize the connection between drinking behavior and their complaint that spouse and children don't follow orders, but with adolescent alcoholics we might emphasize their refusal to clean up after themselves at home, or to call when out after an agreed-upon time, or to complete schoolwork on time, etc. That is, the primary task of the therapist working with the adolescent is often to empower the parental figures to successfully set healthy expectations and limits that can only be met through the adolescent's elimination of excessive drinking.

So often in families with adolescent substance abusers, there are conflicts that limit the parents' mutual disciplinary effectiveness, and there are interpersonal functions that the adolescent's drug use has come to serve. These conflicts and functions must be taken into account through prompt parental, and often sibling, involvement in therapy. Without an early commitment by family, little lasting change will occur in adolescent substance abusing behavior, with or without residential care. Howe has taken the position that drug abuse for the adolescent is usually a problem for everyone *but* the abuser. He suggests that

> "the adolescent drug abuser who is in treatment can profitably be seen as a co-therapist in the initial phases.... Whomever *he* identifies as having a problem should be included in the treatment session.... When the group is assembled, it usually becomes clear that the boy's drug use is, in some significant ways, as much a solution for the family as it has been a problem." (p. 93).

Howe cited a case in which a boy's paint-sniffing served to increase his own power over that of his parents and also to unify them and sidetrack them from their conflicts. "Thus, each time the family started to approach a critical level of anxiety, the boy would be cued to go out and sniff paint and be caught" (p. 96). Hence, he has described substance abuse as a prototype of a "safety-valve" mechanism, "bleeding off" the anxiety that threatens the system's functioning.

Howe supported this notion further by observing that usually when the anxiety is brought to a level that is tolerable for everyone in the system, the cues for delinquent behavior will disappear, and the behavior will cease rather abruptly" (p. 98) (1).

Jay Haley has offered a full-length case summary, with transcripts from selected sessions, of a way of empowering parents in a conflictual relationship to help their substance-abusing son (2). The therapist for the case was Sam Kirschner. The case summary deals with a heroin-addicted young man and emphasizes the setting, through parental cooperation, of behavioral expectations which can only be met off drugs. I recommend it highly as an example of a family approach that can also be used, with highly effective results, with adolescents and young adults who are alcoholic.

Residential care would be used only in those cases in which the mobilization of family resources has been inadequate or impossible or there is too imminent a chance of self-destruction. The latter is sometimes but rarely the case with alcohol abuse alone, but is frequently the case with the all-too-common mixed or poly-drug-abuse problems of adolescence, particularly those involving daily or almost-daily use of marijuana, PCP, or other psychedelics, or cocaine.

References

1. Howe, B. Family therapy and the treatment of drug abuse problems. *Family Therapy (The Journal of the Family Therapy Institute of Marin), 1* (1974), 89–98.
2. Haley, J. *Leaving Home*. New York: McGraw-Hill, 1981.

CHAPTER 11

HELPING THE INDIVIDUAL OVERCOME THE HABIT

Often family work alone leads to the leverage and support which may be sufficient for a member to stop drinking. Sometimes, however, even when the family is available as a resource and the therapist is skilled in systems interventions, the most appropriate locus of change is the individual. In an integrative therapy, ideally the therapist can intervene at both individual and relationship levels, as well as use different modes of systems intervention at different stages. This chapter offers a model for understanding steps an individual traverses in overcoming a substance abuse habit, and describes some individual treatment implications and recent innovative treatment interventions.

Just as habits come to serve functions in interpersonal relationships, as described in Chapter 1, habits also come to serve functions at the individual, intrapsychic level. Altering the interpersonal system of the alcoholic in such a way that alcohol use is no longer needed for its old functions may be a powerful enough intervention in itself. Educating the individual alcoholic to enhance problem-solving skills, social skills, and employee relationship skills may be sufficient to satisfy—post-abstinence—the functions of previous alcohol-using behavior. Sometimes neither is enough. There may be functions, unique to each individual, that are critical to the question of whether a person can either choose an abstinence approach, or sustain one.

Alcohol, like other mind-altering, dependency-producing drugs, can generate dissociative states in individuals. A corollary to this point is that state-dependent learning occurs, learning that is only recoverable by the individual while the same mind conditions are operating as were operating at the time that learning occurred. The common, alcohol-induced dissociative state is more complete than the dissociative states usually associated with some schizophrenias or with hysterical paralysis. In both the latter, there may be the ability to simultaneously experience incompatible, intrapsychic phenomena; and there may be the ability to concomitantly express oneself incongruently, as, for example, with the hysteric's "belle indifference." Those alcoholics who are known to have personality changes between dry and wet states are generally consistent and congruent in their own behavior and thinking from one dry state to the next and from one wet state to the next. Their dissociation is what John Grinder and Richard Bandler have referred to in an innovative presentation on this subject as a "sequential incongruity"(1). Hence, in the alcoholic, there may be the added hurdle to overcome—that *bona fide* internal resources available to the individual at some times are not accessible at others. If he or she has learned, for example, to act gregariously (or passionately or more eloquently, etc.) only in the wet state, or to feel self-confident or assertive only in the wet state, it might be inconceivable to the same person because of the sequential dissociation, that those resources still could be available if that person stopped drinking. Like the person with a true split personality, there may be little or no integration within the self of the emotional and behavioral resources of the wet and dry personalities. For the alcoholic, then, there may be a belief—in fact, an absolute conviction—that a highly valued part of the self can exist only in the wet state. Probably the only thing that would shake that belief would be to have the valued kinesthetic state experience of self when sober.

Without the alcoholic's awareness in the dry state of the valued wet internal state or even the belief that such an awareness is possible, the next essential step in habit change is thwarted. That next step involves identifying functions that the habit has come to serve and either substituting alternative behaviors for them or making the functions unnecessary. Integrating the wet and dry dissociative states, then, is sometimes a prerequisite to addressing these functions.

How the wet and dry states can be integrated elegantly is best described in the last chapter of *ReFraming*, a 1981 book drawn from the transcriptions of certain workshops on Neuro-Linguistic Programming (NLP) by Bandler and Grinder (1). The first step is elicitation simultaneously of the dissociated internal states, one associated with being dry and the other with being wet. Drawing upon an NLP technique modeled on Milton Erickson's style of hypnotherapy, the therapist establishes an anchor, that is, a conditioned stimulus, for an intense awareness in all sensory modalities—visual, auditory, kinesthetic and perhaps gustatory or olfactory—of one state (wet or dry) and then another anchor for the other.

For example, using good hypnotic, suggestive technique, the

therapist might talk a dry-state patient into an intense awareness of a positive state previously experienced only after some but not too much drinking. At the moment (of trance) at which the patient is clearly strongly involved in the newly recollected state, the therapist might firmly take the patient's right wrist between the therapist's own left thumb and little finger and squeeze firmly in a reproducible way that comes to serve as an anchor or trigger for that wet-state awareness. The therapist would repeat the procedure, anchoring the "dry" internal experience to the patient's left wrist. The therapist now has the means to elicit rapidly each of the two states. (One does not have to squeeze a wrist or even apply a touch to establish anchors. A highly specific, well-timed, and reproducible sound or visual stimulus might serve as well or better in many cases. The reader is referred to the case illustration in Chapter 13 and to other sources on NLP for further explanations of anchoring (2,3,4). Anchoring is frequently presented in workshops in NLP and in Ericksonian hypnotherapy, sometimes referred to as the "New Hypnosis.")

Having anchors for two previously disassociated, powerful states, we can "collapse anchors" by applying them simultaneously, eliciting the two states simultaneously, and thereby inducing an integration of a wet and dry state.

At this point, the patient is uniquely able to consider in a dry state just what functions drinking has come to serve, to acknowledge that there is a part of the self that can be appreciated for serving those valued functions, and to search within, with guidance from the therapist, for resources to draw upon for alternative behaviors to serve these same functions. Reframing one's experiences to highlight their most useful facets, as a transitional step toward finding new behaviors, either from within one's own behavioral resources or from learning, has been described well under the heading of a "6-Step Reframe" in Leslie Cameron-Bandler's book on NLP entitled *Solutions*(2). The internal check used in the 6-Step Reframe was drawn from Gestalt Therapy. The patient is first asked to establish contact with that part of the self that came up with the use of drinking as a way to serve certain needs or functions, and is then asked to appreciate fully what that part has been trying to do and to thank that part for its intent (reframe). A number of my patients have identified some form of social ineptness when sober, through this process, and drinking behavior as a sort of compensation.

Next, alternatives are generated by the patient's creative part. The ecological check involves going back inside in one's own thoughts to reestablish contact with that part of oneself that has assumed the now positively defined protective role and to ask if it can accept these new alternatives to drinking under all circumstances under which drinking now continues. Sometimes the answer is a clear, "Yes!" If it is not, or even if it is an equivocal "yes," that is useful information of a different sort. Within any reservations at the subconscious level lie fundamental answers as to the specific nature either of context or of desired outcomes that must be accounted for by alternatives to drinking.

In one case using this procedure, the patient adamantly concluded that the alternatives arrived at through his arduous efforts and my elegant guidance were flatly unacceptable to that part of him that had drawn upon drinking to take care of certain of his needs over the years. Fortunately, I had long since accepted the belief that whatever happens is feedback rather than failure and, therefore, was only momentarily shaken but not crushed. Pursuing the reasons for the rejection of a seemingly appropriate, creative alternative to drinking led to the hitherto elusive solution. In his case, further investigation revealed a cyclical mood change toward mania that preceded binges. The protective part of him knew that he required chemical assistance, for which alcohol had previously been the only known remedy. Lithium became the alternative of choice.

What are the sources of alternatives to drinking? The best resource is often the patient's own creative part. That is, we all have some experience with creativity. Most patients will readily acknowledge that they have at one time in their lives had a creative thought or two. Having done so, they also will find it hard to reject the notion that there is a creative side or part to them, and they will accept an instruction to "go inside and now establish communication with, or draw upon, your creative part and ask it for at least three alternatives to drinking in the contexts desired, for the purposes for which that first part, when you were younger, had previously come up with only drinking." In doing this, creativity can be facilitated in several ways. The therapist can educate while guiding, making comments about either typical ways others come up with, or ways the therapist can think of that might be specific to the patient. What can also be suggested is that the patient think of some creative person and imagine what that person might create to serve the intent the first part has been trying to serve through drinking. A person must have several optional behaviors to enable genuine flexibility of response under any given condition. If the condition is one that previously always triggered the behavior of drinking, the alcoholic is first asked to come up with at least three alternative behaviors that would serve the function drinking was serving under that condition, and then asked to do an "ecological check" that takes into account the impact of using these alternatives on the alcoholic's own psyche and own interactions with the social environment. New alternatives are kept only if an internal check reveals no adverse consequences to oneself if they were employed.

To this point we have covered ways to identify functions drinking may have come to serve and techniques for developing truly acceptable alternative behaviors to serve the same functions. Before going on to another layer of individual functioning that often needs to be addressed, it should be added that these new alternatives, even if well integrated, need to be tested. Testing can be done in the office by "future pacing." That is, the therapist may have the patient imagine dealing with a number of situations that might come about, which previously had been drinking situations. If the patient can run through them in as much sensory detail as feasible, and be confident now without alcohol and with new alternative behaviors, success in real life is more likely than if not so rehearsed. The ultimate test is in actual exposure to the drinking conditions. The therapist can go to the bar with the patient. If the bar is not the essential context, create the context that is. If the most challenging situation is likely to be a particular interpersonal exchange, invite the other parties in, or enact the role yourself.

For example, I once disagreed vehemently, out of the blue, with a woman who had previously always gone for a drink at the start of an argument but who had just rehearsed handling an argument well—lovingly but assertively. She stayed to talk the issue through with me to a reasonable mutual resolution before a friendly end to the session. Subsequently she went home and surprised her husband with her consistent readiness to talk things through rather than drink.

If the new alternatives are sufficiently integrated into the alcoholic's behavior, they will now override the urge to drink. Prompt, successful testing enhances the chances that the alcoholic will be prepared for subsequent, unplanned drinking opportunities.

In addition to or instead of substituting alternative behaviors to serve the identified functions of drinking, often it is necessary to install cognitive mechanisms to delay the automatic impulse to drink. Aversive conditioning, such as establishing an electroshock impulse as a conditioned aversive stimulus to taking a drink, something I do not choose to do, would be a form of delay mechanism that might cause automatic avoidance of alcohol or cause someone "to think twice" before drinking. There is a certain percentage of alcoholics who have been helped by this approach. The principle is important. To the extent that drinking has become an automatic response in the presence of certain cues, helping someone to think a little longer, when previously they would have acted automatically to get a drink, can be the little extra change it takes to stop drinking. Delay can come about in many ways. Perhaps the most widely used delay technique is the voluntary use of disulfiram (Antabuse). The case example in Chapter 13 describes a woman who had decided to stop, had greatly reduced her drinking, but under certain conditions drank anyway, until she used Antabuse. Taking Antabuse gave her a little extra moment of thought about the negative physical consequences of a drink. That was all she needed to prevent drinking in the few remaining circumstances in which she drank seemingly automatically, even though she and her family had so significantly changed that old functions of drinking were were no longer there to be served.

Strictly speaking, as it is generally used now, taking Antabuse is not an example of classical aversive conditioning, in which one has to actually experience something negative brought on by a physical stimulant at least once. When first introduced, Antabuse usually was used that way; that is, a doctor would give a patient a loading dose of Antabuse, then enough to drink to feel nauseated. Later, it was learned that once someone had a clear picture and/or verbal understanding of what could happen, that was just as likely to keep them from drinking while taking Antabuse: A negative anchor had been established for the thought of taking alcohol under certain conditions. Hence, the manner in which Antabuse came to be used provides a nice, natural example of the streamlining that can occur, through the use of anchors, in classical conditioning.

Relaxation and other non-drug, mind-altering techniques provide for some patients another avenue of delay. Deep relaxation, guided imagery, and meditation and self-hypnosis may provide that extra option, between impulse to drink and acting on the impulse, that enables choosing a non-drinking alternative. Occasionally, installing these self-generated methods of relaxation will alone serve to overcome problem drinking. Usually they will not, presumably for all the reasons discussed elsewhere in this book. That does not mean that they are not valuable adjuncts for many recovering alcoholics.

An innovative delay technique derived from NLP, involves the installation of a specific new thinking strategy for moments that previously led to drinking automatically. Borrowing from Robert Dilts (5), I have offered the following type of strategy to some alcoholics and to some regular but not necessarily very heavy drinkers: When the (characteristic) stimulus to drink occurs (it might be a thought, it might be seeing alcohol in some specific form or location), stop! (anchoring the self-command by a forceful tone of voice or even a specific touch) and say, "I have a choice. I can take it, or I can leave it," and do one of several alternatives (preferably already developed through education and/or a 6-step Reframe). I may instruct the patient, "First visualize taking a drink and become aware of how that will feel right away (F1), and then how that will feel a while later" (F2—at an unspecified time or a time selected by the patient as optimal for this purpose, e.g., 4 hours later, or 24 hours). "Then go back and picture leaving the drink (for one of the alternatives of your choice) and imagine how that will feel both immediately (F1') and a similar period of time later (F2'). Next compare only the "while-later" feelings (F2/F2'), and on the basis of that comparison, tell yourself whether you will take a drink or leave it. Act on what you decide." When someone has practiced this sequence well in the office and has imagined using it effectively in a wide variety of previously automatic drinking situations (i.e., future-paced—via the new strategy), they are ready to test it outside the office. Learning to install such a strategy well in a patient requires skills in the therapist not usually gained from traditional therapy or counseling training. Recommended special training would include reading Dilts, et al. *Neuro-Linguistic Programming*. Vol. 1. (6) and selected workshops in NLP techniques and in Ericksonian hypnotherapy. A more general technique of visualizing or walking through a slip is also taught in AA.

The reader will no doubt recognize the specific strategy just described as a formula for controlled drinking, that is, followed optimally, the strategy includes all the steps necessary to enable a rational choice of whether to drink or not, based on both short and long-term consequences that are specific to the individual who is making the choice. There is also implicit in the newly installed strategy the belief that "I have a choice." This poses a dilemma if you believe, as virtually everybody associated with Alcoholics Anonymous does, and as I do, that most recovering alcoholics can never drink without eventually getting out of control again. The woman in the case example in Chapter 13 used this strategy well to largely stop drinking. It did not lead her to choose not to drink in every situation; and when she resumed drinking under certain circumstances, she could not stop in those circumstances until she drank to excess, even though the strategy had enabled her to choose alternatives to drinking under most conditions. Taking Antabuse enabled her to avoid drinking in even those few remaining situations.

In my experience, the only people who should attempt to rely solely on this type of strategy are those (many) regular drinkers who would not usually be considered truly alcoholic but who have come to abuse alcohol. For example, a woman had been drinking two to three drinks at bedtime for many years and rarely drank alcohol at any other time. She was aware, as more women than men seem to report at that level of drinking, that each morning she was not at her best and that she was chronically a bit irritable and depressed, though not enough so to be given a psychiatric diagnosis. She knew from attempts to stop drinking for one to three days at a time that she promptly had a higher energy level and better mood but could not tolerate the bedtime headaches and difficulty sleeping, so she would resume drinking. Teaching her some nighttime relaxation alternatives and then installing the strategy just outlined, so that she could choose the new alternatives over drinking, enabled her to promptly stop her bedtime drinking while still having the option to occasionally take a drink socially, in situations where she had never had a problem with excessive drinking. She also reported having consistently more energy and less irritability. For heavier-drinking, multi-problem alcoholics, this strategy can be an aid and sometimes fosters abstinence in itself. If it does, fine; but I do not recommend using it as an alternative to abstinence in the treatment of alcoholism.

The strategy presented above also has proven useful with a number of alcoholics who adamantly resisted all efforts to get them to accept an abstinence approach, even while they acknowledged that their own pattern of drinking was detrimental to them and/or their families. In those, usually child-focused, cases—where I have been unable to alter, even with great efforts, a parent's belief that some drinking is a necessary ingredient of living, and where I have concluded that less drinking is essential to accomplishing agreed-upon goals for the child(ren)—I have decided that the better part of valor is to offer the alcoholic parent this strategy for more controlled drinking. I do so reluctantly and with an openly stated experimental orientation, believing that partial success for the family is better than no change and that later there will be more leverage to work toward abstinence as necessary.

In concluding this discussion of new directions in individual approaches to the alcoholic, a brief return to the subject of beliefs is in order. Changing beliefs is a central motivating factor in recovery from alcoholism. A traditional approach to belief change in the alcoholic has been offered in Chapter 5 with regard to confrontation as to the definition of alcoholism and to the consequences of one's drinking. Recently there have been qualitative leaps made in the development of psychotherapeutic methods for altering dysfunctional beliefs. Methods are available that enable rapid elicitation of the major (unique) criteria upon which any given individual relies (7). What would someone die for? What are their most highly valued criteria? One can quickly rank-order these criteria by forcing choices.

For example, we can ask what conditions would have to pertain to override a person's highly valued criterion; and what then would have to be present to get the person to abide by the criterion even though that condition pertained. If being loving to one's children is a highly valued criterion, under what conditions would one *not* act loving toward them? If that condition existed, what other conditions would have to be present so that one could act loving toward them anyway? And if that condition existed, what else would lead one to be unloving with them in spite of that? Etc. This would go on until the person answers congruently, "None." The same process would apply equally if the highly valued criterion were quite different, such as financial independence.

Having established a patient's highest one or two or three criteria, one can utilize them to cause the alcoholic to question his beliefs concerning the value of continued drinking. For example, take a hypothetical alcoholic man of Irish ancestry who may believe deeply that all "real men" of Irish origin drink. Assume that it is vitally important to this man to perceive himself as a "real man." In fact, being a "real man" turns out to have value for him second only to defending his country, for which he is prepared to give his life. Such a person might be motivated to seek help to stop drinking by suggesting (perhaps hypnotically) compelling arguments that the defense of Ireland requires that all real men maintain optimal physical health and clarity of mind. Since, clearly, mind-altering, toxic substances are incompatible with such striving, surely no one who dedicated life to country could possibly use alcoholic beverages.

Of course, the foregoing logical exercise would be totally wasted on someone for whom defense of country was less than at or near the top of their criteria ladder. But then another top-level, valued criterion could be ferreted out and used in its stead.

In summary, then, for the therapist in whose patient individual intervention is indicated, we have offered some suggestions—through the use of NLP etc.—for helping that individual overcome the drinking problem.

References

1. Bandler, R., & Grinder, J. *ReFraming: Neuro-Linguistic Programming and the transformation of meaning*. Moab, UT: Real People Press, 1982.
2. Cameron-Bandler, L. *Solutions: Practical and effective antidotes for sexual and relationship problems*. San Rafael, CA: Future Pace, 1985. Revised version of *They lived happily ever after: A book about achieving happy endings in coupling*.

3. Lankton, S. R. *Practical magic: A translation of neuro-linguistic programming into clinical psychotherapy.* Cupertino, CA: Meta Publications, 1980.
4. Davis, S. L. R., & Davis, D. I. Neuro-linguistic programming (TM) and family therapy. *Journal of Marital and Family Therapy 9 (1983):* 283–291.
5. Dilts, Robert. Personal communication.
6. Dilts, R. B., Grinder J., Bandler, R., DeLozier, J., & Cameron-Bandler, L. *Neuro-linguistic programming: Vol. I: The study of the structure of subjective experience.* Cupertino, CA: Meta Publications, 1980.
7. Cameron-Bandler, L. Workshops on "Metaprograms."

CHAPTER 12

BRIEF SUMMARY OF AN INTEGRATIVE APPROACH: A MODEL FOR HABIT CHANGE

Numerous approaches to the treatment of alcoholism have been mentioned in the preceding chapters. Some have addressed the interpersonal system of the alcoholic, and a rationale has been provided for intervening at the family systems level. Others have been directed at the individual alcoholic, with the explanation that some factors influencing drinking behavior reside within the individual and, at times, can or even must be addressed substantially at that level. Regardless of the level of intervention, or the school of therapy drawn upon, certain underlying structures and dynamics operate in the effective resolution of problem drinking. In Table 1, I have summarized what I believe these are.

Each of the elements listed in Table 1 has been described more fully earlier in the book. They are not all of significance to the treatment of all alcoholics. Each has proven critical with some alcoholics, usually in combination with several other elements. Whether it might be possible to extract from this list one or two or three universal operating principles, which, when acted upon elegantly, can be counted upon to produce recovery, I do not know yet. Nor is it known yet whether all that is called alcoholism is more usefully conceived of as one entity or several. I offer this list in summary of the elements I have come to regard as often critical to the successful alcohol recovery process. Categories are grouped under only two broad headings, "Belief Change" and "Habit Control." It is taken for granted that interventions made in any one of the categories listed will impact on all others.

Table 1
Summary of the Critical Elements in an Integrative Approach to the Treatment of Alcoholism (and other substance abuse):

Belief Change (interacting with)	*Habit Control*
	(Mechanisms of delaying hitherto automatic behavior)
Confrontation 1) Consequences of drinking (family, marital, individual) 2) Criteria (identifying and utilizing alcoholic's own against use of alcohol). 3) AA, Al-anon, Alateen (concepts) of hitting bottom and alcoholism as an illness; (spirituality). 4) Family interaction in family therapy.	Support AA, other support groups; Detachment (on part of others in system); Al-anon, Alateen; Family Therapy Aversive conditioning Strategy installation
Integration of wet and dry state Collapsing anchors Reframe 1) Separation of intent or function from behavior 2) Elicitation of alternatives (or obviating need for) a) Individual level b) Interpersonal level 3) Ecological check (Are the new behaviors safe under some or all circumstances; is it all right to stop drinking?) a) Individual level b) Wider systems levels	Other pattern interruption 1) Interpersonal (marital, family, network therapy) 2) Individual Treatment of co-existing and aggravating conditions (e.g. recurrent mania) Residential Care

I will not attempt to reiterate all that has been said before in the book about each item in Table 1, but offer only a few comments for clarification. First, "Belief Change" is one of only two main headings. The reason is that all useful interventions for alcoholism, other than modifying or substituting for a specific conditioned response (forms of Habit Control), can be reduced to some version of a belief change procedure. One can alter the habitual drinking response, and if the consequences are experienced positively, the alcoholic will maintain the new behaviors. One can alter people's belief that alcohol is either good for them, or necessary, or a right to be maintained at all costs, or whatever—to a new belief that alcohol is destructive for them, or was good for them then but not now, or that there are now better ways to do what alcohol used to do for them. When the critical belief changes occur, some people decide to stop drinking. Others decide to seek whatever further help is necessary to overcome their habit, now convinced that it is all right to stop drinking.

Confrontation is the tried and true way to change beliefs in dealing with alcoholism. It is difficult to go often to AA meetings, and not come around to the belief, "I am an alcoholic." The belief that one "hits bottom"—that there is a personal point of self-destruction from drinking that an alcoholic must reach before truly deciding to quit drinking—and the belief that alcoholism is an illness are also central to the recovery process through AA. Confrontation by doctors, therapists, and counselors takes the form of convincing alcoholics: 1.) that there already are significant negative consequences to their particular use of alcohol, whether to health, social, vocational, legal, marital or family areas of living; and 2.) that if the drinking continues then clearly there is a disorder of function. Chapters 5 through 8 provide clinical examples of useful confrontations with alcoholic families.

Often delineating these consequences is not enough to alter an alcoholic's belief either that he or she is a normal drinker or that alcohol is a necessary part of life. A more complex approach to confrontation involves first identifying the criteria the alcoholic holds highest. To briefly summarize what was said in chapter 11, this can be elicited by questions about determinants of the patient's own behavior, for example, questions starting with, "What is something you would never do?" And then, "What would have to happen to make you do it anyway?" Then, "If that happened, what would make you not do it even so?" The questions end when the answer is a believable "nothing." The second part of the confrontation involves utilizing the patient's own criteria in the service of altering beliefs about the value of drinking. For example, a person who would never compromise mental alertness when responsible for others (driving, children, etc.) was helped to acknowledge how the use of alcohol was incompatible with that person's own high criterion. That is, framing one's behavior as incompatible with one's own criterion, having elicited something that person would never do and then showing that he or she is doing that very thing as a consequence of drinking, can be a very powerful confrontation. Another method is to dramatize the impact of drinking on important relationships, through family or marital interventions that include the alcoholic member and that demonstrate interactional consequences of alcohol abuse. This type of confrontation can be verbal, with other family members affirming to the alcoholic and to one another their beliefs that alcoholism is present and a concern indirectly in all of their lives; or it can be nonverbal, through psychodramatic techniques such as family sculpting (a good example of which is given in Chapter 2), which may generate powerful depictions of the differences in relationships when alcohol is present in the family system versus when it is not. Family therapy can be used to assign mutually agreed-on desirable tasks that the alcoholic agrees he can do if not alcoholic, and then deal with the all too frequent failure to complete the task.

After "Confrontation," in Table 1, comes "Integration of wet and dry state." This is not yet a widely used element of alcoholism treatment, probably because the majority of therapists are not yet experienced in the use of NLP, as described in Chapter 11, or hypnosis. Nonetheless, I have included it because it simply may be an essential step for some alcoholics to undergo before they can believe that it is possible for them to give up drinking, or before they can accurately identify the functions that drinking is serving for them and consider and effectively imagine using viable alternatives.

The final three items under Belief Change are each subsumed under the general heading, "Reframe." The NLP 6-step Reframe technique described in Chapter 11 offers an efficient way to accomplish all three of the items listed. Each, however, deserves to be identified as an important, sometimes critical element in its own right.

Separating the intention and function of drinking from the behavior of drinking and then eliciting alternatives to accomplish the former (thereby making the function unnecessary), are often key steps in the treatment of alcoholism.

A recent example of mine was the alcoholic husband who discovered when newly abstinent for occasional months that his wife seemed more at ease with him drinking even though she was also distrustful of him. It evolved that she had gone almost directly from living with an alcoholic father to marrying an alcoholic husband and was, in fact, confused and anxious over how to act with a man who warranted trust. Reframing his drinking as having come to serve a protective function for his wife, and teaching her how to act more at ease with a trustworthy man, were necessary steps to freeing him up to give up his drinking.

The concept that alcoholic behavior comes to serve certain functions in family systems, which my colleagues and I have called the "adaptive consequences of drinking," has been illustrated in more depth in Chapter 1. These functions may have nothing to do with the cause of drinking. It is assumed that, regardless of etiological factors, the drinking behavior of the alcoholic comes to serve certain functions that are there to be served in the system of the alcoholic. Through either family intervention or individual techniques, such as the 6-step reframe, the therapist either can enable the substitution of new, non-drinking-related behavior patterns that serve the function previously served mainly by drinking; or can convince alcoholic and family system alike that that function no longer needs to be served. Either way, a powerful belief is ultimately being altered. The separation of intent or function from drinking behavior, overtly or covertly, can lead to a reframing of drinking in the thinking of the alcoholic and of his family as truly serving some positive role. This belief change can in turn serve as a critical transition toward accepting both the need to find alternatives to drinking and the possibility of doing so. Actually coming up with suitable alternatives and trying them out successfully does more, of course, to alter the alcoholic's beliefs about the necessity or inevitability of drinking, than anything else. Both family and individual techniques, overt or covert, can accomplish this step, especially when the way has been prepared cognitively through attention to the steps noted above.

The final item under Belief Change is an "ecological check." Is substituting new behaviors for drinking a safe and a sound change with respect to the ecology of the alcoholic, the family, and the wider community system? In good Gestalt fashion, the 6-step reframe provides for an ecological check of the safety of alternatives to drinking by including a step in which alcoholics communicate with that part of themselves that is providing for a certain aspect of their welfare through use of the behavior of drinking, and asks for reassurance from within that the new behaviors would be acceptable under all circumstances where, previously, drinking occurred. At the family level, a paradoxical "go slowly" prescription might facilitate a similar ecological check. An exploration of all the interactions that could come about to undo a family member's newly achieved abstinence addresses the same issue. The successful outcome of an ecological check may be another changed belief. The original belief, often unconscious, may have been that something bad could happen if the drinking stopped. The result of the ecological check should be the conviction that abstinence offers viable and safe alternatives.

In the case of the alcoholic husband whose wife became anxious dealing with an abstinent, trustworthy man, an ecological check revealed not only the belief that his abstinence would make her anxious but also the new belief that they could learn effective ways to overcome that reaction to his abstinence.

Some people come to believe that they are alcoholic, believe that they and their families can adapt safely to their abstinence, practice acceptable alternatives in previously drinking contexts, and still slip. These people need help in the category of "habit control." Under certain conditions, there are sufficient cues to trigger drinking automatically. Anything that successfully introduces a longer pause between the impulse and its satisfaction is likely to help. This is especially true when the alcoholic already has the beliefs to support choosing abstinent behaviors. In Table 1, Habit Control is the general heading under which have been placed a widely diverse collection of therapeutic measures, which have in common that their success occurs through the mechanism of introducing delay and thereby choice, where previously only automatic drinking occurred.

The most common form of habit delay is through seeking the company of supportive others at times when one might previously have been carrying out the habitual behavior. Remembering to contact someone is an example of a learned or newly installed strategy. For the drinker, Alcoholics Anonymous is the relevant support group now almost universally available. Its use as part of the integrative family approach to alcoholism is elaborated in Chapter 9. Suffice it to say that knowing that one has a completely understanding, non-drinking group to join, and very likely (ideally) a supportive individual sponsor to call 24 hours a day who will talk when the urge to drink arises, is a sobering thought that often stands between an impulse and its corresponding action.

Learning detachment is another prime example of gaining strategies to delay habitual behavior. Here the effect is usually brought about through a change in the thinking and consequently the behavior of the non-alcoholics in the patient's system. Their behavior is habitual too, for example, their automatic reactions to their alcoholic family member taking a drink. Remaining neutral, going on with their plans or business, or in other ways eliminating their reactions to the alcoholic's drinking removes all outside justifications for continued drinking, causes confusion and anxiety, and inevitably leads to adaptations by the alcoholic that often foster recovery. Such detachment can be taught well by family therapists and through family members' attendance at Al-anon and Alateen, as discussed at greater length in Chapter 9.

Aversive conditioning is another mode of introducing habit delay, discussed particularly in Chapter 10. Briefly, taking a drug such as disulfiram (Antabuse), the only function of which is to predictably lead to feeling sick if one drinks, is the most common example of this category of habit control. One comes to think about the new negative consequences of even one drink as an intervening cognitive step between impulse to drink and taking the drink.

Explicit strategy installation is a direct approach, described briefly in Chapter 11, to introducing new cognitive steps between the first thought of taking a drink and the formerly automatic end-decision point. Both strategy installation and aversive conditioning can be thought of as specific forms of pattern interruption. "Other pattern interruption," in Table 1, is listed as a separate sub-category of "Habit Control," to include all other forms of pattern interruption that can be created uniquely to suit the needs of each individual case. Patterns leading up to taking a drink can often be detected and at any level of behavior: individual, couple, family, wider network. For example, he says "a," she says "b," someone else does "c," she says "d," . . . , and he takes a drink. A deletion of, or substitution for, any step by any person can lead to an alteration in the previously automatic sequence and consequently delay the drinking behavior.

Habit control sometimes requires the effective elimination of an aggravating condition. This is not usually the case; but when it is, it is foolish to disregard the compounding factor. The case of the hither-to treatment-resistant alcoholic who required treatment for cyclical mania is mentioned in Chapter 10 as an example of a coexisting condition, the treatment of which enabled a patient to think twice before periodically disregarding non-drinking strategies which were already functional under normal mood conditions.

Finally, residential care of any duration offers an enforced time-out from alcohol for the length of stay in the program. It is a form of habit control but is time-limited and ultimately ineffectual without attention to enough of the other critical elements of the integrative approach to suit the needs of a given individual and that individual's network. Ideally, the enforced time-out buys time to regain clarity of thinking, to eliminate the worst physiological craving, to acquire new beliefs, and to try out new behaviors without competition from the option of the drinking behaviors. Optimally, the family is incorporated in these changes, so that new learning is not limited to the residential context. Hospital or other residential placement is not a treatment in itself. Its utility depends—as much as does outpatient care—on the principals advanced herein for effective habit change. Residential-based care for alcoholism with adequate post-discharge care and the use of the integrative approach, is highly effective. Since outpatient care utilizing the integrative approach is also highly effective and usually much more cost-effective, it is incumbent upon the treatment fields to offer more and more care for alcoholic patients outside of residential care facilities, limiting the use of such facilities to severe cases in which there is serious organic mental impairment, or high potential for serious withdrawal symptoms, or imminent danger of major self-destructive behavior.

CHAPTER 13

"I NEED HELP TO STOP DRINKING": AN INTEGRATIVE FAMILY THERAPY APPROACH TO THE MANAGEMENT OF A FAMILY IN EARLY RECOVERY

I pull out all the stops in the treatment of alcoholism. My natural propensity for integrating diverse schools of therapy, which is a challenging luxury in many cases, seems a necessity when I work with families with one or more actively drinking alcoholic members. Maybe that is why I have chosen to write about a case that stands out for moving along rather smoothly and clearly successfully. I hope that in writing it I have not gotten mired in a description of a series of crises, and instead have been able to show and stay in touch with the essential issues and interventions in this family therapy case that are archetypal of my experience with the treatment of alcoholism.

Before I describe the case a little background will be offered that will also provide a brief summary of the central issues covered in this book. After some eight years of rather intensive experience with alcoholism clinical research and treatment, I approached this case with some very definite postulates. One was that, regardless of how it started, the heavy use of alcohol came to serve certain important functions in the family of the alcoholic. These were unique to each family, and would need to be substituted for or eliminated. A second was that, while one person was coming in asking for help, I could be more effective and indeed more ethical by working with at least the whole family currently living together at home. A third was that Alcoholics Anonymous (AA), Al-anon, and Alateen could be compatible with and supportive to family therapy. A fourth assumption was that the use of alcohol by the alcoholic had to be very well controlled or preferably stopped before even a very skillful family therapist could be effective and, therefore, that family therapy skills had to be applied directly to eliminating the drinking problem as early as possible, even if many other problems that usually respond well to therapy were identified.

I view alcoholism as a final common pathway disorder. By this I mean that one can develop it through multiple pathways, both environmental and physiologic. From my reading of the research literature, I have also concluded that the single most important etiologic factor is exposure to heavy use of alcohol. In short, I suspect anyone can become alcoholic, though some are more predisposed on a familial basis than others, and it really is not useful to pursue how one got started. We must deal in the present with the physiological aspects of alcoholism, tolerance and withdrawal, the conditioned stimuli to drink, the functions alcohol has come to serve for the drinker and his or her family in their interactions, and any developmental impairment that is a consequence of chronic heavy drinking.

My own approach to family therapy is an integrative one. By integrative I mean that in my training and practice, and teaching, I have attempted to learn, in some depth, to utilize and transmit diverse theories and techniques. While I have described my relevant background at some length in the Preface, a summary here of the theories and techniques to which I have been most exposed should help to clarify further what I mean when I use the term integrative. My training has included intensive work with first-generation teachers Jay Haley, John Grinder and Richard Bandler, and their colleagues. Earlier, there were also prominent psychoanalytic teachers whose influence is surely extant in my thinking, but rarely is consciously activated in my practice. My training has included a lesser but nonetheless serious exposure to first- or second-generation teachers of Bowenian cross-generational approaches, individual and marital behavioral schools of therapy, and a smattering of an infinity of other concepts of change of both Eastern and Western origin that I plagiarize rapaciously out of the conviction that the more concepts and skills we add to our treatment repertoire, the more issues we can address usefully in our clients. Gurman surmised in his exhaustive reviews that there is no one school of therapy, individual or family, that had demonstrated itself to be clearly better than all others for all conditions (1). At the same time some approaches do appear better for certain conditions, for example, structural family therapy for the treatment of certain psychosomatic disorders and drug abuse and functional family therapy for the treatment of juvenile status offenders. (2,3) I believe it would be a shame for a modern therapist not to be able to call upon existing effective techniques for a given condition because he or she is only skilled in one, necessarily limited school of therapy. Multiple schools exist because different seminal thinkers primarily addressed different dimensions of human experience.

My version of integration involves adding together the theories and techniques from diverse schools that together begin to deal adequately with all of the dimensions of experience along which we may want to intervene in therapy. Nowhere has this effort to integrate proven more valuable to me than in the comprehensive treatment of alcoholism. I believe this is so precisely because alcoholism, even though its consequences look so familiar time after time, can occur in so many different preexisting contexts.

The J. Family and the First Interview

This is the story of a relatively brief intervention with the J. family, a nuclear family of six. Mr. and Mrs. J. (Ann and Bob) were each 47 years old. For more than six years, both had been very heavy daily drinkers. Then one winter day, Bob stopped altogether. One month later Ann started to go to AA meetings. Over several months, she continued to go to AA, and she managed to cut down her drinking greatly, but at times she still drank to oblivion. In the early fall, Ann went to her family doctor and asked for Antabuse (disulfiram). Her doctor was one of several family practitioners with whom we work closely at the Family Therapy Institute of Alexandria. Ann arrived at his office intoxicated. Because of her intoxication, he declined to prescribe Antabuse. Instead he told her to see me. In making his referral, her doctor also may have been influenced by the frequent visits to his office of two of Ann's children. He had seen 13-year-old Freddie often for headaches, and 17-year-old Carrie, just as often, for stomach aches.

When Ann first called me, she said she had been going to AA for about nine months and couldn't stop drinking entirely. She could go two to three weeks without a drink, then would drink again for two months or more. She wanted to come in herself to get help to stop drinking. I told her I could usually be most helpful if I had a chance to meet other family members as early as possible. We agreed that she and Bob would come in together at first and that their children might also be invited in, if we were to continue to work together.

As is my custom in most first interviews, I asked Bob and Ann each to tell me briefly in their own words what they would like to accomplish from talking with me. They were way ahead of most alcoholics in family therapy in that they didn't deny, skirt, or minimize alcohol as a problem, nor did they even debate the merits of achieving abstinence. Ann simply said she was seeking a way to stop drinking. And Bob blandly confessed that he only came because Ann had asked him to. He, too, only wanted Ann to be able to stop drinking.

Here I confess that this family is not typical. In dealing with alcoholism, usually I spend much of my energy—and exercise most of my wiles and craft—with most families just to reach the point at which this family began. But I have written about that elsewhere in this book. Here I want to focus on and grapple with the (often simultaneous) phase of therapy that deals with making other changes, changes within a family system that has had plenty of time to make its adaptations to alcoholic parents.

The initial request for Ann's and Bob's desired outcomes had taken only several minutes. I spent the rest of the first session looking for issues in the family that were in need of attention. In particular, I went after drug problems in the children and interactional deficiencies between Ann and Bob. The likelihood of the former I knew was high; the latter was a certainty. I also thought that Bob would only return and the children would only come in if I could establish a good reason for their involvement before the end of the first session. Otherwise, they as a family, like many families, would be happier to deposit the identified problem person in the family, Ann, for help with her drinking and leave well enough alone.

What I found in my brief but highly tailored search was the epitome of the catalogue of complications one finds in the family with alcoholic parents. In this family there were no immediate crises to obscure the more subtle, wide-ranging issues always present. Bob had a decent government job. The children were not in trouble with the law, and there was no talk of divorce. Money was tight, but there were no imminent foreclosures or debt crunches. Yet everyone, as individuals and in their relationships with one another, was functioning below their own previous best levels.

Ann's main complaint was that "I can't sit and talk with my husband like everybody else does" (referring to other couples). She felt that she had been able to talk with him until about seven years earlier, when she had started drinking daily before Bob came home from work. Bob had begun drinking heavily about the same time. Neither really knew if one had increased before the other. Ann also noted that their sexual activity had decreased over the heavy drinking years. They typically had intercourse now less than once a week. The exception was that the past summer, when Bob was dry and Ann had temporarily stopped drinking, they had had intercourse twice a week as they had had in the past.

Regarding their four children, Ann reported that the extent of her yelling at them, and they at her, varied according to the level of her alcohol intake. This had become most apparent when Bob had stopped drinking. The yelling between Ann and the kids had persisted at its customary high frequency until Ann, too, cut down on alcohol. Since she was still drinking at the time of the first session, the yelling was still present but to an extent commensurate with her reduced alcohol intake.

This much of their story I believed because it fit with my experience with families and with my reading of studies in the literature. That is, when one or both spouses/parents drink heavily, talking and sexual intimacy become impaired and there is increasing yelling and disrespectful behavior between children and parents. And when drinking stops or even diminishes, there is some improvement. In fact, there may be a return, at least on the part of the parents, to the previous most mature level of relating, a level which a therapist may not be able to predict well while drinking persists. Achieving abstinence itself does readily produce some lasting improvements in family relationships. Unfortunately, the opposite is not true. Attempting to produce lasting gains in family interactions while leaving the drinking of an alcoholic member unchanged is usually futile and a long and arduous task at best.

Other impressions Ann and Bob attempted to leave with me, I brushed aside. Chief among these was the notion that it was evident everything would be fine if Ann just stopped drinking. This required the assumption that Ann's and Bob's previous most mature interactional behavior was all they needed even at this stage in their lives. Couples with an alcoholic spouse almost always fail to resolve, or even to develop the mechanisms necessary to resolve, the inevitable differences all couples will have, so my guess was that this notion was false.

A corollary to this seemed to be Ann and Bob's assertion that, while the kids had some problems, we really didn't need to discuss them in therapy. That kids' problems either are nonexistent or don't need direct attention is not unheard of, but I required proof. By doggedly probing about the children, I rapidly exposed the children's needs for intervention and at the same time easily observed Ann and Bob's interactional barriers to dealing effectively with certain issues.

I learned that 13-year-old Freddie, entering his freshman year of high school, had frequent headaches—as mentioned earlier—for which he had made many visits to the family doctor. His headaches had become less common over the previous year but still occurred. Seventeen-year-old Carrie, now starting her senior year, had used marijuana in unknown amounts, but frequently, for years and had suffered stomach aches that necessitated many trips to the family doctor. Like Freddie, she had also shown some improvement in symptoms and in school work over the preceding year. Bob, Jr., at 18½, had managed to graduate from high school the year before but still lived at home, and remained a regular heavy user of marijuana and beer. His few friends were also substance abusers. While he did have a job from 3 P.M. to 9 P.M., it had no future. In addition, Ann got him out of bed at 2 P.M. each day and drove him to work. She resented doing it but felt guilty if she didn't. Ann found herself being very defensive with Bob, Jr. when she preferred not to drive him as he wished, so she did what he wanted. Besides, it was unsafe for him to drive their car, and he could not afford one of his own. There had been a recent decrease in yelling and swearing between Bob, Jr. and each of his parents. As for the oldest child Annie, aged 20, I was told she was "okay," had a job and was living in her own apartment. It was not until I could talk with the other children in person that I learned that the younger siblings worried about their oldest sister's drinking habits.

Through asking Ann and Bob to talk to one another in my presence about what behavior they expected of Bob, Jr., I learned also in the first session the limits of their ability to problem-solve and communicate effectively. I noticed that Bob gave terse responses in a tone of voice that Ann took as anger (sometimes mistakenly) whenever they explored dealing with Bob, Jr. on anything. There was much guessing or mind-reading about what the other one meant and also little or no feedback offered, or clarification sought or provided without my instigation. There was, however, little animosity. The problem as Ann and Bob saw it was in Bob, Jr. I was witness to their best level of communication. It was a relief to them again to be talking that well with one another after years of yelling that alternated with long silences. I suspected they had managed adequately until one or two children had entered the teenage years. Then the children's challenges to their togetherness had exceeded the capacity of their communication skills to jointly resolve family issues, and their drinking had increased sufficiently to prevent them from making the time and energy commitment needed to stretch their coping skills (enough to accommodate their normal developmental transition).

I made no attempt to explore the historical evolution of their problems. For me, it is enough that I see, hear, and sense what behavior is occurring that enables the problems to persist in the present, and that I have some concept to guide me as a working hypothesis. Then I intentionally intervene. The consequences of my intervention will either confirm my hypothesis or rapidly allow me to refine and improve upon it. Successful change will often, though not necessarily, be accompanied by considerable understanding on the part of individuals or the entire family. I welcome the understanding as a confirmation of progress that is also apparent in behavior. I pursue, though, relevant change in behavior by the most efficient means available. As in their case, I usually intervene in the first session, even when I state that the first two sessions are just an evaluation, at the end of which I will make my recommendation. By the time I make a recommendation, I want the family to have some idea how I will work with them and to have already experienced some positive outcome from therapy.

With Ann and Bob, the interventions in the first session were twofold. One was that I saw to it, through coaxing them into giving feedback and clarifications, that they carried their discussion of how to deal with Bob, Jr. a little further toward mutual understanding and resolution. The second was that I went on record confirming for them that they were, in fact, dealing with alcoholism/substance abuse in themselves and in at least one child.

Phase One: Ann Alone

I chose to meet with Ann alone the next two sessions on purely pragmatic grounds. While I had planted the seeds of concern over couple's issues and child substance abuse, I had no illusions. Bob and Ann were still wedded to the notion that if Ann stopped drinking they would have all that they wanted from therapy, or perhaps, better stated, all that they could hope for. So I had been consciously engaged in raising their expectations. As part of that, I withheld Antabuse. I had surmised in the first session that Ann wanted to take Antabuse and probably would have used it safely and effectively. Family life would then have become more tolerable before Bob or Ann had sufficient motivation to continue therapy, even to get help with their substance-abusing son. And Ann would not have learned how to talk over a difference with Bob without the urge to drink. Hence, I suspected that she would remain unnecessarily dependent on Antabuse.

So I respected the presenting problem, which I do not always do (but I recommend that one have an awfully good reason if one does not). In each of the two sessions with Ann, I relied largely on Neuro-Linguistic Programming (NLP) skills which I have discussed in Chapter 11 and, with Susan Davis, in recent papers (4,5). The second session (the first one with Ann) focused on giving Ann a new thought strategy for delaying action when she had the desire to take a drink. In the third session, I took on the task of installing an "I can stay to talk (with Bob) and feel okay" state in place of her previous "uptight, knot-in-stomach" state in response to hearing Bob sound angry.

In that first session with Ann alone, then, I dealt exclusively with her drinking habits. More specifically, I learned how her thinking perpetuated her alcohol abuse and then taught her an alternative sequence of thoughts, which she was sent home to practice. I learned that she could go for hours or even days at times without interest in alcohol, then, all of a sudden (with sufficient cues or conditioned stimuli) she would become aware of a feeling, which she called a "desire," that she would like to have a drink. Next she would say to herself, "Don't think about it," which predictably led to a doubling of the intensity of the desire. This cycle would inevitably lead to the desire becoming strong enough that she would act on it. Having done so, she usually drank until she fell asleep. I offered her another set of thoughts as soon as she got the "desire." The sequence I gave her was taken directly from a conversation I had with Robert Dilts, first author of *Neuro-Linguistic Programming, Vol. 1*, which I recommend as the best background resource on thought strategies and strategy changes, (6). The use of this type of strategy is also discussed in Chapter 12. With Ann, this strategy was, first, to have her say to herself as soon as she felt the desire for alcohol, "What are my choices?" She was then taught, in sequence, to say to herself, "I have two choices," and to picture each choice in another sequence. First she pictured taking a drink and thought how she would feel immediately (good, relieved, etc.) and how she would feel a little while or sometime later (regretful, etc.). Next she pictured leaving the drink, not taking it, and how that would leave her feeling immediately (disappointed, craving) and a while later (relieved, self-confident, etc.). Next she compared only the while-later feelings of taking or leaving the drink and was instructed to tell herself, on the basis of that comparison, either "I'll take it or "I'll leave it" and to act on whichever she said.

At the next sesssion, Ann reported having used alcohol on only one occasion but, at that time, consumed a whole bottle of wine.

Fortunately, this one drinking incident was precipitated by an interaction with her husband so I could move swiftly and naturally into changing certain of her responses to her husband, in preparation for a couple-oriented phase of therapy. The precipitant in this episode had been Ann's hearing Bob sound angry at her, followed by his walking out overnight. In response to perceiving his tone as angry, she reported, she (typically) got "uptight," had a "knot in her stomach," and didn't know how to talk to him. When alcohol was around, she would then drink "so I can talk to him okay." In the present incident, she feared that if she had used her new strategy and not taken a drink, she would not have known how to talk to him and he would have prolonged his anger at her, whereas the current sequence of hearing anger, drinking, saying something to Bob and having him walk out could be relied upon to cool things off by the next day. Knowing this sequence, I went looking for something to replace (and improve upon) the function of alcohol when Ann heard Bob sounding angry.

What I sought and found within Ann were her own internal resources for knowing how to talk to someone without knots in her stomach. Drawing upon NLP techniques for rapidly associating new internal states with conditioned stimuli that previously elicited dysfunctional responses (4,5,7), I elicited certain positive states from Ann's own past in which she was confident she could talk over issues effectively. Having established an "anchor" for these states, I could then quickly reelicit these positive states in association with her recollections of recent times with her husband when he sounded angry. When she was able to reexperience these times and imagine how she could have handled them differently, more effectively, and to her complete satisfaction, I then had her anticipate future confrontations with Bob. When she could imagine handling those well in the future, she was sent home to test it out and with instructions to bring Bob with her to the next session.

Phase Two: The Couple

Sessions four, five and six were conjoint couple's sessions spanning four weeks (because I was away one week between sessions five and six). Improving communication skills or, more specifically, learning to stay with a discussion over differences to the point of feeling understood and reaching a resolution without regret, was the main focus of these sessions. At first I emphasized their working out strictly couple's issues. That progressed so rapidly that I quickly guided them to parenting issues in preparation for subsequent family sessions. So often in my experience, this type of family would come in around a child-focused problem, such as on the oldest son's substance abuse and underachievement in school or one of the other children's psychosomatic problems. In that case, I would have been moving from parenting issues to couple's issues. In this case, I was very consciously reversing that order. There is a growing literature on the importance of moving toward couple's therapy with child-focused initial complaints but not enough yet on the need to move toward parenting interventions when the initial client/patient is an adult. This is particularly important with chemically dependent parents.

Couple's work moved rapidly because, according to both Bob and Ann as well as my own observation, Ann had changed her behavior dramatically following the anchoring in, in session three, of certain new responses to an angry tone. "I didn't even hear him get angry this week!" said Ann at the start of session four. This was said in spite of Bob's impression that he had not been different that week. In fact, Bob recalled at least one incident at a family dinner when he positively was annoyed and reported that Ann had not given her usual angry look or response. Both had been pleased with their handling of that situation.

I'm getting used to such heretofore fantastic accounts. When a new state has been effectively installed where previously a negative conditioned response had always occurred, the typical report is like Ann's, "He/she didn't even do it this week!" I don't know whether the changed response is so sensed by the spouse that the spouse's behavior is immediately altered or if it is just that one's internal state is so changed that the old behavior is no longer experienced as having the same intent. Perhaps it is both.

In any case, Ann was now more flexible in her response to either inferred or actual anger from Bob. This, of course, made it much easier to teach both of them the basis of giving feedback and seeking clarification. Having had them practice in session four, I sent them home with the assignment to use every issue as an opportunity to practice more feedback and clarification. This assignment was given with the proviso that they only practice when neither had had anything to drink. I also warned them that if Ann stopped drinking she was likely to demand more of an equal say in family matters, for example, how money was spent. This was said to make the inevitable prove palatable by associating it with health. As I do in nearly every session, I had inquired in session four, too, about drinking in the past week. Ann had drunk earlier the day of the session. She no longer drank in response to anger from Bob or any other family member. But there were still some other cues that were sufficiently potent to override her (increasingly utilized) new strategy for delaying drinking.

Ann's changed response to anger from Bob had quickly generalized to her children. She reported that, for the first time, she was now firm without overreacting to Freddie. For example, she had successfully insisted that he stop watching a football game on television one evening and clean up his room instead, and to her amazement he had, even so, kissed her before bed. Pursuing these changes further, in session five I had Ann and Bob apply their growing communication skills to resolving certain differences over limits to be set with 17-year-old Carrie regarding use of the family car. At this point, I also introduced some structural intervention. Bob had been the only one to effectively present limits, and the kids had treated Ann with a lack of respect characteristic of many children with their alcoholic parents. Hence, I assigned Ann to tell Carrie the new rules "that she and her father had agreed upon."

Two weeks later, in session six, Ann reported that she was pleased that she and Bob were not fighting, and that they were talking more and their sex life was fine. She had taken a drink one day the previous week for no known reason, and, as typically happened, that led to finishing a whole bottle of wine. There had been no other drinking incidents. I spent some time on couple's issues. I assigned going out at least one night per week, without the children, for six weeks. At least one of these times was to be with "new" people. By that they knew I meant that they were expected to reach out, to begin to make some social ties with non-problem-drinking acquaintances. Like most long-time heavy drinkers, their social lives had dwindled away or become limited to a circle of others who were also problem drinkers. I wanted to increase intimacy, but also to establish a non-problem-drinking social circle. Ann still attended AA, but it was not serving that purpose for them.

During this same session, regarding children's issues, I spent a part of the time raising the parents' expectations of Bob, Jr. We confirmed that, in fact, he drank and smoked pot excessively every day, had had several minor skirmishes with the law, occasionally tyrannized younger brother Freddie, and was going nowhere in a career. I got the beginning of an agreement that they really did expect more of him. Then it was agreed that the family, minus Annie who was living out of their home, would all come in together starting the next week.

Phase Three: The Family

The remaining sessions were all family sessions. They included both parents and between one and all four of the children. There were four weekly sessions before a four-week hiatus, (over Christmas and New Year's), and five weekly sessions after the break.

For session seven, the first family session, I invited the three children living at home, who were told by their parents that they were expected to attend. Carrie and Freddie came. Bob, Jr., lied about having some work to do and stayed away. His absence received belabored attention from me, with the end result being an assignment for each of the other family members to tell Bob, Jr., how he/she had wanted him at the family session for their own sakes. The rest of my efforts were spent in educating Carrie and Freddie about dealing with alcoholism in parents. First, I told them that kids don't cause alcoholism in their parents. And, like so many kids of alcoholics, they admitted they each truly suspected it was their fault. Next, I told them about Alateen and how going there would teach them more than I could about how to take responsibility for their own reactions to a parent's drinking, and not for the drinking itself.

Bob, Jr., did join the others for the next session. Much of the session was spent assessing and then confirming his substance-abuse problem. The whole family had been playing down and thereby colluding in his alcohol and pot abuse. I saw to it that I documented and explicated my opinion as a professional that Bob, Jr., was chemically dependent and that I got all the other family members to commit themselve that Bob, Jr., was, in their opinion, an alcoholic and a pot abuser, as well. My main device in accomplishing this objective was a plodding, ponderous set of inquiries into his daily drug-use habits. In the end I could summarize that he currently drank a six-pack or more of beer a day and smoked a joint of pot a day. He had used much more of each up until the month before. In addition, he had one traffic accident while drinking and had frequently missed morning work at various jobs because of hangovers. Again, I described and strongly promoted Al-anon and Alateen. I had already given information on when and where meetings were held. Finally, I gave Ann and Bob the assignment to come up with explicit expectations of Bob, Jr., while he continued to live in their home.

Bob, Jr., did not come to session nine. But some of his behavior at home was different. For a change, he had kept his room straightened up and came home by 11 P.M., and there had been no known incidents of drinking and driving the previous week. Also, Carrie and Ann had gone to an Al-anon meeting and liked it. Bob had planned on going to an Al-anon meeting with Ann, but had not because "she drank that evening." I instructed him to go by himself, for himself in the future, regardless of who drank when.

I found myself able to attend now to some more subtle communication problems and to a hierarchical reversal. In the session Carrie raised an issue her mother had brought up to her that was directed at changing her father's behavior. Not only was she acting as a go-between, but was doing so by pointing a finger at her father in a scolding fashion. I promptly interrupted Carrie and asked Ann to speak for herself to Bob. I persisted in keeping Ann and Bob talking over issues between them while Carrie only listened. One issue emerged through this process that particularly interested me. It turned out that Ann had known that Bob, Jr., had no intention of coming to this session, and she had neither told Bob, nor had let Bob, Jr., know she was disappointed in him. They mutually agreed, by the end of the session, that she would speak up to her son and would keep her husband informed in the future. How she would do this was rehearsed and then assigned for the ensuing week.

Ann did her assignment so well the Bob, Jr., showed up at session ten even with a *bona fide* case of flu. Also, on his own, Bob had picked up on my interactions with Carrie and had asserted himself twice with Carrie over the past week. He had disciplined Carrie effectively, precipitating a useful discussion that led to acceptance of his wish by Carrie both times. I was told these were first-time-ever experiences. I kept up the pressure on Carrie in this session and the next. I was determined to see her in a child role, and her parents sharing full parental responsibility. So when, in session ten, she told her brother Freddie what to do, I interrupted. And when she tried to lead her mother, through questioning, into opting for alcohol in the house over the holidays just to be "festive," I made her rephrase what she had said in the form of a request. Then I supported and encouraged Ann telling her daughter that she wanted no alcohol around, and there would be none. This was stated even though Ann and I had just agreed that she would now start taking Antabuse, and neither she nor I was afraid she would drink over the holidays.

Why Antabuse and why now? Like most alcoholics, with Ann a little drinking inevitably led to more frequent and heavier drinking. Ann's new strategies for delaying drinking had helped but had simply not reduced her drinking to zero. The occasional drinking was creeping up, and Ann and I feared it would soon snowball. That in turn would set back the structural family changes immensely, especially with four weeks vacation coming up. Interestingly, Freddie and Carrie did not want their mother to take Antabuse, ostensibly out of fear she would either take an accidental overdose or drink while on it. My response to that was simply to ask Ann if she had either of these concerns for herself. She said no, and I promptly gave her a prescription for one 250 mg.-tablet of Antabuse to be taken daily.

Four weeks later, Ann and Carrie and Freddie returned, all smiles. Bob and Bob, Jr., failed to come, for work and for unspecified reasons, respectively. Ann had taken Antabuse daily and had had no alcohol for a month. The kids were very pleased with their relationship with their mother, and each reported that their grades in school were, all of a sudden, improving.

Their only issues now were that they felt guilty or angry when their father "looks" and "sounds" critical of them to a greater extent than seems warranted at a given moment. I told them that, especially since father wasn't present, I couldn't really change his look or tone of voice, but that we could alter their own reactions when they truly had nothing to feel guilty or angry about except his look or tone. With Carrie watching intently, I then went to work in NLP fashion with Freddie. Using anchoring plus a visual-kinesthetic dissociation technique, which is useful with phobic-type reactions, I installed what Freddie termed his "happy with myself" state in the context of hearing and seeing in father what seemed to Freddie to represent unwarranted criticism. He could then in his imagination think of alternative ways he could have, in the past, and could, in the future, respond to father appearing and sounding that way. For example, he could imagine asking, "You sound angry at me. Are you?" and feeling okay as he did so. What works in a session may not carry over to home without adequate anticipation of actual challenges the client must face outside the office. The best preparation is to test out the persistence of new behavior in real life immediately. In the absence of father, I had Ann act as father, using the kids to prompt her until she got the look and tone of voice just right. Carrie had been instructed to do all the same things I was helping Freddie do "for herself," so I was testing both of them. By the end of the session each was able to handle Ann's well-simulated presumed critical look and tone with aplomb.

Ann, Bob, and Carrie came for session twelve. During the week, Freddie had said he had gotten what he wanted from therapy, and Ann had excused him from this session to accept an invitation with a friend. Bob, Jr., had relayed through Carrie that he wouldn't come to the session because he "doesn't like how his father talks to him." Oldest sister Annie had said during the week that she would come to the session but then failed to show. In the session itself. Carrie clearly was more comfortable talking with her father. Ann said life at home was sufficiently improved that she wondered about reducing the number of sessions to twice a month. While I agreed that much was improved, I chose to emphasize the failure to come in on the part of Bob, Jr., and now Annie. I was curious, I said, how they could reconcile proposing less frequent sessions on the same day that both their oldest children had failed to come in as promised. The rest of the session was spent helping Ann and Bob collaborate further on limit-setting with Bob, Jr. The understanding at the end was that all of the family would come in next, and sometime after that we might be able to discuss less frequent sessions.

Annie came in for the first and only time to session thirteen. That proved to be enough to reintegrate her into the family and foster her catching up with the changes that others in her family had made. Bob, Jr., still refused to come in, and he never did return. The time of session thirteen was evenly divided between a focus on Annie herself and further practice among family members at carrying on a discussion over differences long enough to achieve mutual understanding and resolution. I wanted Annie to see and become a part of this process. First, though, and even more important, I wanted family members to express to Annie whatever concerns they had about her behavior. What came out was that each person had their own private worry over Annie's use of alcohol. Bob admitted he worried that Annie drank and then drove. He gave more than one example. Freddie and Ann told Annie of their secret concerns over the many bottles of liquor in her apartment. Each went on record that they feared Annie was developing an early problem with alcohol. I found out from Annie that she routinely had four or more drinks a day and six to eight or more socially with her similarly heavy-drinking friends. I told her that I was concerned about her drinking, and then I promptly moved on to facilitating others' working out their differences. I felt the point about alcohol had been made, and now it would be good for her to hear and see how others could and had made changes. The discussion moved along easily and well. I was particularly pleased to see Carrie and Freddie jointly take on their parents on typical adolescent issues. Carrie was clearly no longer in a quasi-parental role, and father was no longer reacted to as an ogre just because he expressed his most earnest thoughts in a deep voice.

Session fourteen included mother, father, Freddie, and Carrie. They talked well and didn't need me much. Freddie and Carrie reported they had stopped fighting with one another. Bob noted that he and Bob, Jr., were talking more and cooperating more with one another. In the session, Bob got Ann to agree more explicitly to bring issues to him directly rather than telling them first to one of the kids who then served as a go-between. To foster this, I assigned Freddie to say, "tell Dad," should his mother come to him with an issue meant for Bob. Similarly, I assigned Ann to say, "tell Dad," if one of the kids came to her with a gripe meant for their father. I finished with a proposal that we assess, at the next session, whether or not to continue therapy.

The same four returned for session fifteen. All said they felt "closer" to one another. Even Annie was phoning her sibs and parents more and, at times, inviting some of them over. They noted how each was now able to talk one-to-one with any other family member well, with only one exception. Freddie described what I summarized as a recurring "war dance" with his older brother. For example, he would ask Bob, Jr., to play ball wtih him and get a disparaging or sarcastic response. Freddie would then get furious or upset, and they would start yelling at one another and, of course, not play ball. Bob, Jr., was not available, but I knew from experience that Freddie was receptive to my anchoring in him his more positive resources under circumstances where previously he had lost his cool. I knew also that Freddie had been very impressed with the change in himself in response to his father and that he attributed it to my intervention. So I moved over next to Freddie and took a few minutes with him while the others watched and listened. I elicited in him what he called the "in-control" state that he wanted to have when his brother taunted him. I established an anchor for it so that I could quickly reelicit it in him and had him imagine how he would handle his brother's taunts differently with that "in-control" resource of his. When he could imagine himself doing that well, I had his father play Bob, Jr., saying "Go away, or I'll break your legs" to Freddie. And Freddie kept his cool.

Then I asked if there was anything more they wanted to work on that they felt they couldn't handle themselves. They agreed there might be, but they wanted to try things on their own. I proposed scheduling a follow-up session sometime hence, and they picked a date nine weeks from then. Ann and I agreed that she would continue to take the Antabuse at least until the follow-up session.

Follow-up

I have follow-up information from two contacts with the family. One was the scheduled session, which by mutual agreement by phone was scheduled for six months after the initial interview. Ann, Bob, Carrie, and Freddie came in for the session. All reported they were each and collectively "doing well." Neither Ann nor Bob had had any alcohol. Ann had reduced her Antabuse to alternate days. She felt that was sufficient to give her a little extra time to delay the occasional impulse to drink. She wanted to continue using Antabuse that way at least another three months, and I completely supported that. Carrie had brought her grades to all *A*s and *B*s and was on the honor roll. Neither child had had any trips to their medical doctor, except that Carrie had discovered that prescription glasses would relieve occasional headaches after reading. Annie seemed, to them, to be drinking less and visiting them more.

Bob, Jr., had been given specific limits at home and consequences if he failed to adhere to them. He had broken the rules regarding no pot or alcohol use in the home and, as a result, had been living out of their home for the preceding month. He lived with a friend, had a job, and was totally supporting himself. His friend had been arrested during that month on a DWI (Driving While Intoxicated) charge.

We all agreed, that, while the family still had issues to work on, they were now capable of taking them on without help. No future sessions were scheduled. I made clear that any one or all of them were free to contact me at any time in the future and that I would be interested in hearing about them from time to time.

My second source of follow-up information was from my phone call to Ann six months after the last session, or one year after they first came to see me. I phoned out of curiosity. I think of doing that often with families I've seen, and actually do it occasionally. Ann answered. Bob was out. Ann and I talked about twenty minutes. I began by telling her I was simply curious how they were doing and decided to call and find out, adding that I do that with people I've seen in therapy from time to time. She opened with, "We're way ahead of a year ago." Then she followed with a few supporting examples. Next we got into what remained to be worked on. Personally, she had stopped using Antabuse several months earlier and remained abstinent. She was also pleased that she had lost twelve pounds, and wanted to lose only twenty more to reach her ideal weight. Interestingly, it was Bob who had had one slip with alcohol. One day on a business trip out of town—he had volunteered to her—he had taken a drink and ended up having a few more. The next day he stopped drinking again. That had happened two months prior to my call and had not recurred. Between Bob and Ann the only remaining issues were occasional actions with the kids by one parent before both had really agreed. The example given was that Bob had gotten Freddie a moped while Ann was still reluctant about it. Freddie had then had an accident on his moped, which didn't hurt him too much but resulted in several hundred dollars' expenses. Since they had not really jointly shared responsibility for the moped, the impulse, not acted upon, for Ann to tell Bob, "I told you so," was great.

Aside from the accident, however, Freddie was doing quite well in his life. In school he had gotten all *A*s at last report, except in language where he had requested and gotten some tutoring. Carrie had graduated high school and gone to summer school to make up for some deficiencies earlier in high school. She was now enrolled full-time and doing well in a local community college with the realistic goal of transferring the next year to the state university. To my moderate surprise, both Bob, Jr., and Annie had moved back into their parents' home. Annie was working as a waitress and had a good chance soon to move up to being the bookkeeper for the restaurant. Drinking was no longer seen as a problem for her. Bob, Jr., was not using pot or alcohol in the home. There were, at times, beer cans seen in his car. On the bright side, he had been promoted to assistant manager of a clothing store and was taking an evening business class at the same community college that Carrie attended. I congratulated Ann on their success and agreed with her on the nature of the issues still to be addressed. I thanked her for the follow-up. That was the extent of my phone conversation with Ann.

Summary

In the treatment of this case, I moved from couple to individual, and again to couple and then to family, and back to individual and again to family. Each member of the family became my patient no less than the referred patient. I drew upon structural and strategic family therapy techniques, communication skills training, behavioral assignments, Neuro-Linguistic Programming and no doubt more; the choice of approach depending on which would allow me most efficiently to achieve my intermediate or enabling objective at a particular phase of therapy. Had I continued with Ann and Bob as a couple, I had already considered pursuing work with each on their relationships with their families of origin. But I elected to support their interest in working together independent of a therapist, confident that they would return if they got stuck. All of the above is characteristic of what I think of as my "Integrative Family Therapy" approach, not just to alcoholism but to any case.

What is unique to my treatment of alcoholism is the dogged return to issues around drinking. I do not assume the drinking will go away if I just do some nifty, even if arduous, family intervention. And if it doesn't go away (or,in rare cases, become at least genuinely controlled), I do assume that my most elegant interactional accomplishments will not hold up. So I ponderously establish the extent of the use of alcohol and other drugs by each family member and the personal and interpersonal consequences of that use to date. Then I bug people during each session about AA, Al-anon, Alateen; about setting and meeting goals for drug use; and about current limits on drug use in the home.

The only other point I would underscore about what is special to my family therapy for alcoholics is that it almost always requires that I draw upon multiple schools of theory and techniques. That is often but not as consistently true when I treat people dealing with issues other than substance abuse. One may encounter alcoholism cases that might seem a bit more intransigent than the present case. The main difference from these cases is that the various phases of therapy may take longer to traverse. Still the treatment needs of this relatively brief case justified multiple modes of intervention and at family, couple and individual levels.

References

1. Gurman, A. S. Dimensions of marital therapy: A comparative analysis. *Journal of Marital and Family Therapy 5* (1979) 5–18.
2. Gurman, A. S. & Kniskern, D. P. Research on marital and family therapy: Progress, perspective and prospect. In S. L. Garfield and A. E. Bergin (Eds.), *Handbook of psychotherapy and behavior change: An empirical analysis*, 2nd ed., New York: Wiley, 1979.
3. Olson, D. H., Russell, C. S. Sprenkle, D. H. Marital and family therapy: A decade review, *Journal of Marriage and the Family 42*: (1980) 973–993.
4. Davis, S. L. R. & Davis, D. I. Neuro-linguistic Programming (TM) and family therapy. *Journal of Marital and Family Therapy 9*: (1983) 283–291.
5. Davis, D. I. & Davis, S. L. R. Integrating individual and marital therapy using neuro-linguistic programming. *International Journal of Family Psychiatry*, 6(1):(1985) 3–17.
6. Dilts, R., Grinder, J., Bandler, R., Cameron-Bandler, L. & DeLozier, J. *Neuro-linguistic programming, Vol. I: The study of the structure of subjective experience.* Cupertino, CA: Meta Publications, 1980.
7. Cameron-Bandler, L. *Solutions*: Practical and effective antidotes for sexual and relationship problems. San Raffael, CA: Future Pace, 1985. Revised version of *They lived happily ever after: A book about achieving happy endings in coupling.*

APPENDIX A
SUBSTANCE USE AND ABUSE SURVEY (SUAS)

PLEASE FILL OUT THIS QUESTIONNAIRE WHETHER OR NOT YOU HAVE HAD ANY PERSONAL EXPERIENCE WITH DRUGS OR ALCOHOL. PLEASE ANSWER ALL THE QUESTIONS.

1. ______Age

2. ______Sex

3. Marital Status

__(1) Married __(2) Separated __(3) Widowed __(4) Divorced __(5) Never Married

4. Do you live alone?

______Yes, for ____years
______No
If yes, please skip to #5. If you do not live alone, *check* which of the following people you live with *right now*. Check *all* that apply at this time, *and* write in the number of years you have been living with them.

______Live with husband/wife for ____years.
______Live with parent(s) or in-laws for ____years.
______Live with brother(s) and/or sister(s) for ____years.
______Live with other relatives for ____years.
How many? __________
______Live with children for ____years.
How many? __________
______Live with friend(s) for ____years.
How many? __________
______Live with other(s) for ____years.
Please specify ____________.

5. What is the last level that you completed in school?

____(1) 8th grade or less
____(2) Some high school
____(3) High school graduate
____(4) Some college
____(5) 4-year college graduate or beyond

6a. What kind of work do you do? ______________________________
(If you are not working now, please write in the most recent work you did.)

b. What kind of place do you (did you) work in (school, factory, store, etc.)? ______________________________

c. If you are not currently working, please check if you are receiving income from one of the following:

______Retirement, pension, social security
______Public assistance
______Other (please specify)

7. Who is the *chief* wage earner in your household?

______(1) Myself (If you checked "myself," please skip to question #9.)
______(2) Husband/Wife
______(3) Both myself and husband/wife
______(4) Parent(s)
______(5) Other. Please specify ______________________________

8a. What kind of work does the chief wage earner do? ____________

b. What kind of place does he/she work in? ____________________

c. If the chief wage earner is not currently working, please check if he/she is receiving income from one of the following:

______Retirement, pension, social security
______Public assistance
______Other. Please specify ______________________________

9. How many cups of coffee (regular coffee, not decaffeinated) or tea do you drink a day? PLEASE WRITE IN THE AVERAGE NUMBER OR CHECK NONE.

______cups of coffee   ______None
______cups of tea   ______None

10a. HAVE YOU EVER USED ALCOHOL, i.e., WINE, BEER OR LIQUOR?
______Yes   ______No
If no, please skip to question #11.

b. How old were you when you first tried alcohol?
______Write in your age at that time.

c. Have you used alcohol in the past month?
______Yes ______No
If no, please skip to question #11.

d. ______How many days in the past month did you have something alcoholic to drink?

e. ______When you drink alcohol, how many drinks do you usually have at one time?

f. On the days that you drink, how many times a day do you usually have something alcoholic to drink?
______Once
______Twice
______Three or more times

11a. HAVE YOU EVER USED MARIJUANA/HASHISH?
______Yes ______No
If no, please skip to question #12.

b. How old were you when you first tried marijuana/hashish?
______Write in your age at that time.

c. Have you used marijuana/hashish in the past month?
______Yes ______No
If no, please skip to question #12.

d. ______How many times have you used marijuana/hashish in the past month?

e. For how many months have you been using marijuana/hashish about this often?
______months

f. Do you often use marijuana/hashish and alcohol together?
______Yes ______No

12a. HAVE YOU EVER USED INHALANTS (such as glue)?
______Yes ______No
If no, please skip to question #13.

b. How old were you when you first tried inhalants?
______Write in your age at that time.

c. Have you used inhalants in the past month?
______Yes ______No
If no, please skip to question #13.

d. How many times have you used inhalants in the past month?

e. For how many months have you been using inhalants about this often?
______months

13a. HAVE YOU EVER USED LSD OR OTHER PSYCHEDELICS (DMT, STP, mescaline, etc.)?
______Yes ______No
If no, please skip to question #14.

b. How old were you when you first tried LSD or other psychedelics?
______Write in your age at that time.

c. Have you used LSD or other psychedelics in the past month?
______Yes ______No
If no, please skip to question #14.

d. ______How many times have you used LSD or other psychedelics in the past month?

e. For how many months have you been using LSD or other psychedelics about this often?
______months

14a. HAVE YOU EVER USED HEROIN/METHADONE OR OTHER OPIATES?
______Yes ______No
If no, please skip to question #15.

b. How old were you when you first tried heroin or other opiates?
______Write in your age at that time.

c. Have you used heroin or other opiates in the past month?
______Yes ______No
If no, please skip to question #15.

d. ______How many times have you used heroin or other opiates in the past month?

e. For how many months have you been using heroin or other opiates about this often?
______months

15a. HAVE YOU EVER USED COCAINE?
______Yes ______No
If no, please skip to question #16.

b. How old were you when you first tried cocaine?
______Write in your age at that time.

c. Have you used cocaine in the past month?
______Yes ______No
If no, please skip to question #16.

d. ______How many times have you used cocaine in the past month?

e. For how many months have you been using cocaine about this often?
______months

QUESTIONS 16–18 ARE ABOUT DRUGS THAT DOCTORS PRESCRIBE TO MAKE PEOPLE FEEL BETTER. SOME PEOPLE ALSO USE THESE DRUGS *OTHER* THAN AS PRESCRIBED OR WITHOUT A PRESCRIPTION, JUST BECAUSE THEY MAKE THEM FEEL GOOD. PLEASE ANSWER ALL THESE QUESTIONS. CHECK AS MANY AS APPLY.

16a. Have you ever used STIMULANTS (such as amphetamines—speed, uppers, bennies, dexies)?
______(1) Never used
______(2) Used *ONLY* as prescribed
______(3) Used *OTHER* than prescribed
______(4) Used *WITHOUT* prescription
If never used, please skip to question #17.

b. How old were you when you first tried stimulants?
______Write in your age at that time.

c. Have you used stimulants in the past month?
______Yes ______No
If no, please skip to question #17.

d. How many times have you used stimulants in the past month?

e. For how many months have you been using stimulants about this often?
______months

17a. Have you ever used BARBITUATES (such as phenobarbital, Nembutal, Seconal-downers)?
______(1) Never used
______(2) Used *ONLY* as prescribed
______(3) Used *OTHER* than prescribed
______(4) Used *WITHOUT* prescription
If never used, please skip to question #18.

b. How old were you when you first tried barbiturates?
______Write in your age at that time.

c. Have you used barb turates in the past month?
______Yes ______No
If no, please skip to question #18.

d. ______How many times have you used barbiturates in the past month?

e. For how many months have you been using barbiturates about this often?
______Number of months.

18a. Have you ever used other SEDATIVES OR TRANQUILIZERS (Valium, Librium, Serax, Quaalude)?

______(1) Never used ______(2) Used *ONLY* as prescribed
______(3) Used *OTHER* than prescribed ______(4) Used *WITHOUT* prescription

If never used, please skip to question #19.

b. How old were you when you first tried sedatives or tranquilizers?
______Write in your age at that time.

c. Have you used sedatives or tranquilizers in the past month?
______Yes ______No
If no, please skip to question #19.

d. ______How many times have you used sedatives or tranquilizers in the past month?

e. For how many months have you been using tranquilizers about this often?
______months

IF YOU DO NOT DRINK ALCOHOL OR USE DRUGS, PLEASE CHECK "NO" TO THE FOLLOWING QUESTIONS. DO NOT LEAVE OUT ANY QUESTIONS.

19a. Have friends or relatives ever raised any questions about your drinking? ____Yes ____No

b. Have friends or relatives ever raised any questions about your use of drugs? ____Yes ____No

20. Have you ever attended a meeting of Alcoholics Anonymous (AA)? ____Yes ____No

21a. Have you ever lost friends or girlfriends/boyfriends because of drinking? ____Yes ____No

b. Have you ever lost friends or girlfriends/boyfriends because of any other drug use? ____Yes ____No

22a. Have you ever gotten into trouble at work or school because of drinking? ____Yes ____No

b. Have you ever gotten into trouble at work or school because of other drug use? ____Yes ____No

23a. Have you ever neglected your family for two or more days in a row because you were
(1) drinking? ____Yes ____No
(2) using other drugs? ____Yes ____No

b. Have you ever neglected your job or school for two or more days in a row because you were
(1) drinking? ____Yes ____No
(2) using other drugs? ____Yes ____No

24a. Have you ever had delirium tremens (DTs) or severe shaking, heard voices, or seen things that weren't there, after heavy drinking? ____Yes ____No

b. Have you ever had withdrawal symptoms after other drug use? ____Yes ____No

25a. Have you ever gone to anyone for help about your drinking? ____Yes ____No

b. Have you ever gone to anyone for help about your use of other drugs? ____Yes ____No

26a. Have you ever been in a hospital because of drinking? ____Yes ____No

b. Have you ever been in a hospital because of other drug use? ____Yes ____No

27. Have you ever been arrested for drunk driving or driving after drinking? ____Yes ____No

28a. Do you use alcohol to help when you feel nervous, upset or depressed? ____Yes ____No

b. Do you use other drugs to help when you feel nervous, upset or depressed? ____Yes ____No

29a. Have you ever smoked cigarettes?
______Yes ______No
If no, please skip to questions #30.

b. On the average, how many cigarettes do you smoke each day?
______None
______Less than 5 cigarettes per day
______About 1/2 pack per day
______About a pack per day
______More than a pack per day

c. If you used to smoke but have now stopped, about how long ago did you stop?
______Within the last two weeks
______Within the past six months
______Within the past year or longer

30. For what problem did you come to the Medical Center? ________
____

31. Do you feel that alcohol or drug use has to do with why you came to the Medical Center?

______Yes   If so, in what way? ______________________________
____

______No

APPENDIX B
THE ACCEPTANCE AND VALIDITY OF THE SUBSTANCE USE AND ABUSE SURVEY (SUAS)

By KAREN KUPETZ, M.S.W., MICHELINE KLAGSBRUN, D.C.P., DEBORAH WISOFF, B.A., JUDITH LA ROSA, R.N., and DONALD I. DAVIS, M.D.

During the past fifteen years, studies have shown the spread of drug and alcohol abuse throughout most segments of the population. There has been a concomitant increase in medical problems associated with or caused by the abuse. Even the moderate use of certain drugs (prescribed or not) or alcohol, when taken in combination, can produce serious, possibly fatal, medical complications. Nowhere are the effects of this abuse more dramatically evident than in medical settings. Recent literature has shown the need for readily accessible information about patients' substance use. Such information would both draw the attention of the medical community to substance abuse problems and facilitate their management.

With these factors in mind, we have designed a self-assessment questionnaire that is easily understood and may be rapidly completed. This provides comprehensive information on:

1. the type, extent, and pattern of drug and alcohol use or abuse,
2. any social consequences of abuse, and
3. relevant demographic data about the patient and his family or significant other(s).

This instrument is useful in a variety of settings with minimal staff assistance. The development of the instrument, its acceptance, and the methods we have utilized to assess validity are describd in this paper.

Setting

The setting for this survey was a medium-sized, urban university medical center, which includes a 530-bed hospital, outpatient facilities, and a health maintenance organization. Medical center patients represent a broad cross-section of the D.C. metropolitan population.

The instrument was used on:

1. internal medicine group
2. obstetrics and gynecology
3. gastroenterology
4. general surgery
5. orthopedic surgery
6. psychiatry
7. health maintenance organization
8. student health service
9. emergency room[1]
10. inpatient services corresponding to the outpatient service listed above

The questionnaire was administered in outpatient waiting areas (and on inpatient services, at the bedside) by university students hired as field workers and trained by the project staff. To reduce potential bias, field workers were regularly rotated throughout the various services. Subjects took five to fifteen minutes to complete the questionnaire.

Patient Acceptance

Patient's voluntary participation in alcohol and drug surveys is often questioned by medical personnel. While it is also one of the most important factors in assessing the utility of an instrument, documenting patient acceptance is of primary importance in itself. Four methods were employed to assess acceptance:

[1]The self-assessment questionnaire was not suitable for this type of setting and was discontinued. The resulting numbers are too small to indicate trends, and are therefore retained as part of the general population sample only.

1. field workers' retrieval forms
2. consent form data
3. verbal reports from field workers and medical personnel
4. on-site observation by project staff

Of the 11,857 people considered as potential candidates for sampling, 5,338 (45%) were excluded as ineligible for the following reasons:

1. 22 percent had been sampled previously during the survey
2. 4 percent were either too ill or incoherent
3. 8 percent were foreign speaking or under age
4. 12 percent were missed due to time factors or field worker's inability to reach them[2]

Table A-1 shows the breakdown of the 6,519 (55%) people considered eligible for participation.

Five thousand seven hundred and forty-five (88%) of those eligible participated in the survey. This is considerably higher than the 80 percent participation rate generally accepted in survey studies. Certainly higher compliance can be achieved but at a disproportionate cost in terms of time and manpower. We feel that our rate of 88 percent compliance is an important asset of this instrument.

The second method of assessing patient acceptance is the consent form. This form, designed to meet HEW requirements for informed consent of human subjects, was detached from the questionnaire to ensure confidentiality. During the latter part of the survey, to provide information for a future follow-up study, space was included on the consent form for patients' addresses and telephone numbers. Patients showed willingness to be recontacted for the future study by including the additional information. Of the 2,444 people who completed the questionnaire during this time, 79 percent gave complete information (name, address, and telephone number), 9 percent signed only their name (no recontact), and 14 percent remained anonymous. Again, this demonstrates a high degree of comfort with the instrument. While some degree of field worker error was expected in recording patient participation, their data proved to be consistent with that of consent forms.

Verbal reports from field workers and medical personnel, while

[2]Throughout the paper, totals may be less or more than 100 percent because of rounding.

Table A-1
Survey Participation

	Number	Percentage	Cumulative percentages
Complete	5,267	81	81
Incomplete	478	7	88
Refused	813	13	100
Total	6,519	100	

subjective, provided an important evaluation of patient response. Project staff periodically visited each service site to observe field worker performance, personnel response and patient attitudes.

Prior to implementing the survey, some medical personnel were reluctant to allow their patients to be sampled. The most common reasons given were:

1. patients would themselves reject the intrusion of drug-related questions; and
2. the content of the survey would be inappropriate for patients who presumably had no drug use.

Our high degree of acceptance refutes the notion that patients are not willing to answer questions of this nature, and findings of substance abuse indicate that medical personnel are not always aware of substance abuse problems and/or do not document them.

Overview of Literature

While the majority of studies in the literature are on inpatient groups only, a very small number of studies investigate both inpatient and outpatient populations (2,3). Thus, there are few precedents for surveying large and divergent numbers of outpatients, even though our experience showed that there were fewer problems in the actual administration of the survey to outpatients than to inpatients.

A few brief screening instruments do exist for assessing problem drinking but even these are not consistently used in a self-assessement format (4,5). Studies utilizing a self-assessment method to gather data on drug use (except student populations) are even less evident (6). This may be related to the fact that, until very recently, few investigators have rigorously systematized their criteria and scoring for drug abuse to enable conversion of an instrument to self-assessment form.

The literature consists mainly of investigations of either alcohol or drugs; few investigate a wide range of substances. Out of 18 general surgical and medical studies, twelve focused on alcohol and six on other drugs. Of 19 studies describing substance use among psychiatric patients, 4 dealt primarily with alcohol, 13 with other drugs, and 2 investigated combined alcohol and drug use (7,8). The related literature on obstetrical patients was almost equally divided between studies of:

1. the potential teratogenicity of a wide range of drugs; and
2. the association between maternal intake of alcohol and abnormalities of offspring.

Thus, inclusion of comprehensive polydrug measures and their integration in a survey format was another area with few precedents.

Criteria for defining substance abuse include a wide variety of concepts such as quantity-frequency, duration of drug use, reasons for drug use, and effects of drugs. Surveys tend to focus on one of these measures to the exclusion of others, with a few exceptions (9–23). We felt that the incorporation of both quantity-frequency and social-consequence criteria would add to the breadth of the survey and offer new information concerning the relationship between these two sets of criteria.

Questionnaire Construction: Principles of Scoring

The SUAS instrument is a six-page questionnaire consisting of the following categories of questions:

1. demographic
2. quantity-frequency of alcohol, marijuana/hashish, inhalants, psychedelics, opiates, cocaine, stimulants, barbiturates, and sedative use
3. social consequence scales for alcohol and other drugs
4. coffee/cigarette use
5. chief complaint

All questions are yes-no, check off or open-ended with a number of brief phrases required for completion. A repeat pattern for quantity-frequency questions of all drugs was used, as well as skip pattern for abstainers and non-current users. Cross-check, disarming, and lie-detector questions were initially considered, but omitted for practical reasons of length. The emphasis here will be on the construction and modification (and scoring) for the criterion questions (categories 2 and 3 above) which identify substance use.

The *Quantity-Frequency Index* (Q-F) is one of the most common methods for assessing *alcohol* consumption. It was developed by Straus and Bacon and later adapted by other investigators (14). In the past decade, Cisin, Cahalan and their colleagues have further refined this method and used it extensively in their large-scale studies. "The Q-F Index estimates the approximate amount a person drinks over a period of time by multiplying the amount he reports he usually drinks (on an average occasion) by the reported frequency over a stated period, such as a month." (15) Alcohol Q-F scores are arrived at by considering:

1. the number of sittings (number of days when drinking occurs multiplied by number of times per day); and
2. the number of drinks per sitting.

On the basis of these two factors (giving more weight to the second factor) an alcohol consumption score is determined which places each subject into one of six groups: abstainer, very infrequent, light, moderate, heavy, and very heavy. Where either quantity or frequency responses are missing, the most conservative estimate is made, based on available information.

To keep our questionnaire simple enough for self-administration, no attempt was made to assess drinking patterns over time. This was also consistent with our emphasis on current use.

Quantity-Frequency criteria of *drug* use were modeled after a system used by Cohen and Klein (16). Their three criteria were:

1. frequency of use,
2. length of use at this frequency, and
3. the number and combination of drugs used.

The first two criteria result in an ordinal rank score (mild to heavy) for each drug used. The third criterion is used in determining an overall score of polydrug abuse. Since Cohen and Klein's scoring system for polydrug use does not include alcohol use, we developed our own system for this purpose. For individual drug use, however, their system appeared the most appropriate in the literature for our screening purpose. Not only did it provide an ordinal ranking system relevant to severity of dependency, but these rankings could be derived with a limited number of questions available on a self-assessment questionnaire. Furthermore, their scoring system had been used in the study of a medical (psychiatric) population, thereby allowing for comparison with our own findings.[3]

The second modification of the scoring system was an elaboration of Cohen and Klein's drug use categories of mild, moderate and heavy. Very low and very heavy use are usually clear-cut, with the intermediate range less reliable. Since we anticipated a large sample, we felt it would be possible to examine gradations of use more fully. The scoring tables for each drug were therefore redesigned to distinguish four categories: mild, moderate, high risk, and heavy.

Drugs other than alcohol were divided into those that are basically used illegally and those that may be taken by prescription. In order to prevent patients from excluding questions regarding drugs used only by prescription, specific categories were developed permitting patients to indicate whether they had "never used" the drug, "used only as prescribed," "used other than as presribed," "used without prescription," or in any combination of the last three ways. This distinction is important in enabling our study to address itself to drugs which are overprescribed and represents further modification of Klein's criteria which are based on non-medical drug use.

The *Social Consequences* section of our instrument was included in response to numerous reports of success with use of the Michigan Alcoholism Screening Test (MAST). This instrument was first described by Selzer in 1971 as "a consistent, quantifiable, structured interview instrument for the detection of alcoholism that could be rapidly administered by nonprofessional as well as professional personnel" (18). The MAST consists of 25 yes-no questions relating to social consequences of drinking. The questions are intended to be more neutral and less threatening to subjects than direct inquiry about quantity of alcohol consumption. Scoring of the instrument is weighted with the highly discriminating questions receiving two points, the three diagnostic questions five points and others one point.

Recently published accounts describe modifications of the existing MAST questionnaire for use in self-administration (19–21). Use of the MAST for diagnosing early stages of alcoholism is considered superior to the usual examinations in clinical practice, and ease of administration is emphasized (19). Except for Kaplan's criticism as to

[3]In a 1976 discussion with one of the authors, Cohen indicated that several new reliability studies on the instrument have now been completed. Preliminary findings using correlations and Kappa analysis indicated that the instrument has high reliability (17).

what the MAST actually reflects (22), all other studies utilizing some form of the MAST have found it a useful instrument, showing up favorably in validity assessments (20,21,23).

The social consequences section of our questionnaire was modified from the Brief MAST (5). Of the ten questions found on the Brief MAST, six were retained exactly as originated (nos. 3,4,7,8,9,10), along with their assigned weights (either a 2 or 5 for positive responses). The first question was omitted due to patients' inability to define the concept of "normal drinking," and questions 2 and 5 were modified to make the questionnaire more conducive to self-administration. Question No. 6 was divided into two parts which made our possible total score (29 points) the same as that of Pokorny's scale (5). After studying the distribution of responses, a score of six points was selected as the criterion for "problem drinker."

Since no instrument comparable to the MAST exists for assessing the social consequences of drug use, parallel questions for drugs other than alcohol were developed. In this way, the inclusion of an entirely different social consequence scale for drugs, which would have fragmented the questionnaire and made it difficult for self-administration, was avoided. From our modified version of the Brief MAST two questions had no drug counterparts (attendance at AA and arrest for drunk driving). The eight remaining questions were scored according to their discriminating power, distributions assessed, and a score of five out of a possible twenty selected as positive. Using both the Social Consequence Scale and the Quantity-Frequency Scale increases reliablility by permitting convergence of data from two sources and places less reliance on any one instrument.

Validity Checks: A Chart Review

A random review of medical charts of subjects completing the self-assessment questionnaire was made for the purpose of checking the validity of the research instrument. The procedure for chart review involved comparing the medical record of every fifth subject sampled with the self-assessment questionnaire, until an adequate baseline number had been reached.

To facilitate comparison between the two sources of information, individuals in the highest category of quantity-frequency alcohol use (without social consequences) were included as abusers. Even though many studies of general populations have maintained a definite distinction between heavy alcohol use with and without social consequences, confining the term "abuse" to the former, we consider a

Table A-2
Documentation of Substance Use in a Random Review of Medical Records

	A. Documented in history					*B. Primary diagnosis*			*C. Both diagnosis and history*		
	1	*2*	*3*	*4*	*5*	*1*	*2*	*3*	*1*	*2*	
	No alcohol use	*No alcohol or drug use*	*Alcohol use*	*Drug use*	*Alcohol and drug use*	*Alcohol*	*Drug(s)*	*Alcohol and drug(s)*	*Primarily alcohol*	*Primarily drug(s)*	*Total number of cases with substance documentation*
Inpatient (n = 133)	6	3	59	5	3	0	0	0	7	8	82
Outpatient (n = 412)	8	0	34	44	7	6	1	1	2	0	95
Total	14	3	93	49	10	6	1	1	9	8	177

medical population qualitatively different in this respect. Heavy alcohol use is always a complication for the provision of good medical care. This topic and our relevant findings will be discussed more fully in succeeding papers in this series.

Extent and type of documentation

Table A-2 summarizes the extent and type of documentation found. "Documentation" includes any note on the chart concerning a patient's use of alcohol and/or other drugs, with the exception of those drugs clearly prescribed for medical treatment. Thus, "use" in columns A 1-5 refers to any degree of use, ranging from "occasional" or "social" through "light" and "moderate" to "heavy." One-third of all records reviewed contained some documentation; however, the rate of documentation was much higher on the inpatient services (62%) than on the out-patient services (23%).

Alcohol is by far the most frequent documented drug, mentioned in 67 percent of all documented cases. In 52 percent of documented cases, use of alcohol was recorded in patient's medical history, and, in an additional six percent, combined drug and alcohol use was mentioned. Alcohol abuse was the primary diagnosis in 8 percent of documented cases in 5 percent with a history and 3 percent without a history).

Drug abuse was recorded as the primary diagnosis in 5 percent of the charts, and drug use mentioned in 28 percent of the histories. Mixed drug and alcohol abuse was the primary diagnosis in only one case, and none of the charts reviewed contained a secondary diagnosis of alcohol or drug problems. Overall, the frequency of drug use documentation was about one-half that of alcohol use.

Comparison of Questionnaire and Charts

All chart reviews done on Medicine Outpatients (n=26) and Ob-Gyn Outpatients (n=93) were matched and compared to their corresponding questionnaires. Because of the large number of charts with no substance use/abuse documentation, only partial checks were done on the remaining services. For these checks, only the charts with the documentation were compared to the self-assessment questionnaire. From the standpoint of questionnaire validity, it seemed more essential to see how well the questionnaire matched with positive findings on the charts, than to assess total numbers of abusers that were missed in the charts.

In 183 cases, there was no chart documentation and the corresponding questionnaires were not checked. Consequently, tables A-3 and A-4, based on the remaining 362 cases, provide a conservative estimate of the questionnaire's screening power as it compares with that of medical charts.

In tables A-3 and A-4, information from both charts and questionnaire is dichotomized into *"abuse" and "non-abuse,"* since the identification of abuse is the purpose for which the questionnaire was designed. The following narrative descriptions, found in the charts, were considered equivalent to "abuse": "heavy," "very heavy," "alcoholic," "primary diagnosis," "secondary diagnosis," "chronic drinker," "binge alcoholic," or reported quantities that met questionnaire criteria.

The summary statistics in each table are defined as follows[4]:

[4]The authors are indebted to Drs. Perry and Cisin for their suggestions of these statistics.

Table A-3
Alcohol Abuse: Questionnaire vs. Charts

Charts	*Questionnaire* Alcohol abuse	No alcohol abuse	*Total*
Alcohol abuse	28	10[a]	38
No alcohol abuse	30	294	324
Total	58	304	362

[a]Includes seven incomplete questionnaires (three in Emergency Room, Major Side).

Prevalence (Q)	16%
Prevalence (C)	10%
Percent Agreement	89%
Detection (C→Q)	48%
Detection (Q→C)	74%
Power (C)	56%
Power (Q)	85%

Prevalence (Q): percentage of all cases identified as "abuse" by questionnaire

Prevalence (C): percentage of all cases identified as "abuse" on charts

Percent Agreement: percentage of all cases in which charts and questionnaires agree

Detection (C→Q): of the cases identified as abuse by questionnaire, percentage detected on charts

Table A-4
Drug Abuse: Questionnaire vs. Charts

Charts	*Questionnaire* Drug abuse	No drug abuse	*Total*
Drug abuse	17	5[a]	22
No drug abuse	15	325	340
Total	32	330	362

[a]Includes two incomplete questionnaires from Emergency Room Major.

Prevalence (Q)	9%
Prevalence (C)	6%
Percent Agreement	95%
Detection (C→Q)	53%
Detection (Q→C)	77%
Power (C)	59%
Power (Q)	86%

Detection (Q→C): of the cases identified as abuse on charts, percentage detected by questionnaire

In order to simplify this presentation, twenty-one cases of mixed drug and alcohol abuse have been reported in both Tables 2 and 3. In all but one of these mixed cases,[5] the questionnaire identified both components of the abuse. One-third of the twenty-one cases were also fully identified in the charts. However, in five cases (24%) the charts recorded alcohol abuse only, and in two cases (10%), drug abuse only. In six cases (29%) neither abuse appeared in the charts.

Table A-5 compares charts and questionnaires on the three summary statistics, which may be considered as measures of the efficiency of these two indicators of substance abuse. It is clear that the questionnaire has the advantage on all three measures—it revealed a higher prevalence of drug and alcohol abuse; it missed roughly one-half as many substance abusers as were missed by the charts; and its ability to label abusers, measured in terms of all potentially identifiable cases, is impressive.

For the purpose of validating the questionnaire as a screening instrument, it is clear that medical charts are not the ideal source of information for comparison. Various factors contribute to the lack of documentation in medical records. For example, all cases of substance abuse missed by charts were found in outpatient services, even though due to chart location the outpatient review had to be done in close proximity to the medical personnel, potentially alerting them to the research project. It must be assumed that outpatients are less likely to receive a comprehensive medical history-taking. Many of these patients are seen in consultation rather than for primary care, and substance use might not be viewed as a relevant area of inquiry. Another important factor is the concern of medical personnel about documenting substance use/abuse. It is reasonable to assume that there are a number of physicians, nurses, or other health care personnel who choose not to record confidential information regarding substance use, especially illicit use, due to third-party and legal implications.

Despite these factors, this type of chart review remains the only feasible method for validation on this scale, and the results appear most favorable.

In addition to the comparison of charts and questionnaire as indicators of substance abuse, the information yielded by these two

[5]An incomplete questionnaire administered in the Emergency Room, Major Side.

Table A-5
Summary Statistics Comparison

	Charts	*Questionnaire*	*Difference (Advantage)*
Prevalence			
Alcohol	10%	16%	6% (Q)
Drugs	6%	9%	3% (Q)
Detection			
Alcohol	48%	74%	26% (Q)
Drugs	53%	77%	24% (Q)
Power			
Alcohol	56%	85%	29% (Q)
Drugs	59%	86%	27% (Q)

sources on the *extent of use* was evaluated. This evaluation was limited by the difficulty of translating medical notes into an ordinal scale. For example, alcohol use was given a variety of descriptions such as, "occasional drinker, social drinker, weekend drinker." Nevertheless, an attempt was made to assess the amount of "underreporting" as defined by the following criteria:

1. a finding of moderate use with no mention in the corresponding chart or questionnaire; or
2. heavy use reported as moderate or social; or
3. moderate use with social consequences reported as light or occasional use.

Using these criteria, three members of the research staff independently compared the information from the 362 documented charts with the corresponding questionnaires. Reliability was high, with only occasional differences between the judges. The results (taking the average in the case of inter-judge differences) are presented in Table A-6.

Although these results are based on highly subjective judgments, and must be treated with caution, they appear to lend considerable support to our positive evaluation of the questionnaire. Of all cases of "under-reporting," 93 percent were found in the charts, and only 7 percent in the questionnaire data. The difference is even more striking for alcohol use (95% to 5%) than for drug use (78% to 22%), although

Table A-6
Underreporting

	"Underreported" by charts	*"Underreported" by questionnaire*	*Total*
Alcohol use	89	5	94
Drug use	7	2	9
Total	96	7	103

the small number of under reported drug use cases precludes any reliable comparison.

Additional Validity Checks

For a small sample of subjects, identified as substance abusers by questionnaire criteria, and recontacted to participate with their families in a family interaction pilot study, data from two research instruments (Harford Schedule[6] and Record-Keeping procedure) are available for comparison with the information given on the survey questionnaire. The Harford Schedule, as modified for this pilot study, consisted of a 30-40 minute structured interview which inquired into the nature and social context of the respondent's recent drinking and drug-taking events. The Record-Keeping procedure was a log or ongoing diary of drinking and drug-taking events, kept by each family member for a 2-3 week period between research interviews. Although the number of subjects completing these procedures was small, it seemed important to use this unique opportunity to evaluate the questionnaire against the comprehensive and thorough investigation that these techniques provided.

Tables A-7 and A-8 summarize the information from these two comparisons.

Our impression from these data is that the self-assessment questionnaire functions as a remarkably effective survey instrument, far more economical of time and manpower than the Harford, yet yielding comparable information for the purpose of distinguishing abusers from non-abusers. It is important to note that four of ten abusers identified by this procedure were picked up on their Social Consequences Scale Scores alone, indicating that this Scale serves as an important screening adjunct to the Quantity Frequency Scales.

[6]Unpublished instrument and data on it was made available by Tom Harford to the authors in 1975 and is accessible from Harford at the National Institute on Alcohol Abuse and Alcoholism.

Table A-7
Comparison of Substance Use and Abuse Survey (SUAS) and Harford Schedule (H.S.)

	SUAS	*H.S.*
Number of available comparisons (i.e., individuals[a] completing both procedures = 20)		
Number of abusers[b] identified		
Alcohol	7	5
Drugs	3	3
Number of abusers missed (identified by other procedure only)		
Alcohol	2	4[c]
Drugs	0	0

[a]Individuals include identified abusers and other family members.

[b]Individuals in the highest category of quantity-frequency use (without social consequences) are defined elsewhere as "heavy users," however, they are included here for purposes of the validity checks.

[c]Two of these individuals were self-identified alcoholics who had begun a trial of abstinence between the time of administration of SUAS and that of H.S.

Conclusions

The SUAS proved an effective instrument in assessing the substance use patterns in over 5,700 subjects in a medical setting. This sample of 5,700 represents a compliance rate of 88 per cent. The high degree of cooperation demonstrates that patients are willing to give information about alcohol, licit, illicit and prescription use of drugs,

Table A-8
Comparison of SUAS and Record Keeping (R-K)

	SUAS	R-K
Number of available comparisons = 12		
Number of abusers identified		
Alcohol	4	1
Drugs	3	4
Number of abusers missed (identified by other procedure)		
Alcohol	1	3[a]
Drugs	1[b]	0

[a]Two of these individuals were attempting abstention during the R-K period.

[b]This individual recorded in the R-K extensive use of a compound tablet containing a barbiturate. It is possible that she was ignorant of the content of this tablet, which would explain the omission from SUAS. (As in Table 7, the small numbers preclude any firm assessment of the validity of the SUAS, yet the overall impression is a positive one.)

thereby providing an accurate assessment of total drug use quickly and simply without a great deal of personnel assistance.

The SUAS was far superior to patient charts in identifying heavy drug and/or alcohol use, especially when both quantity-frequency and social consequences criteria were taken into account. Even when compared with lengthy interviews and weekly logs, the SUAS did at least as well in simply identifying current heavy use of substances, although the numbers are too small to permit definite conclusions.

An examination of internal validity (the correlation of various parts of the SUAS) is not included in the validity section of this paper. We found quantity-frequency scores to be significantly correlated with social consequences scores for both alcohol and other drugs combined. Although this is a crucial topic, the extent and complexity of such a discussion warrants a separate publication.

There were no incidents attendant to filling out the questionnaire. Patients did not complain about being asked to answer the survey questions. Perhaps the inference that can be drawn is that patients could be asked most of the same questions routinely by health professionals. Since, if medical charts are any indication, that does not seem to be happening yet, the foremost utility of this survey might well be to serve as a model for health professionals to supplement their history taking. We feel this survey instrument has usefulness as a screening device to detect patterns and degrees of substance abuse that should influence care.[7]

In addition to its clinical utility, the acceptance and validity of the SUAS as a self-assessment procedure has demonstrated that large-scale-survey research of this type can be carried out efficiently in a medical setting. Studies of the data collected with this instrument are in preparation for publication at this time, and include the following:

1. A comparison of the power of different questions and groups of questions to detect problem use of substances. This will include quantity-frequency (QF) *vs.* social consequences (SC) questions as a group for both alcohol and other drugs; and it will also include single questions such as those on chief complaint (No. 30), drug-

[7]It is worth nothing that the physician may gain useful information with the SUAS for even the 12 percent of patients who may not complete the questionnaire. As was footnoted in tables 3 and 4 in the Validity Section of this paper, among the few abusers on medical charts that were missed by the SUAS, there was a very high percent of incomplete questionnaires (7 of 10 for alcohol, 2 of 5 for drugs, or a total of 9 of 15 = 60%, which is much greater than the expected 12%). These numbers are small, but striking enough to allow us to suggest that heavy or problem use of substances may be suspected among patients who fail to complete the questionnaire.

related reasons for medical care (No. 31), and use as a medicine (No. 28 a,b) *vs.* QF and SC criteria.

2. A comparison of the extent and specific nature of social consequences of various degrees of use of alcohol and of other substances of abuse.
3. A comparison among a variety of general medical and specialty services of current prevalence of substance use and abuse.
4. A study of the relationship between certain distinctive demographic factors, such as the nature and duration of the current living arrangements, and substance use and abuse.
5. A study of the relationship of use and degree of use of common drugs, such as caffeine and cigarettes, to heavy use or problems associated with use of less common drugs, such as sedative-hypnotics.

References

1. H. Parry, Personal communication, 1976.
2. D. Raft, J. Davidson, T. C. Toomey, R. F. Spencer, & B. F. M. Lewis, Inpatient and outpatient patterns of psychotropic drug prescribing by nonpsychiatrist physician. *American Journal of Psychiatry, 132* (1975): 1209–1312.
3. D. G. Mayfield, & D Morrison, The use of minor tranquilizers in a teaching hospital. *Southern Medical Journal, 66* (1973): 589–592.
4. D. Mayfield, G. McLeod, & P. Hall, The CAGE questionnaire: Validation of a new alcoholism screening instrument. *American Journal of Psychiatry, 131* (1974): 1121–1123.
5. A. D. Pokorny, B. A. Miller, & H. B. Kaplan, The Brief MAST: A Shortened Version of the Michigan Alcoholism Screening Test. *American Journal of Psychiatry, 129* (1972): 342–345.
6. C. Shearn & D. Fitzgibbons, Patterns of drug use in a population of youthful psychiatric patients. *American Journal of Psychiatry, 128* (1972): 1381–1387.
7. M. A. Plant, Young drug and alcohol casualties compared: Review of 100 patients at a Scottish psychiatric hospital. *British Journal of Addiction, 71* (1976): 31–43.
8. J. Westermeyer, & V. Walzer, Sociopathy and drug use in a young psychiatric population. *Diseases of the Nervous System, 36* (1975): 676–677.
9. R. Barchha, M. A. Stewart, & S. B. Guze, The prevalence of alcoholism among general hospital ward patients. *American Journal of Psychiatry, 125* (1968): 133–136.
10. E. S. Gomberg, Prevalence of alcoholism among ward patients in a Veterans Administration hospital. *Journal of Studies on Alcohol, 36* (1975): 1458–1466.
11. W. F. McCourt, A. F. Williams, & L. Schnieder, Incidence of alcoholism in

a state mental hospital population. *Quarterly Journal of Studies on Alcohol, 32* (1971): 1085–1088.

12. J. McCusker, C. E. Cherrubin, & S. Zimberg, Prevalence of alcoholism in general municipal hospital Population. *New York State Journal of Medicine, 71* (1971): 751–754.
13. J. P. Nolan, Alcohol as a factor in the illness of university service patients. *American Journal of the Medical Sciences.* (1965): 135–147.
14. R. Straus, & S. Q. Bacon, *Drinking in College*, New Haven: Yale University Press, 1953.
15. D. Cahalan, I. D. Cisin, & H. M. Crossley, *American drinking practices: A national study of drinking behavior and attitudes*, Rutgers Center of Alcohol Studies: 1969.
16. M. Cohen, & D. C. Klein, A measure of severity of multi-drug use among psychiatric patients, *Internal Pharmacopsychiatrist, 6* (1971): 83–91.
17. M. Cohen, A. Karras, & R. Hughes, The usefulness and reliability of a drug severity scale. *International Journal of the Addictions, 12.*
18. M. L. Selzer, The Michigan Alcoholism Screening Test: The quest for a new diagnostic instrument. *American Journal of Psychiatry, 127* (1971): 89–94.
19. R. B. Breitenbucher, The routine administration of the Michigan Alcoholism Screening Test to ambulatory patients. *Minnesota Medicine, 59* (1976): 425–429.
20. W. M. Swenson, & R. M. Morse, The use of a Self-Administered Alcoholism Screening Test (SAAT) in a medical center, *Mayo Clinic Proceedings, 50* (1975): 204–208.
21. M. L. Selzer, A. Vinokur, & J. Rooijen, A self-administered Short Michigan Alcoholism Screening Test (SMART). *Journal of Studies on Alcohol, 36* (1976): 117–126.
22. H. Kaplan, T. Kanas, A. Pokorny, & G. Lively, Screened Tests and Self-identification in the detection of alcoholism. *Journal of Health and Social Behavior, 15* (1974): 51–56.
23. A. Favazza, & J. Pires, The Michigan Alcoholism Screening Test-application in a general military hospital. *Quarterly Journal of Studies on Alcohol, 35* (1974): 925–929.

APPENDIX C

DIFFERENCES IN THE USE OF SUBSTANCES OF ABUSE BY PSYCHIATRIC PATIENTS COMPARED WITH MEDICAL AND SURGICAL PATIENTS

By DONALD I. DAVIS, M.D., F.A.P.A.[1]

This segment presents findings from a comparison between patterns of use of substances of abuse among a psychiatric population and among a similarly studied medical and surgical patient population in an urban, university medical center population. There have been a number of papers in the literature documenting a high rate of alcoholism in specific psychiatric inpatient settings (7,9,10,15). The combined incidence of alcohol, other drugs, or multiple drug abuse in a psychiatric patient population also has been studied (1,2,4,5,11,-14,16,17). The report of incidence of substance abuse among psychiatric inpatients range from 3 percent (11) to 74 percent (14). There is a report of covert abuse of substances other than alcohol in psychiatric outpatients in the range of 13 percent (6). There are also reports of alcoholism among general medical patients ranging from 8.7 percent (7) to 17.1 percent (10). However, given the widely different population samples as well as criteria for abuse of substances in these studies, it is not possible to determine from the literature how substance abuse in psychiatric patients compares with that among other types of patient groups. It also has not been possible to assess from the literature

[1]Family Therapy Institute of Alexandria, Alexandria, Virginia; and the Department of Psychiatry, George Washington University Medical School, Washington, D. C. The Substance Abuse Survey staff members that assisted in this study were Karen Kupetz, M.S.W., Judy LaRosa, R.N., Micheline Klagsbrun, D.C.P., and Deborah Wisoff, B.A. Hugh Perry, Ph.D., and Ira Cisin, Ph.D., contributed to the development and application of the instrument used for the investigation. Paul Poppen, Ph.D., Chuck Bruder, Ph.D., assisted with the analysis of data for this study.

whether there are differences between degree of use, as opposed to frank alcoholism or other drug abuse, in psychiatric *vs.* other patients.

Subjects and Methods

In the present study, close to 3,000 general medical and surgical patients were surveyed regarding the quantity and frequency of their use of alcohol and eight other categories of drugs of abuse in the previous month. Social consequences experienced from use of alcohol or other drugs were also examined, along with a wide range of sociodemographic variables.

The instrument used was the Substance Use and Abuse Survey (SUAS), a self-assessment questionnaire (see Appendix A of this book) developed for this survey with the intent of providing a state-of-the-art tool suitable for large-scale screening within a medical center. Details of the development and of the validity of the SUAS have been presented in another paper (8; reprinted in Appendix B of this book). Briefly, the SUAS consists chiefly of a composite of previously existing, widely used questions and screening criteria regarding the extent of the use of various substances. For example, questions pertaining to alcohol use provide for categorization of responses according to the criteria for the range of light through heavy drinkers used by Cahalan, et al. in their determination of drinking practices among American men(3). Similarly, the assessment of level of use of drugs other than alcohol was derived essentially from the reported work of Cohen and Klein (4). In addition, social consequences of alcohol use were evaluated by incorporating a slight variation on the widely used Brief Michigan Alcoholism Screening Test (Brief-MAST) (13). No comparable, widely used, or well-validated instrument was found from which to develop a portion of the SUAS that would assess social consequences of the use of drugs other than alcohol. Hence, these items were newly developed. In fact, they correspond very closely to the items in the Brief-MAST, often differing only in the substitution of the words "other drugs" for the word "alcohol."

More has been written elsewhere about the application of the SUAS in one large-scale survey of an urban university medical center (8). In summary, less than one percent of patients asked resisted answering the questions. By and large, patients, unlike a few of their physicians who thought that more of their patients might take offense, believed these types of questions were quite appropriate and relevant to their health care.

It is the intent in this paper to present that portion of the survey findings that pertain to patients on the psychiatric services studied. Findings from the large general medical and general surgical service population will be referred to as well, but only to the extent relevant for comparison with the psychiatry findings.

One inpatient and one outpatient psychiatric service were used for the study. The inpatient unit was a 33-bed, general psychiatry residency teaching unit in a moderately large, urban private university medical center. The outpatient unit was the clinic and private practice component of the same residency program. The SUAS was given to 170 inpatients and 130 outpatients by one of two research assistants, who were trained to explain the consent form and oversee the signing of it, and to offer guidance as needed. Consecutive new admissions (within 48 hours in almost all cases) or new intakes in the case of outpatients were surveyed, with the exception that surveying was stopped while research assistants were not working for brief blocks of time. Both services were comprised of a broad cross-section of patients from primarily middle classes, but with representation from both highest and lowest social classes as well. The ratio of whites to blacks approached three to one, and other racial groups made up less than three percent of the patients surveyed.

Results

Comparison of Psychiatric and General Medical/Surgical Patients

As shown in Table A-9, for each category of heavy and/or problem use of alcohol or one other drug or some combination, the percentage for psychiatric patients is substantially higher than the corresponding percentage for medical and surgical (Med-Surg) patients. All such comparisons are significant at the $P<.003$ level. This is true for both males and females (Table A-9). Medical and surgical data have been presented as a combined average for the purpose of this comparison because the averages of each separately did not differ significantly from one another. The category of abstainers and others, representing all nonusers and normative (nonproblem, nonheavy) users of any one or more of the substances of abuse included in the survey, also reveals a significant ($p<.001$) difference between psychiatric and Med-Surg patients. Again, this is true for both males and females, but it is particularly prominent for males.

The Med-Surg population is more heavily biased toward an

Table A–9
Psychiatric vs. Med-Surg Patients by Categories of Substance Use by Sex

	Polydrug[a]	*Alcohol Only*[b]	*Single Drug*[c]	*Rx Drug*[d]	*Abstainers and Others*
Males					
Med-Surg (N = 1303)	2.1%	20.3%	1.9%	2.9%	72.8%
Psychiatric (N = 116)	15.5%	31.9%	6.0%	8.6%	37.9%
Females					
Med-Surg (N = 1666)	1.6%	10.2%	1.6%	5.3%	81.3%
Psychiatric (N = 182)	8.2%	23.1%	6.6%	10.4%	51.6%

[a]Polydrug = heavy use of two or more drugs (including alcohol) as measured by a quantity-frequency index with or without positive social consequence scale score (modified Brief-MAST).

[b]Alcohol only = heavy use of only alcohol as measured by a quantity-frequency index and/or positive social consequence scale score (modified Brief-MAST).

[c]Single drug = heavy use of only one drug (excluding alcohol) as measured by a quantity-frequency index and/or positive social consequence scale score ("other drug" version of Brief-MAST).

[d]Prescription drug = heavy use of prescription drug(s) (used only as prescribed), as measured by a quanity-frequency index.

[e]Abstainers and others = no current use (never used or no use within past month) or light to moderate use of alcohol or other drugs as measured by a quantity-frequency index and negative social consequences scale score (modified Brief-MAST).

outpatient population than is the psychiatric population. A comparison was made of use categories for psychiatric inpatients *vs.* psychiatric outpatients. When we look at psychiatric outpatients alone for both males and females, the percentage of heavy or problem users remains higher in each category than for Med-Surg patients, with only one exception. The sole exception is that no heavy use by prescription was found in the male psychiatric outpatients. Also, the differences in the category, "Single Drug," are no longer statistically significant. Nonetheless, taking the category, "Abstainers and Others," as an overall measure, the difference between outpatient psychiatric and Med-Surg patients is highly significant ($p<.0011$ for females, $p <.0003$ for males). Also, it was uncommon to find a male psychiatric inpatient who was not a heavy and/or problem user of some substance of abuse (only 29.4 percent were not). Though less dramatic, the finding for females was similar in that less than one half of female psychiatric inpatients were not heavy and/or problem drinkers.

Males vs. Females

For males and females, inpatients and outpatients, "Alcohol Only" is the category of heavy and/or problem use most frequently identified. For male psychiatric patients, "Polydrug" (three fourths of which was found to include heavy use of alcohol as one of two or more drugs involved) had the next highest percentages. "Polydrug" was also next highest for outpatient females; but "Rx Drug" and then "Single Drug" both had higher percentages than "Polydrug" for female psychiatric inpatients.

When we looked at the full range of patterns of use of alcohol (Table A-10), we found that psychiatric and Med-Surg patients differed significantly, not only with regard to "Heavy" and especially "Very Heavy" use, but also in the percentage of "Abstainers." For both males and females, the percentage of abstainers was much smaller among psychiatric patients than among Med-Surg patients.

Use of Cigarettes, Coffee, and Marijuana

A similar phenomenon was found between psychiatric and Med-Surg patients in the comparison of the distribution of patterns of use of cigarettes, or coffee, and, to a lesser extent, of marijuana. Here again, this is true for both males and females. There were significantly more heavy users of cigarettes and of coffee among psychiatric patients, while there was a similar percentage of users among psychiatric

Table A-10
Psychiatric vs. Med-Surg Patients by Levels of Alcohol Use by Sex

	Abstainers	*Very Infrequent*	*Light*	*Moderate*	*Heavy*	*Very Heavy*
Males						
Med-Surg (*N* = 1292)	8.9%	14.9%	16.0%	41.6%	12.2%	6.4%
Psychiatric (*N* = 116)	1.7%	15.5%	16.4%	33.6%	20.7%	12.1%
Females						
Med-Surg (*N* = 1666)	16.7%	17.7%	23.3%	32.6%	7.9%	1.8%
Psychiatric (*N* = 182)	6.0%	21.4%	17.0%	30.8%	17.0%	7.8%

[a]Levels of alcohol use are derived by use of the quantity-frequency index:
1. Abstainer = never had a drink.
2. Very infrequent = did not have a drink in the past month
3. Light = one to three sittings, one to two drinks per sitting, in the past month
4. Moderate = four to 20 sittings, one to two drinks per sitting, *or* one to three sittings, three to four drinks each, in the past month
5. Heavy = four to 20 sittings, three to four drinks per sitting, *or* one to 20 sittings, five or more drinks each, in the past month
6. Very heavy = 21 or more sittings, three or more drinks per sitting, in the past month

patients as among Med-Surg patients at each of the lower levels of use. Specifically, 43.1 percent of psychiatric male patients smoked a pack or more of cigarettes a day *vs.* 26.4 percent of Med-Surg male patients; and 29.5 percent of psychiatric female patients smoked cigarettes that heavily *vs.* 17.1 percent of Med-Surg female patients. Similarly, for coffee use, 18 percent of psychiatric male patients drank five or more cups of coffee per day *vs.* 10.5 percent of Med-Surg male patients. Among females, a divider for a significant difference was three or more cups per day (psychiatric, 30.7 percent *vs.* Med-Surg, 21.9 percent). More than seven cups of coffee a day also readily distinguished between psychiatric and Med-Surg patients but the numbers of subjects in these categories were much smaller.

The Social Consequences of Substance Use

Examination of only life problems (social consequences) associated with alcohol or other drug use revealed differences as significant as those found when quantity and frequency of use were taken into account. Of psychiatric patients, 20.4 percent achieved a positive score for consequences of alcohol use *vs.* 4.2 percent of Med-Surg patients. For social consequences of use of drugs other than alcohol, the corresponding positive findings were psychiatric, 15.5 percent, *vs.* Med-Surg, 2.3 percent.

The category of heavy and/or problem use of alcohol only, shown in Table A-9, can be broken down into three components: 1) patients who achieved positive scores for social consequences of alcohol use and were currently heavy users, 2) patients who were currently heavy users but not positive for social consequences, and 3) patients who were positive for social consequences of alcohol but were not currently heavy users. The data were analyzed separately for males by service, and for females by service. The distributions for the two services among the three components are significantly different, for both males and females. Male-Med-Surg patients who were classified as problem and/or heavy users of alcohol only were most likely to be heavy users, but not achieve positive social consequence scores (73.1 percent), whereas male psychiatric patients were rather evenly distributed among the three possible components (only 35.2 percent of heavy users did not score positively for social consequences). Among females, a higher percentage, 54.8 percent of psychiatric heavy users, were negative for social consequences; but this was still significantly lower than the percentage of Med-Surg heavy users who were negative for social consequences (75.5 percent). The differences between psychiatric and Med-Surg services in the percentages of heavy users who did score positively for social consequences was striking. For males these results were Med-Surg, 10.2 percent, *vs.* psychiatric, 27.0 percent. For females, the corresponding results were Med-Surg, 6.5 percent, vs. psychiatric, 27.2 percent.

Discussion

In any comparison of two different patient groups, there is the question, "Are these similar populations?" This is true even when all subjects are patients in the same medical center, as was the case in this study, for which demographic data were gathered and well-established criteria were used for categorization with regard to age, sex, race, and educational level plus marital status and current living arrangements. What differences were present between the two populations, in ratio of whites to blacks, in age groups, in marital status or education, would not begin to account for the magnitude of differences between psychiatric and Med-Surg populations reported in this paper. In short, further data analysis has revealed a relatively small effect of demographic differences in the findings of heavy or problem use of substances in the present survey.

The finding of significantly greater use and problems associated with the use of various substances of abuse among psychiatric patients when compared with a Med-Surg patient population, and the sheer magnitude of heavy and problem use among psychiatric patients, raise the question of cause or effect; but there is nothing in either the method or results that justifies drawing any firm conclusions about it. We could speculate that patients with psychiatric conditions more readily turn to psychoactive drugs for self-treatment than people in a general medical and surgical population and that, subsequently, these same patients' disturbances are more likely to be compounded by problems associated with psychoactive drug use. This scenario would certainly fit our data, though from the data one could also postulate that problem use, or even heavy use of substances with potential abuse not clearly associated with problems, leads frequently to psychiatric conditions. Most likely, there is an interaction of both factors.

Conclusion

This study was conducted with psychiatric patients screened by the clinical services to minimize, or exclude, clear-cut alcoholism or other drug abuse. Yet we still find much more above-average and problem use of alcohol and other drugs than in our medical and surgical patients. From our demographic data, we assume this population is similar to the mainstream of private and fee-for-service outpatient and inpatient practice. We conclude, therefore, that, in the use by patients of substances of abuse, in this broad population, psychiatry is different from general medicine and surgery.

References

1. Aekimian, L. J., & Gorshon, S. Characteristics of drug abusers admitted to a psychiatric hospital. *Journal of the American Medical Association, 205* (1968): 125–130.
2. Blumberg, A. G., Cohen, M., Henton, A. M., & Klein, D. F. Covert drug abuse among voluntary hospitalized psychiatric patients. *Journal of the American Medical Association, 217* (1971): 1659–1661.
3. Cahalan, D., Cisin, I. H., & Crosley, H. M. *American Drinking Practices*, New Brunswick: New Jersey Center of Alcohol Studies, 1969.
4. Cohen, M., & Klein, D. G. Drug abuse in the young psychiatric population. *American Journal of Orthopsychiatry, 40* (1970): 448–455.
5. Fischer, D. E., Halikis, J. A., Baker, J. W., & Smith, J. B. Frequency and patterns of drug abuse in psychiatric patients. *Diseases of the Nervous System, 36* (1975): 550–553.
6. Hall, R. C. W., Popkin, M. K., DeVaul, R., & Stickney, S. K. The effect of unrecognized drug abuse on diagnosis and therapeutic outcome. *American Journal of Drug and Alcohol Abuse, 4* (1977): 455–465.
7. Kearney, T. R. Alcohol and general hospital patients. *American Journal of Psychiatry, 125* (1969): 1451–1452.
8. Kupetz, K., Klagsbrun, M., Wisoff, D., LaRosa, J., & Davis, D. The acceptance and validity of the Substance Use and Abuse Survey (SUAS). *Journal of Drug Education, 9* (1979): 163–180.
9. McCourt, W. F., Williams, A. F., & Schneider, L. Incidents of alcoholism in a state mental hospital population. *Quarterly Journal of Studies on Alcohol, 32* (1971): 1085–1088.
10. Meletzky, B. M., & Klotter, J. The prevalence of alcoholism in a military hospital. *Military Medicine, 6* (1975): 273–275.
11. Nail, R. C., & Gunderson, K. E. A preliminary study of drug abuse in psychiatric patients. *Military Medicine, 137* (1972): 119–121.
12. Rockwell, D. A., & Asterwald, P. Amphetamine use and abuse in psychiatric patients. *Archives of General Psychiatry, 18* (1968): 612–616.
13. Selzer, M. L., Vinokur, A., & Van Royjen, L. A self-administered short Michigan Alcoholism Screening Test (MAST). *Journal of Studies on Alcohol, 36* (1975): 117–126.
14. Sherans, C. R., & Fitzgibbons, D. J. Drug abuse in a population of youthful psychiatric patients. *American Journal of Psychiatry, 128* (1972): 1381–1387.
15. Stark, M. J., & Nichols, H. G. Alcohol related admissions to a general hospital. *Alcohol Health and Research World, 1* (1977): 11–14.
16. Westermeyer, J., & Walzer, V. Sociopathy and drug use in a young psychiatric population. *Diseases of the Nervous System, 36* (1975): 673–677.
17. Whitlock, F. A., Lowrey, J. M., Edwards, J. E., et al. Drug dependence in psychiatric patients. *Medical Journal of Australia, 1* (1967): 1157–1166.

INDEX

ABOUT THE AUTHOR

Donald I. Davis, M.D., is Director of the Family Therapy Institute of Alexandria, Virginia, Clinical Associate Professor of Psychiatry at George Washington University Medical School, and also formerly a Clinical Associate in the National Institute of Alcohol Abuse and Alcoholism and a Career Teacher in Drug Abuse and Alcoholism.